LEGAL WRITING AND ANALYSIS

IN A NUTSHELL®

FIFTH EDITION

LYNN BAHRYCH, J.D., Ph.D.
Attorney at Law

JEANNE MERINO
Lecturer in Residence
Director, First-Year Legal Research and Writing
Stanford Law School

BETH McLELLAN
Lecturer in Residence
Stanford Law School

WEST ACADEMIC PUBLISHING

444 Cedar Street, Suite 700
St. Paul, MN 55101
1-877-888-1330

Printed in the United States of America

ISBN: 978-1-63460-281-5

In memory of Professor Marjorie D. Rombauer, Emerita, Founder of the field of Legal Writing Education and

For our families,
Max Thomas Bahrych, Glee C. Bahrych, and Shannon Glee Squires;
Marilyn Merino and Fred Merino and Russ, Rico, Rosie and Annie;
and Fred, María, Dan, Will and Maggie Alvarez, and Elinore Kaufman

PREFACE

The first edition of this *Nutshell* reflected the combined efforts of the late Professor of Law Marjorie D. Rombauer, Emerita, and Legal Writing Associate Lynn Bahrych Squires, Ph.D., now Lynn Bahrych, attorney at law. Published in 1982, the first edition grew out of their collaborative efforts teaching legal writing and research at the University of Washington School of Law from 1978 until 1982.

Professor Marjorie Rombauer was a celebrated founder of the field of Legal Writing in the law school curriculum. She combined the specialized discipline of legal writing with legal research and analysis to create a new approach to teaching basic legal skills to first-year law students. Her pioneering work and popular legal textbooks have made her an icon in the fields of legal research, analysis, and writing. We have followed in her footsteps, building on her legacy to our profession, by adding legal analysis to this edition of the Nutshell.

In addition to Lynn Bahrych, the authors of the current edition are Jeanne Merino and Beth McLellan, legal writing instructors at Stanford Law School. Jeanne Merino is Lecturer in Residence and Director of the First-Year Legal Research and Writing Program. Beth McLellan is Lecturer in Residence. Jeanne and Beth are indebted to all former and current colleagues who have taught

Legal Research and Writing and Federal Litigation at Stanford. Each of them so generously shared ideas about legal writing that their insights have become our own. Many thanks also to the participants of the 2015 West Coast Rhetoric workshop hosted by UNLV.

This new edition of *Legal Writing and Analysis in a Nutshell* offers law students and lawyers a practical step-by-step method of analyzing and writing clearly, precisely, and effectively about the law. The chapters that follow will guide the legal writer, whether a first-year law student or a practicing attorney, to a reliable set of practices that will insure successful written communication.

LYNN BAHRYCH, J.D., PH.D.
JEANNE MERINO, J.D.
BETH MCLELLAN, J.D.

Stanford, California
October 2016

INTRODUCTION

Lawyers are professional writers. Writing is an essential part of a practicing attorney's daily work. Rather than decreasing the need for writing, the internet and other data transmission innovations have dramatically increased the flow of written communication. New technologies will continue to change how we write, but the law will always require the certainty of the written word.

Today, lawyers must not only write more often, but also more quickly. This new *Nutshell* offers a method of writing efficiently, without losing clarity, precision, and effectiveness. Our step-by-step method is illustrated in the flow chart in Chapter One. This method is designed to clarify each step you take and to help you make deliberate choices. Each step will be explained in one or more chapters.

This new edition of *Legal Writing and Analysis in a Nutshell* includes legal analysis for the first time. Times have changed since the first edition of *Legal Writing in a Nutshell* was published in 1982. We now use email for most communication, as well as texts for informal messaging. The process of writing has changed in response to this new medium. As Marshall McLuhan wrote in 1964, "the medium is the message. This is merely to say that the personal and social consequences of any medium—that is of any extension of ourselves—result from the new scale that is introduced into our affairs by each extension of ourselves, or by any new technology."

Marshall McCluhan, *Understanding Media: The Extensions of Man 1* (1964). Analysis always comes first—that has not changed—but the compact and fast-moving forms of written communication that deliver analysis today are even more tightly bound to the content of their message than in 1964 or 1982.

The Fifth Edition offers legal writers a practical step-by-step method of both analyzing and writing clearly, precisely, and effectively about the law. Although, as we have noted, the means of written communication continually change, the basic elements of effective legal writing have not changed. Whether the legal writer is crafting an email, a letter to a client, or a brief for a trial court, the same fundamental principles apply. Legal writing requires attention to accuracy, attention to the reader's needs and expectations, and attention to the craft of writing precisely, concisely, and effectively.

The chapters that follow will guide the legal writer to a reliable set of practices that will insure successful written communication about the law. Chapters One to Ten explain the traditional elements of written composition, from organization of a legal document to individual word choices. The most common forms of legal writing, the research memorandum, client letter, and persuasive brief, are discussed in Chapters Six and Seven. Guidelines for writing emails are included in Chapter Six. Tips for editing and polishing your documents are given in Chapter Ten. You will find sample documents in

Appendix A, including a case brief, a research memorandum, and a brief for a trial court. Appendix B provides you with a simple method of analyzing and improving your personal writing style. For readers wishing to improve their understanding of the structure of the English language, diagramming of sentences is also included in Appendix B. A glossary of words commonly misused in legal writing is provided in Appendix C. Finally, Appendix D recommends additional sources that we especially value.

OUTLINE

LEGAL WRITING AND ANALYSIS

IN A NUTSHELL®

FIFTH EDITION

CHAPTER 1

BASIC STEPS TO LEGAL WRITING AND ANALYSIS

§ 1.1 INTRODUCTION

This chapter describes our step-by-step method of legal writing and analysis, as illustrated in the flow chart below. The chart describes the process of legal problem solving for the legal writer. The individual steps are more fully explained in the chapters to follow.

§ 1.2 FIRST STEP: IDENTIFY YOUR GOAL

Your first task is to identify your goal. This seems easy and self-evident, but it is surprising how often we begin a writing project with only a vague idea of our goal. Write down your goal or goals. This first simple step will give you clarity and focus, providing a touchstone throughout the writing and analysis process. Are you communicating legal advice to a client? Are you summarizing current legal authorities for an attorney? Are you crafting a settlement agreement? Are you persuading a court to do something specific? Know precisely what your goal is before you begin.

Part of identifying your goal is to identify your audience. Who will be reading what you write? Anything written to address a conflict may eventually be read by a judge, regardless of the initial audience. Identify all possible readers. Although your writing may be protected by the attorney-client privilege, your client may share it with others, raising the possibility that an opposing party may eventually read it.

Estimate how much time your audience will have to read what you write. This may take some investigation, but will save you time if, as is usually the case, your intended audience will be reading what you write quickly and possibly only once. If your document is likely to be read as email, on a small screen or hand-held electronic device, then your writing must be more like a telegram than a Victorian novel. Keep your busy reader in mind as you write. Also keep in mind precisely what you want your reader to do as a result of your writing.

After identifying your goal and your audience, select the type of document that will serve you best. This may be obvious, for example, if you are writing an appellate brief, but sometimes you have choices. Will your goal be served best by an opinion letter that contains a summary of current law? Or by an inquiry to opposing counsel to determine where common ground may be?

When you know your goal, your audience, and the type of document you will use, identify the deadline or set one for yourself. Next, work backwards from your deadline to draft a timeline for completing your document. Use the steps in the flow chart to construct your timeline.

§ 1.3 SECOND STEP: GATHER FACTS AND ANALYZE LAW

Make a list of the sources of information that you will use. This could include case files given to you, interviews with clients, witnesses, or experts, and legal research. Basically, what facts and law do you need to gather? Determine the order in which you will gather this information. Rarely do we have time to research everything relevant, so the next task is to prioritize sources of information. Starting with the most important first, gather as much information as you find useful within your timeline constraints. Knowing when to stop will be difficult at first, but will become easier with experience. Your goal and your timeline will give you essential guide posts as you gather information.

For excellent guidance on legal research, see Morris L. Cohen & Kent C. Olson, *Legal Research in a Nutshell* (West Academic, 12th ed. 2016).

After you have assembled the facts you need and identified the relevant laws, the next step is to organize the facts into a coherent chronology or story and synthesize the legal authorities. Organizing the facts into a story or objective set of circumstances must come first. Only when you know what has happened will you know which laws apply. You may have multiple sources of law. To synthesize them requires clear understanding of each source, whether case law, statutes, rules, or secondary sources, such as legal treatises. Chapter Two explains how to analyze each of the primary sources of law.

With the story or fact pattern clearly outlined, apply the law as you have synthesized it. Knowing how the law applies to the facts in the most relevant or governing cases you have found, compare your facts to those and to any other comparable cases. Identify significant differences as well as significant similarities. The differences may lead you to further research. The differences will also help you to predict opposing arguments. The similarities will provide a foundation for your legal arguments and ultimately for your conclusion.

The application of the law as you have synthesized it to the facts as you have assembled them will reveal the possible outcomes. There is never just one possible outcome. At this stage, you will need to identify the most likely outcomes, without ignoring any significant facts or relevant law. Chapter Two, Legal Analysis, discusses this step in more detail.

Depending on the possible outcomes, you may need to do further legal research or fact gathering. Fact gathering and legal research is often an iterative process. The more you understand, the more you may need to know.

When you have the facts in order and the law analyzed, the next step is a rough outline or synthesis chart. The details of this are discussed in Chapter Two, Legal Analysis, and Chapter Three, Large-Scale Organization.

§ 1.4 THIRD STEP: DRAFT PRELIMINARY OUTLINE

After you have completed any additional legal research, analysis, and fact gathering, you will be ready to draft a preliminary outline. Your outline will begin with a list of conclusions or possible outcomes. Depending on your assignment, it may also begin with a list of issues. Either way, you should list them in the order of their importance. Check to make sure that you do not have the same or similar subjects in different places. Check the list to ensure that related subjects are discussed as closely together as possible, as well as in the order of their importance. Chapter Three, Large-Scale Organization, provides details about this stage of outlining.

Conclusions normally come first because most types of legal writing provide answers to legal questions. Most readers want to know the answers immediately. This includes clients reading opinion letters and judges reading briefs. Therefore, answers should usually be given first, before supporting analysis or discussion.

The process of outlining may reveal holes in your legal analysis or missing facts. The iterative process of adding further research and investigating facts may continue until you are finished with the document. Outlining and drafting force us to think more precisely and logically, which often results in new insights requiring further research. This process is discussed in detail in Chapter Three,

Large-Scale Organization; Chapter Six, Advisory Writing; and Chapter Seven, Advocacy Writing.

§ 1.5 FOURTH STEP: DRAFT DETAILED OUTLINE

The writing process becomes easier at this stage. You will have completed most of the research and analysis, you will know what your conclusions are, and you will have a clear idea of the most likely outcomes. The preliminary outline, which reflects the large-scale organization of your subject, is ready to be refined.

Your conclusions are based on a logical arrangement of facts which have been analyzed using relevant law. After stating your conclusions, the next part of your outline is normally a factual statement or summary of facts. Each relevant law will then be applied in either logical order or the order of importance to these facts.

Each relevant legal issue will have its own paragraph or set of paragraphs. Chapter Four, Small-scale Organization, provides guidance for structuring and organizing individual paragraphs. In the course of outlining at a smaller scale, you may discover holes in your analysis or fact pattern. Again, this process is iterative. You will discover what you know and do not know in the process of outlining at this smaller scale.

§ 1.6 FIFTH STEP: WRITE FIRST DRAFT

With your detailed outline, you are ready to begin writing your first draft. If this seems daunting, remember that this is merely the first draft. Just write it. Don't worry about getting everything perfect at this stage. Just start writing complete sentences, or even fragments of sentences, if necessary, to expand the outline into paragraphs. In later steps, you will edit, refine, and revise. At this stage, just get your thoughts on paper, so to speak.

The first principle for writing, both at this stage and for your final draft, is to write short sentences. You will save precious time if you develop a habit of writing short sentences. However, as we discuss in subsequent chapters on legal language and sentence design, those short sentences must also be precise. Helpful hints for shortening sentences are offered in Chapter Eight, Sentence Design. Chapter Five, Language in a Legal Setting, will help you select the most precise and readily understood words to populate your sentences. Chapter Six will guide your sentence structure and word choices for advisory writing. Chapter Seven will guide you for advocacy writing.

§ 1.7 SIXTH STEP: LET YOUR DRAFT REST, THEN REVISE

Your timeline should allow you to give your first draft a rest. Turn your attention to other tasks for at least a day, preferably longer. This allows you to take a fresh look at it later. Logical lapses will be easier to spot. Make a topical outline of your paragraphs to make sure that you are discussing the same topic in the same place.

Revision at this point will help you to say what you want to say, clearly, precisely, and effectively. Helpful practices at this secondary drafting stage are described in Chapters Two through Four and Chapters Five and Eight.

Your timeline will have included time to edit and proofread. Editing involves, first, a check for ease of comprehension. Can the reader understand what you have written on one reading? Is every thought clear? Is every statement of fact or law accurate? Is each word precise? If you find that you use too many long sentences, for example, you might select a typical 500-word sample of your final draft to do the Individual Writing Analysis in the Appendix. This will help you to identify and improve your writing habits. Guidance for editing, proofreading, punctuation, and grammar is offered in Chapters Nine and Ten.

After you have revised your draft, you will be ready for the final step.

§ 1.8 SEVENTH STEP: CHECK CITATIONS, QUOTATIONS, AND FORMAT

This last step is often done at the last minute, in a rush. Instead, your timeline should allow reasonable time for a careful final check of the accuracy and form of citation, for the accuracy of quotations, and for the appropriate format for your document. If you are working with format or style requirements, for example in formal briefs, you will make a final check to ensure that you have followed all of the rules. Chapter Ten will guide you through this final check.

This final step is about presentation. Presentation is the first thing the reader notices. As we all know, appearances matter. So does attention to details. After the arduous work of analysis and crafting your document, this last step ensures that your reader will begin reading with confidence that you know what you are writing about.

STEP 1

- Write your goal.
- Identify your audience.
- Know your deadlines.
- Construct your timeline.

➤ *See Chapter One.*

STEP 2

- Gather and analyze facts.
- Research and analyze law.
- Apply law to material facts.
- Reach preliminary conclusions.

➤ *See Chapter Two.*

STEP 3

- Order legal issues and sub-issues.
- Summarize material facts.
- Draft preliminary outline (large-scale level).

➤ *See Chapter Three.*

STEP 4

- Gather additional facts, as needed.
- Do additional legal research, as needed.
- Draft detailed outline (small-scale level).

➤ *See Chapter Four.*

STEP 5

- Write first draft.
- Let that draft rest.
- Revise for organization and analytical content.
- Draft and revise again, as needed.

➤ *See Chapters Three, Four, Six, Seven.*

STEP 6

- Edit revised draft for clarity, precision, conciseness, and effectiveness.

➤ *See Chapters Five, Eight, Nine, Ten.*

STEP 7

- Check citations, quotations, and document format.
- Proofread.
- Proofread a hard copy of your final draft.

➤ *See Chapter Ten.*

CHAPTER 2
LEGAL ANALYSIS

§ 2.1 INTRODUCTION

The legal writing process starts with legal analysis. Before you start writing, you must decide what legal issue or issues you need to analyze to solve a particular problem. Lawyers don't usually analyze the law in the abstract. More commonly, a lawyer must understand what legal remedies or defenses are available to address a client's case, how the law would answer a specific legal question given a particular factual situation, or how a change in the law might affect the rights and responsibilities of a client or a class of people.

When you're in law school or working as a summer intern or associate in a law firm, your supervising attorney may tell you what specific legal issue to analyze. But clients don't usually consult a lawyer for an answer about a particular legal issue. They consult a lawyer to solve a problem. The lawyer's job is to figure out the legal issue.

Three key components determine a legal issue. First, you must know the facts that relate to your client's problem and identify the key facts. Second, you must understand what jurisdiction has authority over your case. And third, you must know the substantive legal rights and responsibilities of the parties.

First, to understand what legal avenues will further your client's interests, you must consider a question of law in a specific factual context. A solid grasp of the objective factual circumstances is an essential first step to legal analysis. Writing, outlining, or even simply listing the facts will help you keep them in mind as you research the relevant law.

Second, you must identify the proper jurisdiction, given the facts in your case. The law is different in different jurisdictions. State law varies: California law differs from New Mexico law. The law even varies in different federal circuit court jurisdictions: the law of the First Circuit differs from the law of the Eleventh Circuit. Because the purpose of the first year of law school is to understand legal concepts, not to understand the law of any particular jurisdiction, you will read cases from all over the country. In Torts you might read cases from California, New Hampshire, and New York. In Civil Procedure you may read cases from the United States Supreme Court that apply to federal courts across the country, but you also will read cases from different circuit and district courts.

When you research a problem for a client, you must research the law of the particular jurisdiction or jurisdictions that will govern your facts.

More than one jurisdiction may have authority over your case. If a client comes to you because her apartment is infested with bedbugs, you must first determine which jurisdiction's law applies to the problem. Because landlord-tenant law is usually a question of state law, you would probably start by researching the law of the state where the apartment is located. If the client is renting an apartment with federal subsidies, federal statutes might affect the parties' rights and responsibilities. For some problems, you should also investigate whether county or city laws add to or modify the parties' rights.

Third, you must consider the substantive law, that is, the legal rights and responsibilities of the parties. In a litigation context, you will research causes of action (the legal theories that form the basis of a lawsuit) and defenses (the legal theories that a defendant in a civil or criminal suit can assert to avoid liability).

Lawyers learn a new area of the law by researching it. When you begin law school, open-ended legal research will be difficult because you will not yet have a basic understanding of the taxonomy of the law. With time and practice, however, you will be able to spot the legal issues in a factual situation with relative ease. For more about the legal research process, consult Cohen and Olson's *Legal Research in a Nutshell*.

The components that determine a legal issue are interdependent. As you research the law, you will need to revisit the facts, investigate for more information, and pinpoint the facts that are material to each legal issue. As you decide which courts have jurisdiction over your case, you will need to research the substantive law of those jurisdictions. The process of fact investigation and legal research is not linear; it is recursive. You will revisit the steps in the process multiple times until you have pinpointed the legal issue or issues you need to analyze.

After finding the law relevant to your legal issue, you must analyze the authorities that establish that law. Before we discuss how to make sense of the cases and statutes, an overview of the United States legal system will help you understand how to resolve conflicts between authorities.

§ 2.2 HIERARCHY OF AUTHORITIES AND CHANGING LAW

A. STARE DECISIS

Legal culture is conservative. Principles of legal analysis restrain the pace of evolution in the law. Our legal system grew out of the English Common Law in which the law was developed by judges deciding individual cases, not by legislatures writing statutes.

In our common law system, individual cases that are decided now will have a precedential effect on how future cases should be decided through the principle of stare decisis. Stare decisis is Latin for "to stand by that which has been decided." It means that like cases should be decided alike. The common law process thus prescribes that judges apply the law consistently with how it was applied in the past. Even though modern legal systems mix statutory law written by legislatures with case law written by judges, the principle of stare decisis still exerts a strong stabilizing force on the law.

Yet the law must change. Changes in technology or social situations may dictate a change in the law. Deciding whether or how the law should change may require courts to compare an old situation with a new situation to decide whether those situations should be treated the same way. That determination often turns on whether the two situations are materially similar or different.

In 2001 the Ninth Circuit was asked to decide whether an online system for downloading music was "fair use" of copyrighted material. The United States Supreme Court had previously decided that using a video recorder to tape a television show for later viewing was "fair use." The Ninth Circuit held that use of the online system was not fair use. The material difference, the court reasoned, was that music downloaded using Napster could be distributed to the general public. *A & M Records, Inc. v. Napster, Inc.*, 239 F.3d 1004, 1019 (9th Cir. 2001).

Sometimes a technological change creates ambiguity in the law where none existed before. The phrase "natural mother" had only one meaning before in vitro fertilization made it possible for one woman to be the genetic mother of a child and another woman to be pregnant with the child. After this technological advance, the California Supreme Court had to decide whether a child conceived using in vitro fertilization has two "natural mothers." *Johnson v. Calvert*, 5 Cal. 4th 84, 87 (1993).

Ambiguity can also arise with changes in our society and culture. In *Lawrence v. Texas,* 539 U.S. 558 (2003), the Supreme Court held unconstitutional a state law criminalizing gay sex, a mere seventeen years after ruling the opposite in *Bowers v. Hardwick,* 478 U.S. 186 (1986). The court held the statute violated the right to privacy because it sought "to control a personal relationship that, whether or not entitled to formal recognition in the law, is within the liberty of persons to choose without being punished as criminals." *Id.* at 567. The Court rejected its earlier position in *Bowers*, and cited "an emerging awareness that liberty gives substantial protection to adult persons in deciding how to conduct their private lives in matters pertaining to sex." *Id.* at 572.

These examples notwithstanding, staying the course is hard-wired into the law. Don't expect a court to agree to change course simply because change would further policy goals or provide the fair result in a given case. You must strategically identify opportunities for change, craft your arguments carefully, and target the right law-creating institutions to effectively argue that the law should be different. An about-face in the law like the one in *Lawrence v. Texas* is rare. As explained below, because a lower court is bound to follow the rulings of a hierarchically superior court, an argument to a lower court not to follow the decisions of a higher court rarely succeeds.

Moreover, although it is axiomatic that a court's job is to interpret statutes, many courts will defer to the legislature instead of deciding a case in a way that stretches a statute's plain language.

B. COURT SYSTEMS AND HIERARCHY OF AUTHORITIES

Of course, our government is much more complicated now than it was in Old England. The U.S. Constitution establishes three branches of government—the legislative, executive, and judicial—each of which plays a role in creating law. The legislature writes statutes, the courts interpret them, and the executive enforces them. But, as explained in **§ 2.3 below,** opinions written by judges and regulations written by executive agencies also have the force of law.

The relationship between the three branches of government is a system of checks and balances that works like the children's game of rock, paper, scissors. Which institution is more powerful than the other two depends on the circumstances. Although this shifting hierarchy is more complicated in practice, the general rules are:

- The legislature can pass statutes that overrule judge-made law, but it cannot overrule a court's finding that a statute is unconstitutional.
- A court can interpret a statute and decide how it should apply to a given situation, but a court can also strike down an unconstitutional statute.
- The executive branch enforces statutes. Administrative agencies are a part of the executive branch. An administrative agency can propound regulations to administer the statutes

the agency is charged with enforcing. Regulations must be consistent with the authorizing statute. If an agency authorized by a statute establishes regulations, the courts usually defer to that agency's interpretation of the statute.

Our federal system of government divides power between the federal government and the state government. The state's power traditionally included the "police power" to enact laws to promote the health and welfare of its people. This broad power is sometimes in tension with the federal government's power under the Supremacy Clause of Article IV of the Constitution, which provides that the federal Constitution and laws made pursuant to it "shall be the supreme Law of the Land."

If a state law conflicts with a federal law, the federal law may be said to "preempt" the state law, in which case the state law has no effect. *Maryland v. Louisiana,* 451 U.S. 725, 746 (1981). To decide whether the federal law preempts the state law, a court considers if the federal statute expressly preempts the state law, if the federal law regulates the field completely, and how much the state's law conflicts with the federal law.

C. STATE AND FEDERAL COURT SYSTEMS

There are at least fifty-one court systems in the United States, one for the Federal Government and one for each of the fifty states. There are also dozens of independent courts that resolve disputes under tribal laws, which will not be discussed here. Each court system has the same basic structure. The federal court system and most of the state systems have three levels of courts. The trial courts (called "district courts" in the federal system) are the first courts to hear a controversy. The losing side of a trial court decision can appeal to an intermediate court of appeal (called "circuit courts of appeals" in the federal system). The losing side at the intermediate court of appeal can petition the highest court in the system (called the "supreme court" in the federal system and many state systems) to review the case. In the federal system, that request is called a petition for "certiorari." Some states only have trial courts and a supreme court.

Twelve of the thirteen federal circuit courts are regional courts that cover particular states. The Court of Appeals for the Federal Circuit has jurisdiction to hear appeals in specialized cases such as those addressing patents or those decided by the U.S. Court of International Trade and the U.S. Court of Claims.

Federal and state trial courts decide both questions of fact and questions of law. If a fact is disputed between the parties, the court listens to both sides and decides what really happened. A trial court also decides questions of law. If the case is decided by a jury, the jury decides the questions of fact, and the judge decides questions of law. In our landlord-tenant example above, the jury would decide whether there were bedbugs in the apartment and whether the bedbugs were the fault of the landlord or the tenant. The judge, however, would decide whether the law of the state recognizes a warranty of habitability that would excuse the tenant's obligation to pay the rent.

An appeal of a lower court's decision is not a complete "re-do." The standard of review determines the amount of deference the appellate court will give the lower court when reviewing the lower court's decision. The court of appeals usually decides questions of law "de novo," as though it was hearing the case for the first time with no deference to the trial court's decision. But generally the court accords broad deference to findings of fact and will not disturb a trial court's decision unless the decision was clearly erroneous.

1. Mandatory Authority

Judges also do not have free reign to decide cases as they choose because they must follow "binding," or "mandatory," authority. Courts are constrained to follow the decisions of hierarchically superior courts. They are said to be "bound" by those decisions. Thus, using the federal system as an example, a district court is bound by the decisions of the circuit court in which it resides and by the U. S. Supreme Court. It is not bound by the decisions of other district courts, not even other district courts in its own circuit. A circuit court is bound by the decisions of the U.S. Supreme Court, but it is not bound by decisions of other circuit courts.

Somewhat counter-intuitively, a federal court is bound by a state court's interpretation of the state's own laws. As you will learn in your Civil Procedure class, at times a court may decide cases brought under the laws of another jurisdiction, but in those circumstances the court is bound by the decisions of that jurisdiction's laws. When a federal district court in San Francisco decides an issue of federal law—say, whether a landlord is liable under the Fair Housing Act for discriminating against a tenant because of her religion—the court is bound by the decisions of the Ninth Circuit and the U.S. Supreme Court. But in deciding whether the landlord is liable for the same behavior under California's Unruh Act, the federal district court is bound by the decisions of the California Supreme Court.

Similarly, a California trial court, called a "superior court," is bound by decisions of the California Courts of Appeal and the California Supreme Court on matters of state law. On matters of federal law, a California trial court is bound by decisions of the Ninth Circuit and the United States Supreme Court.

A court is only bound by the decision of a prior case if the facts are materially the same, even if the prior decision was issued by a hierarchically superior court. Thus, if the facts of the prior case are materially different than the facts of the case the court is deciding, the rule of law expressed in the prior case may not apply. See **§ 2.3** below for details.

2. Persuasive Authority

All law that is not binding, including non-binding judicial opinions and out-of-state statutes, is considered persuasive. Persuasive authority can help you to understand the law. It can be cited in a brief to a court, but, as explained in Chapter 7, you should use binding authority to explain the general rule of the law. Persuasive authority may be used to fill in the gaps when there is no binding authority on point. Persuasive authority may also be used to develop specific arguments. Although authority from outside of your jurisdiction might help you build an argument in your client's favor, a court's interpretation of another jurisdiction's statute will be more valuable if that statute is like your state's statute.

In many jurisdictions, opinions that are not published in case reporters are not binding precedent, even if they are authored by a hierarchically superior court. In California, for example, lawyers are not allowed to cite unpublished California cases in briefs. Federal circuit courts designate many opinions as "unpublished," or non-precedential. If written in 2007 or later, you may cite these opinions in briefs, but court rules may restrict citation of unpublished cases written before 2007. See Federal Rule of Appellate Procedure 32.1(a). You should investigate any restrictions on citing unpublished cases before you start your research.

Commentary on the law that is not the law itself, such as comments found in law review articles, legal encyclopedias, restatements of the law, treatises, and practice guides, is secondary authority. Secondary sources may be help you understand the law, but use caution when deciding whether to cite them in a brief. Some secondary sources are considered to be more authoritative, like a treatise or a restatement of the law. But most lawyers would not cite a legal encyclopedia in a brief. You should only cite secondary sources that have a good reputation for sound legal analysis and for being up to date. If you don't know the reputation of a source, ask a law librarian or a lawyer who practices in your jurisdiction.

§ 2.3 READING AND UNDERSTANDING LEGAL AUTHORITIES

Let's work with an example that illustrates how to understand the law from legal authorities. This example is used throughout this book, including the sample legal documents in Appendix A. Case citations in these documents are formatted according to the *Bluebook*'s style rules for practitioners. These citations also apply our "local rule" that requires citation for official reporters for California cases.

A sixteen-year old named Artie Abrams walks into your office seeking legal assistance. He is a pizza delivery driver in the small town of Scranton, California. About a year ago, he delivered a pizza to the Dunder-Mifflin paper company. When the manager of the company, Michael Scott, tried to pay for the pizza with a two-for-one coupon, Artie informed him that the coupon was not good for take-out pizza. Artie refused to hand the pizza over to the customer when he would not pay with cash for the pizza. Angered, Michael Scott had one of his employees escort Artie to a conference room where Artie was held for ten minutes.

Since this episode, Artie has not been able to return to work. He is afraid to be in confined spaces. He would like to know if he has a legal claim against Michael Scott.

To find out if he has a legal claim, you first gather relevant authorities in your jurisdiction. Then you read them carefully. As an advocate, lawyers read the law to understand not only what the law *is*, but what the law *might be*. Lawyers read cases, statutes and regulations to determine precisely how they constrain the courts and what avenues are open to argument. Reading and understanding the law requires law students to read carefully and attentively. A lawyer must understand more than the "gist" of an opinion to take full advantage of the analytic tools that expand the range of possible arguments.

Not all legal questions require exhaustive research and analysis. Sometimes a legal question can be answered by reading one case or one statute. If the facts are clear, the law is straightforward, and your case falls squarely within the rule of the law, the analytic process is uncomplicated. In our false imprisonment example, you will need to know what the statute of limitations is to make sure your client's claim can still be filed. You can find the statute of limitations with just a bit of research. In California, Code of Civil Procedure Section 340(c) states that "the period prescribed for the commencement of an action . . . for . . . false imprisonment . . . [is] within one year."

Analyzing the statute of limitations on Artie's claim is straightforward:

- Step One: The statute of limitations for false imprisonment in California is one year. (Rule)
- Step Two: Michael Scott held Artie in a conference room on October 11, 2016, less than one year from today. (Facts)
- Step Three: The statute of limitations has not run on Artie's claim for false imprisonment. (Conclusion)

The structure of this kind of logical reasoning is syllogistic and deductive, in which a conclusion is drawn from two premises. The first premise is a general abstract statement of the law. Lawyers often call this the "rule." "Rule" is a catch-all phrase for all of the law relevant to a particular piece of analysis. Sometimes the rule can be stated in a single sentence, as in this example. Sometimes the rule has multiple parts, contains both substantive and procedural aspects of the law, and can take pages to explain. If the cause of action or defense that you're analyzing comes from a statute, the statute is probably the place to start explaining the law. You may then bring in case law to explain how courts interpret the language of the statute.

The second premise is not abstract; it states the specific facts of your case. In the statute of limitations example, the facts fit so neatly to the statutory rule that the material facts—the facts that determine the outcome of the legal issue—can be stated in one sentence. As you see below, however, in complicated cases you may need to say a lot about the facts of your case. You may need to compare and contrast them to the facts of precedent cases to assess how the law would apply in your case.

Deductive reasoning is sometimes referred to as top-down reasoning because it starts with a general rule and then draws a conclusion using the specific facts of a case. In law, this deductive analytic structure is referred to by the commonly-used acronyms "IRAC" and "CRAC." As discussed in more detail in the next chapters, IRAC stands for Issue-Rule-Application-Conclusion and CRAC stands for Conclusion-Rule-Application-Conclusion. In this text, we generally recommend the CRAC paradigm, which tells your reader the legal conclusion that you reach first, before setting out the rule and the facts.

Legal readers typically expect an analysis of the law to proceed deductively, but lawyers often reason inductively. Inductive reasoning draws a general rule from specific cases. If the rule is not clearly stated in a case or a statute, you may be able to glean a principle of law inductively by inferring from multiple cases a rule that is difficult to see from just one case. Some judicial opinions are written inductively. Instead of leading with the general principle of law (the rule), the courts reason by explaining individual cases and then telling the rule that it infers from the cases at the end.

Yet even if you arrive at the rule inductively, most legal readers will find it easier to understand how the rule of law functions if you tell the general rule first, and then use the specific cases to explain the rule. One law professor describes this process as a rule proof. First state the rule that you derive from the cases, and then use the cases to prove that the rule is correct. See references by Richard K. Neumann, Jr., and Kristen Konrad Tiscione in Appendix D, Selected References.

In our statute of limitations example, you could understand the legal rule in just one step. You must take multiple steps to understand the rule for more complicated legal problems. Start by reading each piece of authority carefully to determine what that authority tells you about the law. When multiple authorities bear on a legal issue, a single case or statute may not give you a full picture of the law. Thus, you may need to figure out what multiple authorities tell you about the law. You must first read each relevant authority—statute, case, or regulation—carefully to determine what that authority tells you about the law. Then you must synthesize the legal authorities you have found into a single statement of the governing law.

Try out different techniques to help you synthesize multiple legal authorities. Some lawyers use outlines, while others use charts or diagrams or sketches on a white board, to help them figure out how the authorities fit together in a particular area of law. Don't forget that secondary authorities, like hornbooks and treatises, may also guide you.

A. UNDERSTANDING STATUTES

Our various legislatures have enacted statutes at different points in time. Some statutes were written decades—even centuries—ago. After a state statute is enacted, it is published in the topical compilation for that state, typically called a "code." The United States Code is the compilation of statutes passed by the United States Congress.

Because codes are compiled from statutes written at different points in time, they can be difficult to read. If you do an internet search of the California Code of Civil Procedure 340(c), for example, you will see that the tidy statutory language quoted in subsection (c) is a paraphrase of the original language, enacted in 1872, because it was complicated and difficult to parse.

Consider downloading a complicated statute before you try to analyze it, then formatting it to make the chapters and sections of the statute more obvious. As you read the statute, highlight its different components. Strike through sections or paragraphs that are not relevant to your analysis. Annotate relevant components in track changes, putting the statutory language in your own words. This will help you to thoroughly understand the statute, an essential step in legal analysis.

1. Identify What the Statute Does

Once you have identified the individual provisions that deal with the legal issue you're analyzing, analyze the statutory language to figure out how it works.

- What groups of people are affected by the statute?
- What does the statute require?
- What are the consequences if someone violates the statute?
- Does the statute identify elements or factors of a legal claim or defense?

Determine how the statute applies to your case. In particular, note the statute's effective date, any jurisdictional requirements, and any exceptions to how the statute should apply.

2. Read the Statute in Context

Even when you have identified a statute that is on point for the issue you are analyzing, read it in the larger statutory context. Review the code's Table of Contents to see how the statutory provision you are analyzing fits into the whole. In particular, skim the sections before and after the provision to identify any exceptions.

You must also read the following components if they are contained in the pertinent part of the code:

- The chapter titles of the entire act;
- All definitions, which often appear at the beginning of the act;
- A statement of purpose;

- The penalties for violating the statute and remedies for someone who was hurt by a violation, which often appear at the end of the act;
- The language of other cross-referenced provisions;
- The dates the statute was enacted and revised. Revision dates are important because a more recent version of the statute, or a different statute covering the same issue, will control over a prior version of the statute and over judicial interpretations of the statute.

3. Use Interpretive Aids to Construe the Statute

Most lawyers agree that if the language of the statute is clear and its application makes logical sense, then the language of the statute should govern. But if the language is ambiguous or its application in a new situation doesn't make sense, then lawyers use one of two philosophical approaches to statutory interpretation.

The first approach is to follow the plain meaning of the statute's words, even if the result would conflict with what the legislature would have intended. The second approach is to discern the legislature's intent and interpret the statute consistently with that intent. There are problems with both approaches.

On one hand, the English language is so inherently ambiguous that discerning a statute's plain meaning is often difficult. Even when the legislature tries to be clear, the meaning of words changes with time. New social situations create ambiguity where none existed before. The legislature may write a statute to cover one type of situation, but other situations will arise that the legislature did not consider. Sometimes, if statutory language is a compromise, the legislature deliberately adopts vague language, expecting that a court will clarify it later.

On the other hand, using legislative intent as an interpretive device is also problematic. There may be dozens of legislators who sign onto a piece of legislation who have many conflicting intents. In addition, interpreting the law in light of the legislature's intent may not give people fair warning of how their behavior may be treated by the law.

You should use both approaches to complete an analysis of your issue. Even if you agree with one side in this debate, you are obligated to explore all avenues of interpretation for your client.

a. Where to Find the "Plain Meaning" of a Statute

To find a statute's plain meaning, look first at the provisions of the statute that relate most directly to your legal issue. Then, read the definitions to see if the legislature defined a term that applies to your analysis. Read the statute to see how terms in the provision you are analyzing are used in other parts of the same statutory scheme.

Also look to sources outside of the statute. Research cases to see how courts have applied the statute, looking particularly at how courts have interpreted the statute's words and phrases. Read dictionaries, including legal dictionaries like Black's Law Dictionary and Burton's Law Dictionary, as well as general-use dictionaries like Merriam-Webster's. And last, consider your own common-sense intuition about what the statute means.

b. *Where to Find the Legislature's Intent*

You can look to legislative histories to find the intent of Congress. Each state legislature compiles its legislative history, which you can generally find in conjunction with its statutory code. Read committee reports, see how bills are amended, and consider members' statements in the Congressional Record, which you can find in U.S.C.C.A.N.

Also research the statutory history. The legislature may amend a statute if a majority of legislators concludes that the courts are on the wrong track.

c. *Canons of Construction*

Canons of construction are a set of maxims commonly used by courts to aid statutory interpretation. Here are several of the most common canons.

- *Ejusdem generis* literally means "of the same kind." The canon is used to mean that if a general phrase (*e.g.*, "and other animals") follows a list of specific things ("horses, goats, chickens, and cows"), the general phrase should be limited to the class to which the specific things belong (farm animals).

- *Expressio unius est exclusion alterius* means that expressly including some things in a list excludes all things not listed.
- Statutes in *pari materia* (on same subject) should be interpreted together.
- The *rule of lenity* holds that ambiguous penal statutes should be strictly construed in favor of the defendant.
- Remedial statutes should be liberally construed to achieve their purposes.

B. UNDERSTANDING CASES

A court's opinion can tell you what the law was in its jurisdiction at the point in time the opinion was decided. Think of a judicial opinion as a toolbox to construct your understanding of the law and how it should be applied to a future case. If the opinion is published and has not been overturned by a higher court or a later case or superceded by statute, a subordinate court is bound to follow the holding of the case.

To understand the reach of the holding, read cases actively and creatively. The "law" isn't an objective, immutable truth that looks the same to everyone. Lawyers thus exert influence in the legal system when we read and interpret a case. Together with the courts, we construct the law. Most of the law that we find in judicial opinions started as a legal argument in a party's brief.

Important constraints limit how lawyers interpret cases, but we often have room to maneuver on behalf of our clients. To help you discover the reach of a case, you might read for the positive (what does this case say?), in addition to the negative (what doesn't this case say?).

You may read and brief cases differently for your doctrinal classes than you do in your legal writing course or in practice. Cases in casebooks have been edited to focus on particular issues, but the cases that you will research on your own are not. Cases often address multiple issues, and only some of them may be relevant to your client's matter. You might skim the opinion first to see what parts are relevant to the legal issue that you are analyzing. Be careful, however, because sometimes opinions are not well organized. Information relevant to your issue may be located in a place in the opinion that you might not expect. In legal writing, as in law practice, you must almost always read a case specifically to understand how the rule from the case will affect your client.

Print out any case you need to analyze. Write on your copy of the case. Use highlighters to highlight the different components of the case in different colors: for example, the material facts in yellow, the rules that explain the law in pink, the holding in blue, and dicta in orange.

Write out your understanding of the law in your own words. Take care, however, to incorporate the key words and phrases that the courts use to explain the law. These key phrases have precise legal meanings. Lawyers expect to see these exact phrases used to describe the law.

If you are reading the opinion to prepare a written analysis, take notes to save yourself time when you begin to write. Note the exact page where key ideas appear in the opinion so you can cite the case properly when you draft and edit your document. Quote key phrases and particularly pithy sentences that you might want to quote. Even in your notes, take care to use quotation marks to avoid inadvertently failing to acknowledge the source in your final document.

The formal case brief is a classic tool for analyzing judicial opinions. Your teachers or supervising attorneys may require you to write briefs for particular assignments. You also may find it helpful to prepare a formal case brief for cases that govern an issue you are researching. Regardless of your purpose, writing a case brief assures that you have thoroughly deconstructed and studied a particular case. See Appendix A for a summary of the components of a formal case brief and for an example of a formal case brief.

Law students and lawyers also use shorter, informal variations on the classic case brief. Highlighting and annotating opinions in casebooks—so-called "book briefing"—readily translates to judicial opinions printed out on a hard copy or in an electronic format. Some legal readers compile annotated case lists that organize short squibs of pertinent cases. Distilling key information, case squibs may include material facts, specific holdings, and the most important aspects of the courts' reasoning. An annotated case list may be particularly useful when your assignment requires wrangling a large number of cases.

C. HOW TO READ A CASE

The following components are the key tools in the case toolbox. Analyze the case rigorously by separating the following components.

Read the opinion *Wilson v. Houston Funeral Home* in Appendix A before reading this section. It is binding precedent in Artie's case. We will refer to the case as *"Houston Funeral Home"* since *"Wilson"* is a common name and may lead to ambiguity.

1. Statement of Facts

Each judicial opinion explains how the law is applied to a controversy, but it also tells the story of what happened between the parties. The statement of facts doesn't tell you everything that happened to the parties. The advocates and judge distill the facts to the ones they believe are material to the outcome of the case.

Consider the real-life impact of the ruling and opinion on the parties—the subjects of the opinion. How does the law function to regulate their relationship? Does the outcome make common sense for the parties? Does it make sense for others in future cases who may be affected by the court's decision?

Identify the facts that are material to the court's decision. One way to identify a material fact is to ask whether the court's decision would be different if that fact were changed. In *Houston Funeral Home*, would the court have ruled in favor of the plaintiff if the funeral home director had threatened not to take Ms. Wilson and her daughter to a birthday party if they did not pay him?

2. Procedural Posture and Standards of Review

The procedural posture and the standard of review of the case explain the "lens" through which the court reviews the facts and the law.

In deciding a motion to dismiss for failure to state a claim, for example, a court will not decide what facts are true. It will assume that the facts in the complaint are true (unless, under the federal standard, the facts as pleaded are not plausible.) But if your case has reached a later stage of litigation, the plaintiff may not be entitled to such a favorable standard. The court will grant a motion for summary judgment, for example, to the party that demonstrates it is entitled to judgment as a matter of law because there is no dispute of material fact.

In *Houston Funeral Home,* the court was deciding a demurrer—California's analogue to a motion to dismiss for failure to state a claim. The court articulated the standard of review clearly: "we accept as true the properly pled factual allegations of the complaint." Therefore, the court did not decide if the Wilsons win their case against Houston Funeral Home. It only decided that a jury could reasonably find the Wilsons were falsely imprisoned. Consequently, the court allowed the case to proceed to the next step in litigation.

3. Legal Test

a. Identify the Legal Test That the Court Uses to Decide the Case

Sometimes a court makes this easy. In *Houston Funeral Home,* the court defines false imprisonment twice. The court first quotes the penal code definition of the crime of false imprisonment. Then it quotes a California Supreme Court case that defines the tort of false imprisonment as "[a]ny exercise of force, or express or implied threat of force, by which in fact the other person is deprived of his liberty or is compelled to remain where he does not wish to remain, or go where he does not wish to go."

Most of the legal test is explicit and can be extracted from the first paragraph of the false imprisonment discussion in which the court articulates the legal test. But other parts of the test are more implicit. The court stated, "[e]ven if Willie Houston believed in good faith he was entitled to plaintiff's $5,000 check, the provocation, motive and good faith of the defendant are irrelevant to pleading a cause of action for false imprisonment." Even though this part of the rule was not included in the definition of false imprisonment in the first paragraph of the discussion, you would be right to conclude that the good faith of the defendant is not an excuse for false imprisonment.

The court also stated that "a reasonable jury could also find a period of forty-five minutes to an hour was sufficiently long to constitute false imprisonment." From this statement you may also properly deduce that the length of time a plaintiff is confined is a factor in deciding whether a false imprisonment has occurred.

Sometimes a legal test is so implicit in the law that you cannot be sure that it is a part of the rule from just one case. In such instances, you may see a sufficiently strong pattern from a series of cases that you may be justified to infer a rule from the pattern.

Indeed, one opinion rarely tells all of the law that you need to understand a legal test. You often must synthesize a test or rule from a series of opinions. See **§ 2.3(D) below** for more about how to understand the law from multiple authorities.

b. Typical Structure of Legal Tests

The legal test is the overarching test for a cause of action or a defense as a whole. Legal tests come in typical structures. Familiarity with these structures may help you identify different legal tests.

- *Elements Tests.* In an elements test, more than one enumerated component must each be met to satisfy the test. For example, at common law, the elements of burglary were (1) breaking and (2) entering (3) a dwelling unit (4) at night (5) with the intent to commit (6) a felony. A person could not be convicted of burglary unless the prosecutor satisfied each of these six elements.

- *Factors Tests.* A factors test is a test where a court considers a number of factors, none of which is controlling on its own. Whether a use of a copyrighted work is fair use is determined by a factors test. A court considers (1) the purpose and character of the use, (2) the nature of the copyrighted work, (3) the amount of the work used, and (4) the effect of the use on the market.
- *Totality of the Circumstances Tests.* A totality of the circumstances test is also a balancing test, but the court considers all of the circumstances of the context of the case, not just specific factors. Whether a juvenile's confession is voluntary is determined by a totality of the circumstances test. A court will consider all circumstances, including, but not limited to, the juvenile's age, educational background, and mental status, as well as the entire context of the interrogation, before deciding if a confession is voluntary.
- *Threshold Tests.* A threshold test is a test that must be satisfied before considering a substantive claim. For example, institutions that are not "places of public accommodation" are not required to abide by the ADA. Thus, before reaching the substantive question of whether a business has violated the Americans with Disabilities Act by failing to make a website accessible to a blind person using a screen reader, you must first analyze the threshold question of whether the website is a "place of public accommodation" within the meaning of the Americans with Disabilities Act.

These are the most common kinds of tests. You might create a flow chart or graphic depiction of the language of a statute or opinion to understand the structure of a legal test.

4. The Holding

Stare decisis dictates that courts are bound by the holding of a case. They are not bound by dicta or by a court's speculation about what it would do in a hypothetical case.

If the legal issue raises a pure question of law, the holding simply tells the answer to that question. For example, the holding of the gay marriage cases is that gays and lesbians have a fundamental right to marry under the Equal Protection and Due Process clauses of the Fourteenth Amendment. *Obergefell v. Hodges*, 135 S. Ct. 2584 (2015).

If the legal issue is not a pure question of law, the holding is the court's decision about that specific legal issue applied to the facts of the case. It includes two of the three components that are essential to stating a legal question: the precise question of law and the material facts of the case.

There may be more than one holding related to the same issue in a case. A narrow holding characterizes the facts specifically so that fewer future cases would be bound by the holding. A broad holding characterizes the facts generally so that more future cases would be bound by the holding. One holding of *Wilson v. Houston Funeral Home* is:

> Plaintiffs stated a claim for false imprisonment when defendant funeral home director held them for

> 45 minutes and threatened not to bury their loved one until they paid him.

But this is a narrow holding, which could be viewed as only applying to this case. The following holding is broader:

> Plaintiffs stated a claim for false imprisonment when the defendant held them for a period of time and threatened not to perform professional services he had promised until they paid him.

This last formulation is broader than the first—broad enough that Artie's case seems nearly analogous. Arguably, however, this holding is so broad that it no longer captures the court's reasoning that the plaintiffs were compelled to remain in the bank because "to do so would have been to abandon the remains of their loved one to an uncertain fate."

5. Dicta

Dicta are a judge's comments or explanations that were not required to reach a decision on the case before the court. "Dicta," the plural of "dictum," comes from Latin meaning "a remark made in passing." A judge's statement of how the court would decide a hypothetical case not before the court is dictum. It would be dictum if the court in the *Houston Funeral Home* case had speculated that the plaintiffs would have had no claim if the funeral director had asked them for payment at the burial site. Courts are not bound by dicta, but they can be predictive of how the court would rule in the future.

D. ANALYZING MULTIPLE AUTHORITIES

One authority alone rarely tells a full picture of the law. Lawyers must read multiple authorities together. Sometimes the authorities seem inconsistent. First try to reconcile the authorities, but if you can't, remember the hierarchy of authorities discussed in § 2.2. The hierarchy will help you decide which authority prevails if they conflict.

1. Reason in "Layers"

The ultimate legal question you are analyzing may have multiple independent issues. If, for example, you must analyze whether Artie could maintain a lawsuit against Dunder Mifflin, you would have to analyze whether Dunder Mifflin is liable for the actions of its employee, Michael Scott; whether an action for false imprisonment is viable; and whether other possible causes of action are viable. You also would have to analyze the statute of limitations for each cause of action and Artie's damages under each claim. Because these are all separate legal issues, you would address each one separately.

2. Identify Core Substantive Rule and Ancillary Rules

Some legal rules you extract from a case are the core rules that define the substance of the legal test or explain the meaning of the words in that test. Others are more ancillary rules that explain how the law should be applied. For example, an ancillary rule is that the court should decide the legal issue from an "objective" perspective considering what a reasonable person would think of a situation. Still others are procedural rules, such as the essential standard of review and burdens of proof. You need all these rules to understand how the law should be applied.

§ 2.4 APPLYING LEGAL RULES TO A FACTUAL SITUATION

Once you understand the analytical structure of the legal test, you can analyze whether the facts of your case prove or disprove the elements of your test. First consider whether you should address each component of your legal test one at a time, or if you should address them together. If the components of the legal test are separate elements or factors, you typically should analyze each one separately.

Within each element or factor, identify the abstract rules that describe the law and the facts in the precedent cases that are material to the courts' decisions.

Next, ask what is the legal conclusion that a court must reach to find that element is satisfied? For example, to find that a plaintiff has a valid false imprisonment case, the plaintiff must demonstrate that he was subject to "unreasonable duress" that deprived him of the liberty to leave.

Also, identify how the legal conclusion was reached in the precedent cases by identifying the key facts that support the legal conclusion. For example, in the *Houston Funeral Home* case, the plaintiffs were not physically held at the bank, but they were compelled to stay by Houston's threat not to bury their loved one.

After you identify the precedents' key facts, compare the facts of your case to those in the precedents. Are your facts analogous to the key facts of the precedent cases, or are they distinguishable? Will it be easier to reach the same legal conclusion or more difficult?

Compare Artie's facts to the facts in *Houston Funeral Home* to determine if the duress Artie was subject to was unreasonable. On one hand, Artie was not subject to the same kind or degree of duress as the plaintiffs in *Houston*. The plaintiffs in *Houston* were in an emotionally fragile state, having just lost a husband and father, when they were confronted with the funeral director's threats that the deceased would not receive a proper burial. It is easy to imagine that a jury would conclude that this duress was "unreasonable." On the other hand, even though Artie was under less emotional duress, he is only sixteen years old. It takes less duress to overcome a minor's will. In addition, Artie was escorted to a small room where a big man was posted outside of the door with his arms folded. This display of authority may have been sufficient to compel a reasonable person in Artie's position to stay in the room. Thus, by such deductive reasoning, you can conclude that a jury could reasonably find that Artie's case satisfies the "unreasonable duress" element of false imprisonment.

§ 2.5 REACHING A CONCLUSION

After you have identified the appropriate jurisdiction, the governing law of a specific legal issue, the material facts of the precedent cases, and the corresponding facts of your case, you will be ready to reach a legal conclusion. Your conclusion is an application of the governing law to the key facts. The governing law may come from case law, a statute, a regulation, a binding contract, an ordinance, a constitution, or a treaty. When the governing law is applied to the key facts, you will have a legal conclusion to a specific legal issue.

If you have more than one issue in the case or problem you are addressing, you will need to decide the logical relationship of those issues. Committing your analysis to an outline may help ensure that your analysis is correct and comprehensive. Once you know the legal conclusion or conclusions to your issues, you are ready for large-scale organization of your legal document.

You have now finished with Steps One and Two. You are ready for Step Three in which you will order your legal issues and sub-issues and draft a preliminary outline.

STEP 2

- Gather and analyze facts.
- Research and analyze law.
- Apply law to material facts.
- Reach preliminary conclusions.

➤ ***Next Step, Chapter Three.***

CHAPTER 3

LARGE-SCALE ORGANIZATION

§ 3.1 INTRODUCTION

Legal writers must organize everything we write on several levels. Smaller units of writing serve as building blocks for larger units. Words must be arranged in sentences. Sentences must be arranged within paragraphs. Paragraphs must be arranged in paragraph blocks to present larger units of thought. In longer documents, paragraph blocks and other individual paragraphs must be arranged within sections that are then combined and ordered to produce the complete document. We impose structure at each level to reflect relationships between different parts of the whole and to communicate more effectively with our readers.

We discuss large-scale organization and outlining in this chapter. In Chapter Four, we address small-scale organization, including paragraphs, paragraph blocks, and transitions. We also return to the subject of outlining.

§ 3.2 ORGANIZING ADVISORY AND ADVOCACY WRITING

Both advisory and advocacy writing consist of basic ingredients: facts, issues, authorities, rules, rationales, applications, and conclusions. These ingredients shape the large-scale organization for most legal documents by determining their major sections. These sections typically follow the traditional rhetorical pattern: introduce what will be said, say it, and then summarize what was said.

For example, objective memoranda typically include these major sections: Question Presented, Brief Answer, Statement of Facts, and Discussion. See our Sample Research Memorandum in Appendix A. Longer memoranda may add an Introduction or a separate Conclusion. The substance of these sections is discussed in Chapter Six. This large-scale structure may vary, so be sure to follow the one used at your law school or law office.

Briefs follow a similar pattern: Introduction, Statement of Facts, Argument, and Conclusion. See our sample brief in Appendix A, which is styled as a Memorandum of Points and Authorities. The substance of these components will be discussed in Chapter Seven. Again, the content of briefs may vary in your law school. Moreover, in practice, you must also check any applicable court rules when you prepare a brief, a memorandum of points and authorities, or any other document that you submit to a court.

Note that both our sample memorandum and brief introduce each major section with a heading. Headings tell your reader how you have organized a document, helping her stay on the right track. Headings signal that you are changing topics. Headings also make the document easier for your reader to use.

Our advice for organizing the core analytical sections of a memorandum or a brief follows below.

§ 3.3 ORGANIZING A DISCUSSION OR ARGUMENT SECTION

A. USE AN EFFECTIVE STRUCTURE

The heart of an objective memorandum is its Discussion; the heart of a persuasive brief is its Argument. The discussion and argument sections analyze and argue the issues, the relevant law, and how that law applies to the facts to reach or support specific conclusions. You must choose an effective large-scale structure for these critical sections. You also must communicate this structure to your reader.

Within the Discussion or Argument, legal issues and sub-issues will typically suggest a logical structure. We recommend that you use legal issues as large-scale organizing principles rather than cases or other individual authorities. Organizing case-by-case is usually not effective because that structure makes your reader work harder to understand how the pieces of your analysis or argument fit together.

Your next steps are to choose the appropriate order for these issues and to communicate that structure to your reader. Sub-sections (B) and (C) below contain some advice that can help you take those steps. Our examples assume that you are writing an objective memorandum. But if your goal is to advocate rather than to advise, you may opt to alter these patterns for rhetorical effect. (See also Chapter Seven on Advocacy Writing.)

B. CHOOSE A LOGICAL ORDER

1. Legal Rules or Tests

Ordering legal issues, or sub-issues, by following the structure of the pertinent legal rule or test can provide a logical analytical framework for a Discussion. Our sample research memorandum in Appendix A applies this principle.

Sarah Student is tasked with analyzing whether her client, Artie Abrams, can state a claim for false imprisonment. To do so, she must analyze how the legal test used by the California courts would apply to the facts in Artie's case. That test has four elements: intent, involuntary confinement, length of time, and lawful privilege. Each element raises a corresponding sub-issue that Student must analyze. Student addresses those sub-issues in the order stated in the test, creating a logical structure for the Discussion.

Student communicates this structure to her supervising attorney by beginning the Discussion with a clear roadmap of where her analysis will go. In the Discussion's first paragraph, she states the four-part test (noted with bracketed numbers):

> To determine whether one can make a claim for false imprisonment, courts consider [1] the intent of the defendant, [2] whether the defendant exerted such unreasonable duress as to involuntarily confine the plaintiff, [3] the length of confinement, and [4]

> whether any lawful privilege might excuse the defendant of false imprisonment.

In the second paragraph, Student states her broad conclusion, referring to each element of the test (see the italicized language below) in the same order.

> Artie can likely state a claim for false imprisonment against Michael Scott. A jury would have reason to find that Scott *intended* to *involuntarily confine* Artie for an appreciable *length of time* and that no *lawful privilege* applies in these circumstances.

These two paragraphs are sometimes referred to as "umbrella" paragraphs because they provide a structural cover for the entire discussion section.

Sarah Student divides the rest of the Discussion into sub-sections A through D, tracking the four-part structure that she set up in the umbrella paragraphs. Each sub-section begins with a sub-heading that further reinforces the Discussion's large-scale organization.

2. Interdependent Issues

Sometimes whether or how you must analyze an issue will depend on the answer to another issue. Discussing the issues separately usually makes their interrelationship easier for your reader to understand and will avoid awkward cross-referencing. Here's an example.

> Our client, Sam Seller, sold an office building to Beth Buyer that was destroyed in a fire two weeks after the sale closed. Buyer alleges that shortly before the

sale closed, our client promised to transfer the building's fire insurance policy for Buyer's benefit.

Issue: Can Seller be liable to Beth Buyer for failing to keep his alleged promise to transfer the fire insurance?

This ultimate issue raises interrelated issues of fact and law. The answer to each issue affects the next issue, suggesting the following logical order:

1. Did Seller promise Buyer to transfer the insurance policy? (issue of fact)

2. If Seller promised to transfer the insurance policy, was that promise sufficiently definite to be enforced? (issue of law)

3. If the promise was definite enough to be enforced, would the parole evidence rule allow a court to admit oral evidence of the promise? (issue of law)

Introduce this order to your reader at the beginning of the Discussion and then reinforce it with sub-sections and sub-headings.

3. Chronological Order

If the issues are related to a chronology of events, you may want to discuss them in that order.

Return to the fire insurance example. Assume that Beth Buyer also claims that several months before the closing, our client, Sam Seller made misrepresentations about the building's sprinkler system and that those misrepresentations induced Buyer to sign the contract to buy the building. Seller's misrepresentations could be the basis for a tort claim for fraud.

In addition to separating the issues according to the possible tort and contract claims against our client, addressing the tort claim first would also be logical because that structure would reflect the chronology of events.

> Tort Claim
>
> Did Seller make material misrepresentations regarding the building's sprinkler system that induced Buyer to agree to purchase the building?
>
> Contract Claim
>
> 1. Did Seller promise Buyer to transfer the insurance policy? (issue of fact)
>
> 2. If Seller promised to transfer the insurance policy, was that promise sufficiently definite to be enforced? (issue of law)
>
> 3. If the promise was definite enough to be enforced, would the parole evidence rule allow a court to admit oral evidence of the promise? (issue of law)

Don't forget to give your reader a roadmap at the beginning of the Discussion and to reinforce that map with sub-sections and sub-headings.

C. OTHER CONSIDERATIONS

Our system of federalism may affect large-scale organization. We generally discuss federal and state law issues separately and federal issues first. But federal and state law issues may be intertwined in ways that will lead you to make a different choice.

Our system is hierarchical, so generally constitutional provisions and statutes control over case law. Starting your analysis or argument with the controlling law may be a logical organizing principle in a memorandum or a persuasive one in a brief. But again, depending on your subject matter, you may choose a different order.

For example, whether a state statute raises a state or federal constitutional question may depend on how the statute is interpreted. In that situation, analyzing the statute first may be the best choice. Similarly, courts may prefer to decide a case on statutory or common law grounds if that resolution will make deciding a constitutional issue unnecessary (or "moot").

In a brief, you should choose the most persuasive order. We typically try to frontload our best arguments. For more about the order of arguments, see Chapter Seven.

A senior attorney, or a judge, may ask you to limit your analysis, or argument, to particular issues or to address issues in a particular order. We recommend that you follow the requested order unless you have a good reason not to. If you think the law requires additional analysis or a different order and the request is from a senior attorney, you might discuss your analysis with her before you proceed. If the request comes from a judge, strategies for persuasion may suggest additional argument or a different order, leaving you with a tricky choice to make. (See Chapter Seven.)

§ 3.4 ORGANIZING INDIVIDUAL ISSUES AND SUB-ISSUES

Legal readers expect legal analysis or argument to follow certain patterns. Legal readers are smart, but they are busy and often must read quickly. They must have enough information to exercise an independent judgment about whether your conclusion is sound. Following expected analytical patterns helps a legal reader know where she is going and keeps her on track. Knowing where a Discussion or Argument is going also helps your busy reader absorb and scrutinize your analysis or argument after reading it once.

For issues that require applying law to facts, the expected pattern begins with either a statement of the legal issue or conclusion, followed by a summary of the pertinent legal rule and by an analysis of how that rule applies to the facts. The pattern ends with a short legal conclusion. The basic pattern is sometimes referred to as IRAC (issue-rule-application-conclusion) or CRAC (conclusion-rule-application-conclusion). If you follow the CRAC paradigm, your organization will be syllogistic in which you "prove" your conclusion from major premises (the rules) and minor premises (the facts).

The opening issue or conclusion and the closing conclusion usually are comprised of a sentence or short paragraph. Traditionally, the IRAC paradigm was used in advisory writing, and the CRAC paradigm was used in advocacy writing. Now lawyers are more likely to also begin with their conclusion in advisory writing, so we generally refer to the CRAC paradigm in this book.

The rule section of the paradigm can be several sentences, several paragraphs, or several pages, depending on the law's complexity. You may extract or synthesize the law from primary legal authorities, likes statutes, cases, or regulations, and, in some instances, from secondary authorities, like treatises. The rule section may include statements, explanations, and illustrations of rules and legal principles. The rules and principles must be supported with citations to legal authorities. The application section includes your analysis of how the law applies to your matter or case and will take into account the arguments for all the parties to the dispute. Your analysis or argument will typically end with a brief conclusion.

Some legal writing teachers don't use the terms IRAC or CRAC to refer to the expected patterns in legal writing. But we do agree that, more often than not, legal readers expect you to begin an analysis or argument with a conclusion and to explain the law before you analyze or argue how that law applies.

You may choose to vary the basic paradigms depending on the complexity of your analysis or argument. For example, a rule may have several sub-parts each of which requires a paragraph or more to explain. In that situation, you might elect to introduce the rule, including its sub-parts, and then develop and apply each sub-part. This CRAC variation might be abbreviated as: CR-RA-RA-RA-C. Moreover, different structural approaches may work for the same writing project. Whichever structure you choose, reinforce it with paragraph structure and transitions which we will discuss in more detail in Chapter Four.

§ 3.5 OUTLINING

We strongly recommend that you master the skills of outlining. These skills will help you draft different types of outlines during the writing process that can help you organize effectively at the large and small-scale levels.

A preliminary outline is a particularly useful tool for developing a document's large-scale structure and organizing its analysis. We typically draft a preliminary outline during the research process, as we begin to identify and refine the issues. For example, Sarah Student might have written this preliminary outline after researching her client's possible false imprisonment claim. In addition to her memorandum's major sections, this outline lays out the Discussion's analytical framework and sub-sections.

Question presented

Brief answer

Statement of facts

Discussion

Umbrella section stating broadest rules for false imprisonment and my conclusion

1. Defendant's intent

2. Involuntary confinement

3. Length of time

4. Privilege

Writing is often described as thinking on paper. Thinking about our analysis or argument leads us to redraft and revise. That process can lead us to a clearer view of what we want to say and how we want to say it. That clarity ultimately can lead to effective drafting.

Here's a more developed version of the umbrella and intent sections of Student's preliminary outline. The umbrella section now states the broadest rules that will guide the analysis and notes supporting authorities. Each reference to a case also includes the page of the case supporting that part of the rule. Similarly, the intent section has been expanded to sketch out the rule and application components of the CRAC paradigm.

Umbrella

Definition of false imprisonment. *Fermino* @715, Cal. Penal Code § 236

Four elements of false imprisonment. *Fermino* @715

Confinement's lawfulness generally is question of fact. *Fermino* @723 n. 8

1. Defendant's intent

   a. Rule

      i. Plaintiff must show defendant intended to confine. *Fermino* @715

      ii. Plaintiff doesn't need to show defendant intended to harm. *Id.*

      iii. *Fermino* illustration, employer summoned plaintiff-employee to windowless room. *Id.*

      iv. Defendant's belief that plaintiff owed defendant money not a defense. *Wilson* @1136

   b. Application

      i. Compare employer's statements in *Fermino* to Scott's statements

      ii. Compare failed defense in *Wilson* to Scott's defense about pizza coupons

   c. Conclusion

After settling on a large-scale structure, we build on it to create a detailed outline like our sample outline in Appendix A. We will talk more about organizing these details in Chapter Four.

Outlining has other practical benefits in law school and in practice. Your busy schedule will need to accommodate working on writing assignments over time. Having an outline on your computer that you can gradually expand into a draft can help you pick up where you left off at your last drafting session efficiently. As a practitioner, you often will write complicated documents, like briefs, with other lawyers. Agreeing on an outline will help everyone see the big picture and make it easier to assemble the document into a coherent whole.

You have now taken the first three steps to writing a clear, precise, and effective legal document. You have drafted your preliminary outline and are ready for step four, small-scale organization, which includes drafting a detailed outline of individual paragraphs.

STEP 3

- Order legal issues and sub-issues.
- Summarize material facts.
- Draft preliminary outline (large-scale level).

➤ ***Next Step, Chapter Four.***

CHAPTER 4

SMALL-SCALE ORGANIZATION

§ 4.1 INTRODUCTION

In this chapter we turn to small-scale building blocks: paragraphs and paragraph blocks. A paragraph is a unified group of sentences that address a single topic; a paragraph block is a unified group of paragraphs that develop a topic. We connect these building blocks with transitional words, phrases sentences, and paragraphs. The small-scale structure of your paragraphs and paragraph blocks should help your busy reader understand your analysis quickly and easily. We conclude this chapter with more advice about outlines.

§ 4.2 DESIGNING PARAGRAPHS

A. WHY TO PARAGRAPH

Like the design for a Discussion or an Argument at the large-scale level, legal readers expect certain patterns at the paragraph level. For example, they expect each paragraph to be unified around a single topic, theme, or thesis that will be clearly stated in that paragraph's first sentence.

We design paragraphs to create: (i) logical divisions, (ii) rhetorical effects, and (iii) visual effects. These purposes often overlap. In legal writing, paragraphing typically should reflect logical divisions. Our analysis or arguments depend on proceeding in logical steps. Those steps make up individual paragraphs that may be aggregated into a block of paragraphs.

Paragraphs may also be divided for rhetorical purposes. As discussed in Chapter Seven, advocacy writing uses techniques for emphasis, such as placing key words at the beginning or end of a sentence. Similarly, the beginning and end of a paragraph are natural points of emphasis.

A third reason for paragraph breaks is for visual effect. We can deliberately vary paragraph length or location to draw our reader's eye to particular points in our analysis or our arguments.

B. UNIFY EACH PARAGRAPH

Each paragraph should be unified around a single topic or theme. Unless you use a paragraph break for rhetorical or visual effect, you should state, develop, and close that topic or theme within that paragraph. For example, read the following paragraph from our sample research memorandum, thinking about how it is unified.

> A jury could also find that Artie had been confined for long enough to state a claim for false imprisonment. The defendant must have confined the plaintiff for "any appreciable time, however short." *Wilson*, 42 Cal. App. 4th at 1135. In *Wilson* the court held that a jury could find that forty-five minutes to an hour was long enough to establish false imprisonment. *Id.* Even fifteen minutes can be an "appreciable length of time." *See id.* (citations omitted). Although Artie's confinement was a few

> minutes shorter, a jury could decide that ten minutes was an "appreciable" period of time, especially in light of Artie's age.

This paragraph's unifying topic is the legal issue regarding the length of time that Sarah Student's client was confined. The topic is introduced in the paragraph's first sentence, stating Student's conclusion. Each additional sentence develops the topic, following the order of the CRAC paradigm. Like a period that ends a sentence, the last sentence of the paragraph closes the topic.

C. BEGIN WITH A TOPIC OR THESIS SENTENCE

Start every paragraph with a topic or thesis sentence that states the topic you will discuss or the point you will prove in that paragraph. Our advice applies to all types of paragraphs, including paragraphs in a factual section or in an analytical section like a Discussion or Argument. Return to Student's paragraph analyzing the length of time Artie was confined and re-read its first sentence. That sentence states the point Student proves in the paragraph: "A jury could also find that Artie had been confined for long enough to state a claim for false imprisonment."

D. CONTROL PARAGRAPH LENGTH

To be effective, a paragraph must be the right length. If a paragraph is too short, it may not have enough information to engage and hold your reader's interest. But if a paragraph is too long, your reader may be forced to reread it to understand the theme or point. A busy reader, who doesn't make time to reread, may miss your point.

No "Goldilocks" rule can tell you when a paragraph is "just right," not too long and not too short. But we can offer you two guidelines. If a paragraph is longer than half a standard 250-word page, consider dividing it. If a paragraph is twenty-five words or less, ask yourself whether its short length serves a logical, rhetorical, or visual purpose.

Like a very short sentence, a one or two-sentence paragraph can give your reader a visual jolt, emphasizing your point. A very short paragraph can effectively highlight a major transition, emphasize an important conclusion, or summarize a block of paragraphs. On the other hand, a series of short paragraphs can chop up your theme or point, forcing your busy reader to work harder to understand your meaning. Therefore, you might want to avoid a series of short paragraphs unless that structure serves a rhetorical or visual purpose.

Length matters.

E. TAKE ADVANTAGE OF LOCATION

Put important ideas in positions of emphasis: at the beginning and at the end. Begin each paragraph with a topic or thesis sentence. End each paragraph with an appropriate conclusion or transition.

Location also matters.

§ 4.3 DESIGNING PARAGRAPH BLOCKS

A. ARRANGE PARAGRAPH BLOCKS IN MEANINGFUL PATTERNS

A paragraph block is a group of paragraphs addressing a single topic or theme. A facts section of a memorandum or a brief is typically composed of one or more paragraph blocks. Although a Discussion's sub-section may have only a single paragraph, often you will need to write multiple paragraphs, or paragraph blocks, to explain your analysis effectively. In our sample memorandum, two of the sub-issues are addressed in a single paragraph, one requires a two-paragraph block, and the most complicated sub-issue requires a three-paragraph block.

Just as every paragraph should begin with a specific topic or thesis sentence, paragraph blocks should begin with a sentence or a paragraph that introduces the topic or point that unifies that group of paragraphs. If you use an introductory paragraph, it typically will double as a roadmap for the paragraphs that follow.

One way to think about the optimal structure for a paragraph block is that it's an extended version of the optimal structure for a single paragraph. A single paragraph should begin with a topic or thesis sentence articulating the topic you discuss or the point you prove in that paragraph. In a paragraph block, that single topic or thesis sentence may be expanded into a paragraph. Instead of supporting sentences, a paragraph block features supporting paragraphs. Like the last sentence of a single paragraph, the last paragraph in a paragraph block is a period, closing that block.

B. USE EXPECTED PATTERNS LIKE CRAC

Legal readers also expect paragraph blocks to follow certain patterns, including the CRAC paradigm and its variations.

In the single paragraph example in § 4.2.B above, the analysis was relatively simple, only requiring a sentence or two for each part of the paradigm. But a more complex analysis may require you to use multiple paragraphs or multiple paragraph blocks, especially in CRAC's rule and application components.

Often, even for more complex analytical tasks, you still may be able to state your conclusions effectively in a sentence or two. You may also have a choice about combining these conclusions with another part of the paradigm.

Sarah Student's analysis of Scott's intent to confine Artie illustrates how CRAC can be used to organize a two-paragraph block. This sub-section's opening sentence serves a dual function. First, the sentence states a conclusion that introduces the CRAC paradigm. Student could have styled that conclusion as a one-sentence paragraph.

> A jury could reasonably find that Scott intended to confine Artie in the conference room.

Instead she chose to combine that first conclusion with the rule development for the intent sub-issue.

The second function of Student's opening sentence is to act as a topic sentence for the first paragraph. By including the phrase "intent to confine" in that sentence, Student subtly signals her reader that the rest of the paragraph will explain the rule for intent. Student made sure that her supervisor would understand her signal by identifying "intent to confine" as an element of false imprisonment in the Discussion's umbrella section and by referring to intent in the sub-section's heading. Here is the full text of the first paragraph in the block:

> A jury could reasonably find that Scott intended to confine Artie in the conference room. A plaintiff must demonstrate that the defendant intended to confine the plaintiff. *Fermino*, 7 Cal. 4th at 715. In *Fermino* the court found intent when a "store's personnel manager summoned . . . [plaintiff] to a windowless room and . . . interrogated her concerning . . . alleged theft" from the store. *Id.* But a plaintiff need not show that the defendant intended to cause harm. *Id.* at 715 ("false imprisonments often appear to arise from initially legitimate motives"). *See also Wilson*, 42 Cal. App. 4th at 1135 (citation omitted) (explaining that defendant's "provocation, motive and good faith" do not defeat a claim for false imprisonment). Thus, in *Wilson* the defendant's belief that plaintiffs owed him money was not a defense to plaintiffs' claim that he held plaintiffs in a bank until they were able to cash a check. *Id.*

The second paragraph in this block applies the law to the facts of Artie's case and concludes the sub-section. Note how Student signals her shift to the application in the paragraph's first sentence. That sentence tells her reader the specific point that Student proves in that paragraph, weaving together references to the law, "*Fermino*" and "intended to confine," with references to the parties in Student's case, "Scott" and "Artie." Student presents the application sentences in the same order that she uses to set out the rule, reiterating a small-scale pattern that helps her supervisor understand the analysis more easily.

Again, a conclusion in the paradigm does double duty. Student restates her conclusion: "Therefore, Artie can easily show that Scott had the requisite intent." But this conclusion is in a different position, finishing the CRAC paradigm and also closing the two-paragraph block. Here is the full text of the second paragraph:

> Like the manager in *Fermino*, Scott made statements that show he intended to confine Artie. Scott ordered Schrute to "escort this young man to the conference room," then warned Artie that "you will come out when you decide to give me a discount on the pizza." Moreover, like the defendant's belief in *Wilson*, Scott's belief that he was entitled to a discount would not defeat a claim for false imprisonment. Therefore, Artie can easily show that Scott had the requisite intent.

When you review our sample memorandum and brief, see if you can identify how we have applied, and varied, the CRAC paradigm to organize paragraph blocks, particularly in the discussion and argument sections.

§ 4.4 USING TRANSITIONS

A. WHY TO TRANSITION

A good transition refers to what has preceded and announces what is to follow. Without transitions, a piece of legal writing is like a mosaic without glue: no matter how elegantly designed, nothing holds together.

For substantive coherence, each component of your writing should be connected to the whole. Each sentence should be linked to its surrounding sentences. Every paragraph should be linked to the preceding paragraph, either by theme or by explicit transitional words. If you move to an unrelated topic without also moving to a new section or sub-section, you should tell the reader how this unrelated topic fits into the mosaic.

Transitions between issues, sub-issues, and paragraph blocks must be carefully constructed. These transitions may be (i) paragraphs in themselves, that is, transitional paragraphs, (ii) the first sentence in a subsequent paragraph, (iii) the last sentence in a preceding paragraph, or (iv) a substantive link between paragraphs.

B. TRANSITIONAL PARAGRAPHS

A transitional paragraph may act as a roadmap, connecting discussions of multiple issues in a section or sub-section of a document. A transitional paragraph also can connect paragraph blocks.

We have already seen an example of a large-scale roadmap in an "umbrella" paragraph in Chapter Three. At the beginning of our sample memorandum's Discussion, that paragraph tells the reader how the different sub-issues regarding false imprisonment fit together.

You can apply the same technique to a sub-section of the Discussion or Argument if the law requires you to analyze multiple sub-issues within the section. Using a "mini-umbrella" paragraph, you can tell the reader how several sub-issues or several specific arguments fit together, ideally in the same order in which you will analyze or argue them.

Similarly, you can use a transitional paragraph to introduce the content of a paragraph block. A transitional paragraph at the end of a paragraph block can summarize its content and also introduce the next group of paragraphs. This type of transitional paragraph may call your reader's attention to an important change of topic, to a shift in the logical sequence of ideas, or to a conclusion.

C. TRANSITIONAL SENTENCES

Two successive paragraphs are most commonly linked by a transitional sentence. You must construct paragraphs so that either the first leads into the second or the second refers back to the first. You can make this connection in a transitional sentence.

A sentence briefly recapping or referring to the preceding paragraph can be an effective transitional device. For example, this sentence in the second paragraph of sub-section B of Student's Discussion links two rule paragraphs: "In the absence of physical compulsion, the plaintiff must be subject to such duress as would reasonably overcome his or her free will." The introductory phrase—"in the absence of physical compulsion"—refers back to the part of the rule developed in the first paragraph, making the transition.

Again, keeping our readers in mind, we think the least effective transitional sentences begin with generic place-fillers like these: "The next case to be considered is" or "In addition, courts consider." Conversely, the most effective transitions are tailored and intrinsic to the logic and style of your analysis or argument.

Unlike place-fillers, simple enumeration, such as "First," "Second," or "Third," provides useful information to your reader. For example, this device can identify the elements of a legal rule and help your reader see how those elements connect to the related points in your analysis or argument.

Parallelism is another simple but useful transitional device. To use this technique, construct two sentences containing the same parts of speech and arrange them in the same order. For example: "A good defense is based on more than law. A good defense is based on sound principle." Several sentences with a common subject, with or without parallel predicates, will provide smooth reading as well as reflect substantive links between ideas.

D. SUBSTANTIVE TRANSITIONS BETWEEN SENTENCES

A substantive link can effectively transition between sentences. In each of these examples, just two words do the work.

1. *These holdings* must be carefully compared.

2. Given *this precedent,* the court will undoubtedly affirm the judgment.

3. From *this analysis,* we may predict a similar outcome in our case.

A summary phrase referring to a topic that has been discussed in the first sentence eases the transition to the second sentence in these examples.

1. Plaintiff's position, *that the report is admissible,* is consistent with the government's position.

2. Police officers have a proper alternative for investigating facts when, *as in this case, they suspect foul play but do not have probable cause to arrest.*

3. Just as *the parties made dissimilar claims in these two cases,* they also sought dissimilar remedies.

Repeating or echoing key words or phrases also serves as an effective substantive transition between sentences. Most legal terms of art function as transitions each time they are repeated. Words or phrases such as "evidence" bring to mind a complex concept that need not be restated in full each time the term is used.

Juxtaposing the discussions of two cases presents a common transition problem. Consider using substantive information, like (i) the similarities or differences between the cases, (ii) their chronological or jurisdictional relationships, (iii) the relative importance of the cases, or (iv) some other substantive link. The example below solves the transition problem by using several substantive links. First, the writer suggests the different ways in which the two courts might measure the level of restraint required to support a false imprisonment claim. Second, the writer also flags the decisions' chronological relationship and the courts' different positions in California's hierarchy.

> In the absence of physical compulsion, the Court of Appeal in *Roberson* assessed whether the plaintiff was subject to a level of duress that would overcome his or her free will. On the other hand, five years later in *Fermino*, the Supreme Court recognized that unreasonable duress could constitute sufficient restraint to support a false imprisonment claim.

E. TRANSITIONAL WORDS

1. Choose Precise Transitional Words

Use transitional words precisely. For example, the common transitional words "yet" and "however" are often misused; they signal a change of direction, comparable to "on the other hand." Transitional words that have several possible meanings, like the general utility word "as," are difficult to use precisely, so we recommend that you avoid them. Similarly, instead of "since," which also has a temporal meaning, choose a more precise word like "because," meaning "for the reason that."

Although transitional words with a single narrow meaning, such as "conversely," can be effective tools, they must be used appropriately, as in the following example:

> If an employment contract does not provide for a definite period of employment, the employer may discharge the employee at any time, with or without cause. *Conversely*, an employment contract for a definite period of time is not terminable at will.

In the example, the transitional word "conversely" emphasizes the substance of the sentence it introduces, making an effective transition.

Compare this ambiguous and imprecise example:

> Mr. Shaw could not validly dispose of community property in his will *so that* part of the will is not valid. (Does "that part" refer to a part of Mr. Shaw's will? Or is "so that" a phrase meaning "consequently"?)

This revision clarifies the sentence's meaning:

> *Because* Mr. Shaw could not validly dispose of community property in his will, part of the will is not valid.

2. Prefer Substantive Transitional Words

Use substantive transitional words rather than place-fillers. Like the best transitional sentences, the best transitional words are logical and substantive, rather than imprecise or general. Effective transitional words express the logical connection between what went before and what comes after. For example:

> Plaintiff is factually and legally incorrect. *In addition,* Ms. Stanford was not even eligible for Social Security benefits at the time of her death, *and* she could not qualify thereafter.
>
> *Revised:* Plaintiff is factually and legally incorrect *for two reasons. First,* Ms. Stanford was not eligible for Social Security benefits at the time of her death. *Second,* Ms. Stanford could not qualify after her death.

3. Vary Transitional Words

When you are choosing transitions, you may disregard the general rule that the same word should be used to refer to the same thing. If you use the word "however" or "therefore" six times in a paragraph, your reader will find it irritating, distracting, and finally meaningless. For effective transitions, variety and elegance may prevail over consistency. Nothing prevails over substance, however, so think carefully about the substantive link between sentences or paragraphs.

We have included lists of transitional words in Appendix C to use for introducing, concluding, restating, exemplifying, emphasizing, contrasting, adding or amplifying, comparing, sequencing, cause and effect, time or place, and a list of alternative words for overworked transitions. Our lists are meant to provide you with substantive alternatives for transitional words and phrases. Selecting a precise transition is entirely a matter of context. Each of the transitional words you choose will work well in some contexts, but not in others.

§ 4.5 MORE ABOUT OUTLINING

At the end of Chapter Three, we urged you to master the skills of outlining as tools for large-scale organization. Detailed and reverse outlines also can help you develop and impose effective small-scale structure.

As you begin to work out the details for a document's Discussion or Argument, incorporate those details into your preliminary outline. Like a preliminary outline, a detailed outline is a living document that will change to reflect your evolving ideas about what you want to say and how you want to say it.

In Appendix A you will find a detailed outline for the Discussion in Sarah Student's memorandum. If you compare that outline to the preliminary outline at the end of Chapter Three, you will see that the detailed outline expands the information about the law and the facts for the umbrella section and subsections A through D. A detailed outline also is a tool for sketching out any necessary paragraph blocks in the rule or application sections.

A reverse outline is a tool for assessing a draft's large and small-scale structure. After drafting, create a reverse outline by extracting and aggregating the topic or first sentence of each paragraph. Then check to see whether the resulting outline reflects the logical structure that you have chosen. If you extract the entire first sentence of each paragraph, you also can assess whether each paragraph begins with a sharp topic or thesis sentence.

You have now completed step four in the legal writing process. You have gathered any additional facts or law that you need to analyze your issues and included this in your more detailed outline. You have drafted a detailed outline, including the topics of paragraphs and paragraph blocks. You are ready to begin writing the first draft.

Drafting involves choosing each word carefully, which is the subject of Chapter Five. Drafting involves choosing the right sentence structure for the units of thought you need to convey, which is the subject of Chapter Eight. Choosing the right words and the right sentence structures requires a clear understanding of the purpose of your document, whether it is advisory or persuasive. Advisory writing techniques are discussed in Chapter Six. Persuasive writing techniques are discussed in Chapter Seven.

STEP 4

- Gather additional facts, as needed.
- Do additional legal research, as needed.
- Draft detailed outline (small-scale level).

➤ ***Next Step, Chapter Five.***

CHAPTER 5

LANGUAGE IN THE LEGAL SETTING

At Cornell University, my professor of European literature, Vladimir Nabokov, changed the way I read and the way I write. Words could paint pictures, I learned from him. Choosing the right word, and the right word order, he illustrated, could make an enormous difference in conveying an image or an idea.

—Justice Ruth Bader Ginsburg, "Advice for Living," *New York Times* (Oct. 2, 2016)

Lawyers have only one tool: language. They must love words and use them exactly.

—*Scalia & Garner, Making Your Case: The Art of Persuading Judges 61* (Thomson West 2008)

§ 5.1 INTRODUCTION

Clear, precise, and effective use of language is fundamental to legal writing. As Justice Scalia observed, "Lawyers have only one tool: language." To use language effectively, each word must be intentional and precise. Each word must be necessary. Brevity is not only the soul of wit, but also essential in every form of legal writing.

At first, law students struggle with the new language of the law, where "claim" may refer to a client's cause of action, not a claim, for example, of a party affiliation. After a while, the challenge is no longer just to understand legal language, but how not to get lost in it.

Many published law cases contain archaic legalisms, as discussed below. Law students and lawyers may absorb this vocabulary and repeat it without thinking about its effect on the reader, or even about its exact meaning. For example, "herein" is a commonly used archaic term with no clear reference. In any document, it could refer to the sentence, the paragraph, the section, or the entire document. This chapter will help you to recognize these vestiges of the past and choose clear and precise words instead.

Legal writing must serve a variety of audiences, from lay readers to appellate judges. The tone, style and extent of analysis must be varied to serve each reader's needs. Often legal writers collaborate with others, requiring that styles and tones be matched in the final document.

Regardless of the audience, style, or tone, legal writing needs to be spare. Sometimes there are page limits, as with most court briefs. The best way to write concisely is to ask, for each word: Do I need this? For each thought, ask whether it is necessary to your conclusion or purpose.

Word choice should be intentional, not automatic or reflexive. Often the first word or phrase that comes to mind is a cliché or an approximation of what you mean. In a given context, there is seldom only one "correct" word choice. This chapter is intended to help the legal writer make effective choices as well as correct choices. It includes principles for word selection and a discussion of redundancy in legal writing.

In the Appendix, we have provided a glossary of words commonly misused in legal writing. It contains specific advice about using common legal terms precisely. For example, the Glossary begins with the common word "above":

> **above**, as in the *above* theory. Usage experts acknowledge this use of *above* with a noun to be permissible but prefer reversed order (theory *above*) by analogy to other indicators of place (*e.g., below*). Use of *above* with a verb is more precise (*e.g., above*-mentioned theory, theory summarized *above*) because what has been done *above* is identified. All of these usages are to be preferred to *aforesaid* in legal prose.

Similarly, the common word "among" requires greater precision in legal writing:

> **among, between**. *Among* is precisely used to express a relation of more than two persons: *among the four parties. Between* ("by-twain") is precisely used to express a relation of two persons: *between the two parties*. Therefore, the common contractual language *among and between parties A, B, and C* is not a redundancy. It means: among A, B, and C; between A and B, B and C, and A and C. From its first use, however, *between* has extended to more than two things in some situations and is

the only word for expressing the relation of a physical thing to many surrounding things, as *in the property between the three rivers.*

For new legal writers, reading the Glossary will be a good way to become sensitive to language in the legal setting. Experienced legal writers will also find useful explanations for frequently misused words, such as "affect" and "effect," discussed in the Glossary.

§ 5.2 PRINCIPLES FOR MAKING WORD CHOICES

To say precisely what we mean requires thought: first, we must identify what we mean, and, second, we must decide how best to express it. Many writers use the words that come automatically to mind without giving them further thought. These automatic word choices are not necessarily the best choices. The following principles will help you to make effective word choices rather than automatic word choices.

A. USE WORDS IN THEIR LITERAL SENSE

A common source of imprecision in legal writing is personification, the giving of human qualities to abstractions or objects, for example, "cold-blooded decision." A related source of imprecision is metonymy, the substitution of an attributive or a suggestive word for the word identifying a person or thing, for example, "stage hand" for "stage worker." In some types of writing, this kind of imprecision may be acceptable. In legal writing, precision is essential. In each of the examples below, revising for literal precision results in greater clarity about who is doing what.

1. *Imprecise*: The five points analyze the statute.

Precise: The court analyzes the statute in five points.

2. *Imprecise*: California has so held.

Precise: The California Court of Appeals has so held.

3. *Imprecise*: This Washington case so found.

Precise: The jury in this Washington case so found.

B. OMIT ARCHAIC LEGALISMS

Archaic legalisms are words and phrases, such as "hereinafter," "heretofore," "aforesaid," "forthwith," "herein," "hereby," "for purposes hereof," "notwithstanding anything to the contrary herein," "so made," "by these presents," and "said." Not only are these words obstacles to the lay reader, but they are also imprecise and thus troublesome to the legal reader. For example, if the words "thereof" and "therefrom" are removed from the following sentence, it gains both clarity and readability:

> The following assets for administration under this Article 4, including the proceeds, investments and reinvestments *thereof*, and accumulated income *therefrom*, if any, shall constitute the "trust estate."
>
> *Revised:* The following assets for administration under Article 4, including the proceeds, investments, reinvestments, and accumulated income from the assets shall constitute the "trust estate."

Archaic legalisms may create the appearance of precision, thus obscuring ambiguities that might otherwise be recognized. For example, a question that has been frequently litigated is whether "herein" refers to the paragraph in which it is used, the section, or the whole document. Therefore, after removing the archaic language, consider whether you must add precise references to time, place, or subject matter.

C. USE THE SAME WORD TO REFER TO THE SAME THING; USE DIFFERENT WORDS TO REFER TO DIFFERENT THINGS

Never attempt to improve style by introducing synonyms or other word variations that will create confusion or ambiguity. In the following sentences, the substitution of the word "prevailing" for the word "dominant" creates initial confusion: Is the author going to discuss two views?

> According to the *dominant view*, this article is applied to periodic meetings as well as to special meetings. The *prevailing view* is that Article 237 of the Commercial Code provides the right for minority shareholders to convene either type of meeting.

Similarly, from the following sentence, can we know whether the author is discussing two or three forms of copyright?

> Although under the old Act *a common law copyright* existed in writings until they qualified for statutory protection, the *non-statutory copy*right was extinguished when the *statutory copyright* was created by publication or registration.

A corollary is to use different words when you mean different things. If the same word is used to mean different things, the reader may be momentarily confused.

1. As a final *consideration*, there was no discussion of the contractor's *consideration.*

2. Under our present system of criminal *sanctions*, legislative limits and judicial discretion *sanction* individualization of sentences.

D. USE SIMPLE, FAMILIAR WORDS

When you have a choice between a short, familiar word, such as "call," and a longer word, such as "communicate," choose the shorter, simpler one. Simple words are understood more quickly. Readers prefer words that they understand easily. They require less reading and thinking time.

Simple Words	*Longer Counterparts*
after	subsequent to
before	prior to
begin, carry out	implement, effectuate
happen	eventuate, transpire
inform	apprise
make	render
sent	transmit
think	deem
think, see, regard	envisage

E. USE CONCRETE RATHER THAN ABSTRACT WORDS

Concrete words such as "split decision" are easier to understand than abstractions such as "judicial dichotomy." Legal writers are likely to use abstract, overblown language in part because many of the cases that law students read during their first year reflect an older, overstuffed style that is relatively easy to imitate. Legal writers must resist the old style.

Some common abstractions are simple words that can often be eliminated without loss of meaning, for example, "type," "kind," "manner," "state," "area," "matter," "factor," "system," and "nature."

1. *The central thrust* of plaintiff's legal *position* is dependent on *matters* having to do with three decisions of the United States Supreme Court.

Revised: Plaintiff's argument for summary judgment depends on three United States Supreme Court decisions.

2. The court may not abandon the traditional termination-at-will *manner* of analysis in order to apply a reasonableness *factor* in the *area* of non-employment contracts.

Revised: The court may not abandon the traditional termination-at-will analysis for non-employment contracts in order to apply the reasonableness analysis.

F. USE WORDS THAT CREATE AN APPROPRIATE TONE

All words have connotation (overtones of meaning) as well as denotation (explicit meaning). Since connotation contributes to tone, the word choices in a particular piece of legal writing should have connotations consistent with the practice of law. This generally precludes the use of colloquialisms, most abbreviations ("TV," "ad," "MC," "high-tech"), and slang.

The following except from the fact statement in a brief contains inconsistencies in tone that undermine its credibility:

> A third-party park-sitter, unbeknownst to Plaintiff, contacted said Plaintiff's head with a wine bottle. Plaintiff now has two metal plates and twelve screws holding things together.

G. AVOID EQUIVOCATIONS

Lawyers and law students often hesitate to make direct or dogmatic statements. To protect themselves or to reflect uncertainty, they use either equivocal or qualifying words that undermine their meaning. Typical words and phrases used in this way are: "it seems to indicate," "if practicable," "it would seem," "it may well be," and "it might be said that." If you are uncertain, state the reason for your uncertainty. Otherwise, begin sentences with their subject.

H. USE UNQUALIFIED NOUNS, ADJECTIVES, AND VERBS

Sometimes writers add modifiers to add emphasis to poorly chosen nouns, adjectives, and verbs. The right word ordinarily needs no emphasis. When the following modifiers are removed, emphasis falls naturally where it should: on the noun, adjective, or verb.

absolutely	nearly
actually	obviously
basically	particular
certain, certainly	plainly
clearly	practically
completely	pretty much
deepest	quite
extremely	really
frankly	so (as in "so great")
generally	sort of
given	surely
greatly	truly
in effect	various
kind of	very
more or less	virtually

1. The surface of the material *basically* was *very* rough and extremely discolored.

Revised: The surface of the material was rough and discolored.

2. The tide was *obviously* faster than the owner's engineers had calculated, making the owner

clearly liable for its *completely* inadequate construction plan.

Revised: The tide was faster than the owner's engineers had calculated, making the owner liable for the inadequacy of its construction plan.

Words that convey absolute qualities must remain unqualified if they are to retain their meaning, for example, "perfect," "dead," "absolute," "equal," "essential," "matchless," "mortal," "universal," "supreme," and "unique."

I. USE FEW LITERARY DEVICES

A plain style is usually the best style. If you do wish to use figurative language, do so where it will not interfere with communication of substance. When you edit or revise, consider the sensory dimension of words. Omit rhyme ("however clever"), cacophony ("egalitarian documentation"), conspicuous alliteration ("fallibility of four factfinders"), and unintentional puns ("a case without appeal").

Clichés come readily to mind during writing. Thus, a standard part of your revision should be to remove them or to renovate them. For example, you might play on the common cliché "adding insult to injury" by writing "adding insult to perjury," but remove such clichés as "height of absurdity," "day of reckoning," and "cold light of reason."

J. AVOID JARGON FROM OTHER FIELDS

Words go in and out of fashion. Vague psychoanalytic terms, such as "interaction" and "supportive" were frequently used for a time before they gave way to computer jargon, such as "interface" and "input." Avoid word fads altogether. Words in fashion are quickly degraded; their specific meaning disappears, leaving only a vague colloquial meaning.

§ 5.3 A FEW BRIEF WORDS: REDUNDANCY IN LEGAL WRITING

As most lawyers know, redundant wording has a long and respectable past. Our Anglo-Saxon ancestors gave us word pairings, such as "safe and sound." After the Norman Invasion, French synonyms were added to the Middle English word pairs. Thus many legal terms have come to us in triplicate, for example, "give (Old English), devise (Old French) and bequeath (Old English)." Some word pairings are still commonly used, such as "acknowledge and confess," "act and deed," "deem and consider," "fit and proper,", "goods and chattels," "keep and maintain," "pardon and forgive," "shun and avoid," "aid and abet," "cease and desist," "fraud and deceit," and "null and void." Before automatically adopting an archaic word pairing, consider whether both words are needed.

Unnecessary word pairing continues to be a habit in modern English. If you think about each word you use, you will avoid redundancies such as the following.

basic fundamentals	telling revelation
basic starting point	terrible tragedy
false misrepresentation	true facts
final result	unexpected surprise
if and when	unless and until
sufficient enough	save and except

A more pervasive form of redundancy is the throw-away phrase, such as:

a certain amount of	as a matter of fact
due to the fact that	all intents and purposes
in case of	the nature of the case is
in regard to	the necessity of
the fact of the matter is	with reference to

Watch for these phrases when you edit and gradually train yourself to omit them during initial drafting.

Many other unnecessary words litter professional prose. As an editing technique, ask the question, "Do I need this word?" for each word in your next few writing projects. You will begin instinctively to pare away such unnecessary words and phrases as these:

Wordy	Revised
am hopeful that	hope
at that point in time	then
by means, reason, or virtue of	by
despite the fact that	although, even though

give recognition to	recognize
have knowledge of	know
in accordance with	by, under
in order to	to
in relation to	about
in the majority of instances	usually
is applicable to	applies to
is dependent on	depends on
make application to	apply to
make provision for	provide for
provides with an example of	exemplifies
until such time as	until

While redundancy wastes a reader's time, repetition of key words saves a reader's time. From sentence to sentence, key nouns and verbs should be repeated. The line between helpful repetition and redundancy may be thin, but with experience the legal writer will develop a sense for where that line is.

You have now considered the word choices you will make as you draft your legal document. This is part of Step Five in the legal writing and analysis process. Your next task, as you write your first draft, is to write effectively in either an objective, advisory style or in a persuasive style, as an advocate. Chapters Six and Seven address advisory and persuasive writing conventions and techniques.

STEP 5

- Write first draft.
- Let that draft rest.
- Revise for organization and analytical content.
- Draft and revise again, as needed.

CHAPTER 6
ADVISORY WRITING

§ 6.1 INTRODUCTION

This chapter addresses two classic forms of advisory writing: the legal research memorandum and the client letter. We also address advisory writing's modern form: email. We describe the special features and preferred writing techniques for each genre of advisory writing.

§ 6.2 LEGAL MEMORANDA

A. PURPOSES OF LEGAL MEMORANDA

The legal research memorandum is one of the basic documents used in law offices. Its general purpose is to analyze a problem objectively to help a senior lawyer prepare to give advice or make decisions about the problem.

A memorandum should be tailored to the specific purpose for which it will be used. A senior lawyer may request a memorandum for many reasons, including:

(i) Considering whether to accept a case;

(ii) Preparing to meet with the client to obtain additional facts about the client's problem;

(iii) Preparing to advise the client on which of several courses of action to take;

(iv) Preparing for negotiations with the client's adversary

(v) Preparing to draft a settlement agreement or other type of contract or transactional document;

(vi) Preparing to draft a pleading or a discovery document;

(vii) Preparing for trial; or

(viii) Preparing for an appeal or other review of a court decision.

Even if no dispute resolution process has begun, the memorandum may need to be written with the possibility of mediation or litigation in mind.

A memorandum will typically be written for another lawyer, such as a senior partner or associate. But sometimes, a memorandum will be written for or shared with another professional, such as an accountant or a trust officer. To help tailor solutions to your audience's needs, try to identify the memorandum's prospective readers and its specific purposes as early in the research and writing process as possible.

B. FORMAT

The whole document should be easy to use for quick reference. Divisions should be clearly marked. Sections should be easy to locate.

Memorandum format varies. Your first-year legal writing teacher, firm, or company may prescribe a particular format. If not, a conventional format you can use is:

1. Heading
2. Introduction—Optional
3. Questions (or Issues) Presented
4. Brief Answers
5. Statement of Facts
6. Discussion
7. Conclusion—Optional

See our sample research memorandum in Appendix A. In the next sections, we describe approaches to writing these components.

Some lawyers were taught to begin a memorandum by stating the facts. We recommend a format that gives the reader an overview of the legal problems and solutions addressed in the memorandum before stating the facts.

C. HEADING

The memorandum should begin with a heading that includes the recipient, the author (you), the subject, and the date. If the memorandum (or other written communication) is protected by the attorney client privilege, you should also note that with a legend at the beginning of the memorandum. For example: "Confidential: Privileged Attorney-Client Communication." See our sample memorandum in Appendix A.

D. INTRODUCTION

A memorandum may begin with a separate introduction concisely summarizing the client's problem. An introduction may be more common in a memorandum that is long or is written to a primary reader who isn't familiar with the client's problem (like a senior partner). You don't need to include a separate introduction in every memorandum.

E. QUESTIONS PRESENTED

Identifying the questions presented (or "the issues") is the key to analyzing any legal problem. Sometimes the legal questions will be specified by the person who requests the memorandum. But more often, you must slowly identify these key questions as you research, analyze, and reflect about the problem.

Once you identify these questions in your mind, then you must figure out how to phrase them effectively. Your goal is to communicate your understanding of the questions precisely and concisely to your audience. This challenge is the subject of the following subsections.

1. Draft the Ultimate Question

Revisit what we will call the "ultimate question," the question or questions that prompted the senior lawyer to ask you to write a memorandum. A question may be specific or more open-ended.

If the ultimate question is not specified for you, try to draft one as soon as you begin working on the memorandum assignment. You should expect to revise and edit it continuously until you are finished with the memorandum, so don't worry about perfecting it at this early stage. Just take a shot at the question before you start researching, and continue thinking it about during the research.

2. Organize and Format Specific Questions

If you must answer several questions, state them in this section in the same order that you analyze them in the memorandum's Discussion. You can give your reader a helpful signpost by organizing the questions into a numbered list that corresponds to numbered subsections in the Discussion.

Typically, a question can be phrased as either an interrogatory or a declaratory sentence. If you use a form that begins with "Whether," it's customary to punctuate with a question mark even though the question may not technically be a complete sentence. The punctuation signals the reader that the statement is a question.

Here are examples of two formats that you can use for a specific question. The first format uses the "under-does-when" pattern. The second format begins with "whether." You will see that the facts are stated slightly differently in the two examples.

(i) Under California law, can a 16-year-old pizza delivery driver state a claim for false imprisonment when a company's manager refused to pay for the pizzas he had ordered, then asked another employee to escort the driver to a room, where the driver was kept for ten minutes?

(ii) Whether a 16-year-old pizza delivery driver can state a claim for false imprisonment, under California law, when a company's manager refused to pay for the pizzas he had ordered and had the driver escorted to a room and held there for ten minutes while an office worker guarded the door?

Your question also may be more open-ended:

> Can our 16-year-old client state a legal claim when he tried to deliver pizza to his employer's customer, whose manager refused to pay and then escorted our client to a room where he was kept for ten minutes while another office worker guarded the door?

A question typically will combine a key legal principle, like "a claim for false imprisonment," with key facts. The key facts should make the question specific enough to be understood "standing alone." A question will only be meaningful if it is stated in terms of the problem's facts, not merely in the abstract. Moreover, your reader should not be required to read the full Statement of Facts in order to understand what a question means. Compare the false imprisonment questions above to this abstract question: Does our client have a claim for false imprisonment? Without the key facts, this question could be about any false imprisonment case. A senior lawyer will want your prediction about our client's specific situation.

Because including the facts will add words, a specific question may be harder to understand. In our false imprisonment examples, the facts add more than 30 words to each question. Use a structure, like "under-does-when," which improves readability by keeping the subject and verb close together and by putting facts at the end of the sentence. See the first false imprisonment example above.

Generally, when several facts are included in a single issue, the law is stated before the facts. If the subject matter permits, arrange facts from the most general to the most particular. The question itself should thus move from the general area of law, at the beginning, to the most particular fact, at the end.

Only include key facts. Dates, amounts, and similar details ordinarily are not necessary to make a question meaningful. Moreover, these details will be supplied in the Statement of Facts.

If the key facts are complex or numerous, you can use a format that combines a short summary of the facts and a simpler question. For example:

> Artie Abrams is a 16-year-old who works part-time delivering pizza. A company's manager ordered pizzas from Artie's employer. When Artie would not accept coupons for the pizzas, the manager refused to pay and asked another office worker to escort Artie to an office, where he was held for ten minutes.
>
> Can Artie state a claim, under California law, for false imprisonment?

3. Use Subquestions Effectively

As your research and analysis progress, you may decide to nest subquestions under a question. Writing and rewriting these subquestions will often advance your understanding of the problem and help you develop reliable conclusions.

If you use subquestions, each subquestion should be specific and may incorporate distinct key facts. This technique often reduces the number of facts that must be incorporated in the primary question, making the primary question simpler and clearer.

The form and style of questions will vary with the subject matter. However, never use a single subquestion. If there is a subquestion "a," then there should also be a subquestion "b."

4. Revise and Edit

Expect to revise and edit your questions several times, including a final proofreading when you have finished writing the document. See also Chapter Eight, "Sentence Design."

F. BRIEF ANSWERS

This section should be short. Answer each question in one sentence if possible. Cite legal authorities only if they are the crux of the problem. Even though the Brief Answers precede the Discussion, you often will wait to write these answers until after the Discussion is finalized, or nearly finalized, when you fully understand the problem's analysis and conclusions.

If a memorandum analyzes more than one question, some writers combine the questions and answers into one section. Each question is followed by its brief answer, saving the reader from toggling back and forth between two sections.

G. STATEMENT OF FACTS

The Statement of Facts lays out the basis of the legal problem, objectively. This section tells the reader what happened, as well as when, how, and to whom. You shouldn't reach any conclusions or include any law in this section. Also reserve any characterizations, editorial comments, or evaluations of events for the Discussion.

Include the material facts and enough background facts so your reader can understand what happened. One rule of thumb is to include, or at least refer to, every fact in the facts section that you rely on in the Discussion. Another rule of thumb is to make the facts section complete enough, so that no one will need to duplicate the work you have already done. Follow the practice in your law office or law school classes for supporting the facts with citations.

Keep your audience in mind. If a client will be reading the memorandum, don't repeat facts that she already knows, such as, the general nature of her business. If, for example, you are analyzing a contract, you may want to include the language of its key clauses either in the facts section on in an attachment for your reader's convenience. If you choose to use an attachment, give your reader a heads up by referring to it specifically in the Statement of Facts.

1. Use Effective Style

Present the facts so your reader will be able to understand them, on a first reading, and also remember the most important facts while reading the Discussion that follows. State the facts in simple language without distortion or bias. Distinguish alleged facts from established facts by using appropriate qualifications, such as "alleged," "testified," or "found by the court." Signal significant questions about facts by including inconsistent information.

Brevity is best. You must choose which facts to include. But before you leave out a fact, ask yourself whether the reader will need to know that fact to understand your analysis. Also ask whether your reader will understand what happened without that fact.

2. Organize for Clarity

In objective writing, you can organize facts chronologically or topically. Sometimes you can combine the two approaches.

A chronological narrative is typical, beginning with the key facts in the first sentence or two. This briefly orients the reader to what happened, and when, where, and to whom it happened. The full narration of events follows.

You may use specific dates as organizing principles to determine the section's paragraphs. Signal the reader by incorporating dates or temporal language into the paragraphs' thesis sentences. Follow your office's practice regarding which specific dates to include. Keep in mind that some readers will think each specific date is important and try to remember it. If you include unimportant dates, you may make your reader work harder than she should to understand what happened. You also can use other temporal phrases, like "the next day" or "six months later," to tell her how that paragraph fits into the narrative's timeline.

You may opt for a topical structure to organize a complex set of facts into subsections. Subheadings can identify shifts in major topics. A topical structure is common for multi-party problems, for example, litigation involving multiple plaintiffs or defendants with multiple claims and defenses. Help your reader understand how these topics fit together in the section's introduction and conclusion, and by using specific transitions between subsections.

3. Revise and Edit

Some lawyers draft the Statement of Facts before finalizing the Discussion. Others reverse those steps. Whichever process you choose, don't forget to budget time to revise the facts section so that it includes each key fact in your analysis. Also make time to edit the facts section so it says what you want it to say, clearly and concisely. Here's an example of how editing can clarify facts:

Unclear Statement of Facts:

Artie, a 16-year-old, who works part-time for a pizza business, was acting as a delivery driver when a branch manager of Neighborhood Bank ordered several pizzas from Artie's employer, and Artie was given coupons as partial payment for the pizzas. Refusing to accept the coupons, but insisting on all cash, Artie was escorted into a small room in back of the branch manager's offices and another office worker was posted outside the door for ten minutes while Artie was held inside the small office without permission to leave.

Revised and Clarified:

Artie is a 16-year-old who works part-time delivering pizza.[1] The branch manager of Neighborhood Bank ordered pizzas from Artie's employer.[1] When Artie delivered the pizzas, the manager tried to pay with coupons.[2] Artie refused to accept the coupons. The manager refused to pay with cash.[3] When Artie insisted on cash, the manager escorted him to a small room, posted another office worker outside the door, and held him there for ten minutes.[4]

[1] *One idea per sentence.*

[2] *Short complex sentence using active, not passive, voice.*

[3] *Parallelism (fourth and fifth sentences)*

[4] *Parallelism with a series of verbs ("escorted," "posted," and "held") which add rhetorical emphasis to the main point, which is that Artie was detained in a small, guarded room for ten minutes.*

H. DISCUSSION

This section contains your objective analysis of how the salient law applies to the specific facts of a problem. The senior lawyer who has requested the memorandum will most likely use it to make a decision about that problem. Therefore, while exploring the law in a general or abstract way may be appropriate in an academic paper, that approach is rarely the right one in an office memorandum. Instead, your analysis must be tailored to the particulars of the problem you have been asked to research and evaluate. Lawyers and other legal readers will also expect you to present your analysis by using certain conventions for structure and style.

1. Write Objectively

The purpose of an office memorandum is to explore the possible solutions to a legal problem. Exploration requires objectivity. In your role as an objective writer, you must explain the strongest and most likely arguments for each party in the dispute and then assess their relative strengths. You should express your analysis and conclusions objectively.

As a law student or a new lawyer, you may have trouble writing objectively because that style will be unfamiliar at first. All writers want to express feelings and opinions, especially if they have strongly held views. With practice, however, you will become comfortable with looking at a problem from both sides and with the conventions of predictive legal writing.

2. Write with Your Reader in Mind

For most memoranda, your audience will be a lawyer in your office or on the legal staff of a company or organization that is your client. In this situation, you are speaking as one specialist to another. But even if that lawyer is more experienced, you probably will know more about the subject you have just researched and analyzed than your reader does. Therefore, give your reader the background information about the law and the facts that is necessary for her to understand and appreciate your analysis. Don't assume your reader knows, or will recall, how the law works. Similarly, don't assume that she will know important details about legal authorities, like the holding of a key case or the language of a statute. Include that critical information in your memorandum, so your reader doesn't need to stop reading and look it up in order to understand what you are telling her.

In writing for a lawyer, you can take advantage of many shortcuts. Your reader will be familiar with the forms of legal analysis. See Chapter Two. She also will be familiar with many legal terms of art, freeing you from explaining or defining those terms. As you gain experience in law school and practice, you will develop a sense for how much you can assume your reader knows. But this shared knowledge isn't a license to use obscure jargon, wander off on tangents, or fail to explain or provide logical connections between ideas because they seem obvious to you after your research. Your reader will expect you to communicate your analysis directly, clearly, and concisely in plain English.

If you expect someone who isn't a lawyer to use your memorandum, you may need to forgo some of those shortcuts in order to communicate effectively with your audience. Consider the suggestions about writing for lay persons in Chapter Five.

3. Organize Your Analysis

a. Large-Scale

Organize the Discussion by major issues and subissues, using subheadings to guide your reader. Ideally, the major issues and headings will track the order introduced in the Questions Presented. The Discussion's structure will vary depending on the number of questions presented and their complexity. The sample memorandum in Appendix A shows you how to organize a Discussion by using multiple subissues that are raised by a single question presented.

Subheadings may be topics limited to a word or short phrase. But these "signposts" may also be written as complete issues or conclusions, like they are in our sample memorandum. Whichever approach you choose, we recommend writing and formatting subheadings consistently. Follow the conventions for capitalization and punctuation used in your law school or law office. See Chapter Nine, Punctuation and Grammar. Legal style manuals, which are discussed in Chapter Ten, may also have rules for formatting headings.

Your reader will appreciate roadmaps of the country ahead. "Umbrella" paragraphs and "mini-umbrella" paragraphs can introduce the Discussion's broad analytical framework or the framework for a particular subsection. Your reader will expect you to discuss each part of your analysis in the order set out in your roadmap, unless you tell her otherwise. See, for example, the Discussion's first paragraph in the sample memorandum. That umbrella paragraph introduces the broad analytical framework and the order in which the Discussion will analyze the subissues about false imprisonment. As a result, the reader knows where she's going.

b. Small-Scale

While the IRAC and CRAC paradigms don't apply to a memorandum as a whole, we use them, and their variations, to organize sections of a Discussion. In their simple forms, a subsection's heading or first text sentence alerts the reader to the subissue or subconclusion for that part of the analysis. The "rule" is the next part of the paradigm, followed by the best arguments for each party, the "application." Finally, those arguments must be evaluated in the "conclusion."

In objective writing, we try to explain the law completely before we apply it to the facts of our client's problem. You will see that pattern in subsections A through D of the sample memorandum.

If the rule is long, perhaps several pages, we may use a mini-umbrella to give the reader an overview of the area of law. We may then develop each subrule and its application separately. Sometimes, in order to streamline the rule section of the paradigm, we may incorporate parts of it into the application. For example, if a case is a useful analogy, we might develop the case's details in the analogical argument where it's used rather than in the rule section. However, if you decide to use a roadmap that's tricky to read, consider giving your reader some extra signposts. Varying the expected IRAC and CRAC paradigms can be the best route to take, if you add a mini-umbrella or other directions to make sure your reader gets to her intended destination.

If the arguments are relatively uncomplicated and short, the application can be a short paragraph. See, for example, our sample memorandum in Appendix A. The application paragraph in subsection A of the Discussion is only a few sentences long. When the analysis is more complex, you may need multiple paragraphs or paragraph blocks.

4. Explain the Pertinent Law

Unless you know otherwise, don't assume your reader is familiar with the law. Unlike an academic paper, an advisory document should only explain the law that is salient to your client's situation. Do, however, provide your reader with enough information about the law so she will be able to appreciate your analysis without reading or re-reading the authorities you rely on.

The length and content of your explanation will vary. Although you may only need several sentences or several paragraphs, sometimes several pages will be required. Develop the rule so that your smart, but busy, senior lawyer or client can understand it easily. Be concise and direct. Do the work for her by explaining how the different parts of the rule fit together.

In our sample memorandum, the law is reasonably settled because California's appellate courts, including its highest court, have considered false imprisonment issues in a number of decisions, including relatively recent ones. Sometimes, however, the pertinent authorities will be sparse or old. An issue may be one of "first impression" which has never been addressed by the courts in the controlling jurisdiction. If the law is unsettled, tell your reader that directly as part of your rule explanation.

Generally, the Discussion's rule statement is comprised of the legal principles for an area of law, moving from broad to narrow. You will extract or synthesize these legal principles, also referred to as "rules" or "subrules," from the range of legal authorities, including statutes, regulations, and case law. See, for example, the sample memorandum's first umbrella paragraph at the beginning of the Discussion that describes the broad rule for false imprisonment.

You may be able to further explain the rule by summarizing how courts have applied it in precedent cases. You can also use the specific holdings, key facts, and pertinent reasoning from those cases to make the rule concrete and set up analogical analysis.

You also must prove that the law is what you say it is with legal citations. Follow the practice in your law school or office. See more about using legal authorities and citations in Chapters Two and Ten.

5. Include Complete Arguments and Counter-Arguments

Your analysis should incorporate and evaluate complete arguments for your client. Your analysis also should address counter-arguments. These arguments and counter-arguments may be based on rules, analogies, logic, policies, narratives, principles, and customs. We also consider the consequences of outcomes, sometimes described as "slippery slopes," "floodgates," or "negative impacts on judicial resources." While a memorandum isn't a law review article, you can consider policy arguments, even if those arguments aren't directly addressed in the primary authorities.

6. Use Conservative Style and Tone

Legal writing style tends to be formal. It changes slowly. Traditionally, we've avoided the first person, contractions, and abbreviations in research memoranda. While we have used both the first person and contractions in this book to make our style more conversational, one of us lost the argument to say “memo” instead of memorandum, even though “memo” is what you will call one of these documents at school and at work.

We recommend avoiding slang, “that’s cool,” and colloquial expressions, like “split hairs,” “beat around the bush,” or “miss the memo.” Colloquialisms are easily misinterpreted. It’s difficult to control their tone and effect. Similarly, forgo hyperbole, like “a ridiculous argument” or “an outrageous position.”

Use a tone that won’t detract from the information you want to convey. You can achieve a matter-of-fact tone by packaging that information in straightforward, unequivocal sentences, and by stating your findings and conclusions directly, without apologies or unnecessary qualifications.

7. Use Quotations Selectively

Paraphrase judicial language rather than quoting at length. Isolate the relevant judicial language, quote it directly with necessary context, and paraphrase the rest. The reader should not have to decide what part of a long quotation is important. For more about quotations, see Chapter Ten.

I. CONCLUSION

A separate conclusion ties together the answers you have stated in the Discussion. You may also use a Conclusion to state additional options or recommendations for handling the problem.

Sometimes a Conclusion will be difficult to predict. For example, if the question concerns how a California trial court will apply a California statute, predicting that answer may be difficult if the California appellate courts haven't addressed that issue (an "issue of first impression"). Because you probably understand the subject far better than your reader, you will be expected to state an opinion, however qualified it may need to be.

The Conclusion should not merely repeat the Brief Answer, but it may parallel the Brief Answer. The Conclusion customarily explains your reasoning in more detail than the Brief Answer. Whatever its content, the Conclusion should summarize. Your Conclusion should not introduce new authorities or new information about authorities covered in the Discussion.

In a short memorandum, you may not need to include a separate Conclusion. But you still should signal the reader that the analysis is done. You can do that in a concise, final paragraph at the end of the Discussion.

§ 6.3 CLIENT LETTERS

Lawyers write to clients to give answers to legal questions and to describe possible courses of action and attendant risks. In representing business clients, you may be writing to in-house counsel. But many clients are lay persons who will not typically have special knowledge of the law, its concepts, and its terminology. Because lawyers should write for their clients' benefit and understanding, writing an advisory letter to a client who is a lay person can be a challenging writing task. The first step is to recognize the problem.

Before drafting a letter to a client, ask these questions: What can I assume this client knows? Does the client have any familiarity with the pertinent law? How can I effectively communicate my advice without sounding condescending? Write the letter with the answers to those questions and with the following guidelines in mind.

Be direct. Answer the client's questions directly and give advice or recommendations within the first few sentences. If you can't give direct answers and advice, say so, and explain why.

Be complete. State any advice or recommendations for action completely. State the facts upon which you base your answers and advice, so your client can judge whether you are acting on complete, accurate information.

If the purpose of the letter is to weigh risks or courses of action, as in litigation, then consider theories of liability, possible damages, and the probability of winning. Both the client's case and the opposing case should be outlined and objectively evaluated. Give the reasons for your conclusions and advice in language the client can understand.

Be clear. Your letter to a lay client should be written in plain language. Doing that is more difficult than it may appear. Three of the more important guidelines for plain English are listed here:

(1) Replace words and phrases, including technical terms, with which a lay reader is probably unfamiliar, with familiar words whenever you can do so without losing meaning. For example, instead of "voir dire," write "questioning of prospective jurors." Instead of "statute of frauds," write "a statute that requires some contracts to be written."

(2) Define or illustrate (or both) any technical terms and terms of art that you must use. If a definition would be too difficult for a lay reader, use an example instead.

(3) Avoid terms with both legal and common meanings—like "privilege." If you can't, identify the differing meanings clearly for your client.

Be specific. Give exact times, costs, and other important information whenever possible. If exact information can't be provided, explain why, and state when it will or may be available.

Be brief when the subject matter permits. Short letters need no apology. Don't pad a short letter. And shorten a long letter whenever possible. One way to shorten a client letter is to look for legal analysis that does not directly explain your answer. Clients rarely need or want such information. See Chapter Five about concise word choices and Chapter Eight about shortening sentences.

Be realistic. Unless you are writing a formal opinion letter, leave out analytical details, like case analysis, and legal citations. For most clients, citations will be indecipherable. Before including this technical legal information, ask yourself whether your client will want or will understand it.

Be objective. Lawyers sometimes argue their cases in letters to clients as an unconscious "warm-up" exercise before addressing opposing counsel or a court. Such an argument may have the unhappy effect of leading a client to expect more than the lawyer can deliver. Advisory writing may be argumentative at times, but the argument should have a specific, defensible purpose, *i.e.*, to persuade a client to give up a lawsuit or to change settlement terms based on a prior, objective discussion.

Be considerate and control the letter's tone. Your client is someone with a problem. Try to solve that problem in a sincere and humane way. Being considerate requires controlling your tone carefully. Don't joke about the severity or significance of your client's problems.

Tailor the level of formality to your client and maintain that level throughout the letter. Don't begin with "Dear Charlie" and close with "Very truly yours, Bickerstaff, Edgewater, and Ransom." Don't try to impress your client by using obscure reasoning, legal jargon, or hyperbolic expressions, like "preposterous on its face." Eliminate stilted or verbose language, like "a date certain," "purports to know," or "with matters in this recumbent posture." Remember that your client is paying for this letter and expects to have his or her time and intelligence respected. Here are some examples.

1. *Mixed tone (formal and colloquial), stilted and wordy*: While no advantage to deletion of the provision is apparent, its deletion would not be the end of the world. In the event you wish to substitute another version of the provision, I offer other illustrative provisions for your perusal.

Revised: Omitting the provision will do no harm that I can see. But here are two alternatives that you could use. (20 words instead of 40)

2. *Wordy and indirect*: This will reply to your written inquiry of August 10, 2016, concerning certain aspects of your purchase. My delay in responding is due to overwhelming work for other clients. After extensive, careful research, I am able to consider the issues that you raise in the order that they occur in the letter.

Revised: In response to your August 10 request, I have researched your problem and will answer your questions in the order you have asked them. (24 words instead of 52)

3. *Mixed metaphors and wordy*: Give me a call when you have digested this letter, and we can get our ducks in a row.

Revised: Please call when you are ready to proceed. (8 words instead of 19)

§ 6.4 EMAIL

Email and other electronic methods of communication are essential tools for both law students and practitioners. Although they may seem less important than research memoranda or briefs, lawyers increasingly communicate critical information by means of email and other electronic wizardry. The form and substance of these communications reflect on your professional competence. They also can profoundly affect legal outcomes. Like other forms of legal writing, you will need to adapt your writing skills and practices to these forms of communication.

A. PERILS AND ETIQUETTE OF COMMUNICATING VIA EMAIL AND OTHER ELECTRONIC MEDIA

Email is ubiquitous. Lawyers use it to communicate with clients, with each other, and increasingly with the courts and administrative agencies. Email is widely recognized as the most frequent form of communication among lawyers, for everything from negotiating a settlement to arranging a lunch meeting.

Email is also the least controllable form of communication. Think of your emails as billboard messages. This metaphor may seem extreme. However, as we send emails every day, for everything in our lives, we potentially expose information and ourselves to a wider audience in ways that are hard to fully imagine.

By its nature, email is less formal than other forms of legal writing. Its casual nature and ease of dissemination present challenges that you must consider whenever you write an email in the course of doing business. Remember that you have no control over the distribution of your emails once they leave your phone or your computer. Once sent, any email can be forwarded without your authorization or knowledge. This reminder is worth repeating and highlighting:

> *Even if you mark your emails as "privileged" or as "work product," emails can easily be forwarded without your authorization or knowledge.*

Not only may your emails be forwarded without your permission, they may be read by the email service provider and mined for marketing information. Current case law is ambivalent at best on the right of privacy and attorney-client privilege in email communication. Keep yourself informed about the latest case law on this subject. "Free" email services, such as gmail, yahoo, and hotmail, require customers to accept pages of boilerplate agreements that, among other things, may waive the right to privacy or attorney-client privilege. If you or your clients use an email service that is not encrypted and password-protected, read the terms of service carefully and take all necessary measures to protect your privileged communications.

The same advice applies to texts, tweets, Facebook posts, and other online communications. The internet is the new Wild West. Nearly anything goes, and can come back to haunt you. Unless you take security measures, once you hit "send," you should assume that you have lost control over who may read it.

When you use social media for business, be aware of what psychologists have described as the "online disinhibition effect." It can make you feel anonymous, as if you are writing in a vacuum that won't ever provoke feedback from the recipient. A good way to corral this tendency is to imagine that a federal trial judge will be reading whatever you write—every email, every text, every post.

B. EMAIL ETIQUETTE: TEN SIMPLE RULES

We recommend that you keep these simple rules in mind. We also recognize that sometimes you will decide to break them. But think before you do, and then proceed with caution.

Rule 1: Keep email messages short. Think of each email as a telegram, not as a letter or a memorandum. If you need to write a letter or a memorandum, write it in your word processing program, then send it as an attachment.

Rule 2: Start each email as a new message to avoid unwanted "tails." If you must repeat something from a prior email, then repeat it. If you make a habit of always starting a fresh email, you will avoid the peril of sending confidential material to the wrong person. This disastrous mistake is not only embarrassing, and potentially costly for clients, but it can destroy the attorney-client privilege that protects your confidential communications. The privilege can be lost not just for that message, but for the subject of the message in general.

The rules for electronic discovery are beyond the scope of this book. But if you do break this rule, as lawyers often do, be aware that if one email in a string is discoverable, the entire string may also be discoverable. And that one-line email in the string that you wrote to another associate complaining about how miserable it is to deal with opposing counsel might ultimately be discoverable and read by that opposing counsel, or the federal or state trial judge hearing the case.

Rule 3: Fill in the "Send" box last. This precaution prevents transmitting your message inadvertently before it's finished and ready to send.

Rule 4: Avoid "Reply All" if you are working for a client. "Reply All" increases the risk of violating the attorney client privilege because it increases the number of readers who can forward the message to others who may nullify your client's privilege.

Also be careful about combining the "Bcc" function with "Reply All." If the Bcc recipient replies to "All," that reply will also disclose his or her identity to "All."

Rule 5: Routinely mark emails to clients as "privileged," that is, as subject to attorney-client privilege. You might also include a reminder not to forward the email without consulting you first. Before you hit "send," remember that your client may choose to forward your email anyway. But a reminder about the privilege may encourage the client to reconsider sharing the email. You also have the opportunity to indicate the email's level of importance by using a flag or other device in your mail program. If something needs to be done quickly, flagging your email also could be useful.

Rule 6: When writing to opposing counsel, or in a litigation setting, ask for a "read receipt" to show that your email was received and when it was received. Write the email as if you are copying the judge, or other adjudicating official, because the judge may end up reading it.

Rule 7: Spell check and edit your emails. Make sure that the email is addressed to the right person. The auto-fill function can fill in the wrong address. Assume that your emails will be read critically by readers other than the ones you intend. As part of your editing, delete exclamation marks or emoticons. If you think that emoticon really is necessary, reconsider what you've written. Use the same formal style that you use for letters and briefs.

If you are writing a complex email, you will revise and edit it more effectively if you can let it rest. Similarly, if you are writing an email under stressful circumstances, or at the end of an exhausting workday, consider reviewing it in the morning with fresh eyes, before you hit "send."

Rule 8: For important documents that you don't want altered by recipients, convert them to "PDF's" before sending, being sure to turn off track changes or highlighting. You don't want the world to see your thinking process, your first drafts, or the arguments you decided not to make. If you do opt to send a Word document, take advantage of any program features that allow you to "scrub" the document's metadata.

Rule 9: Observe all of the usual rules governing attribution of sources. Just because it's an email doesn't mean you can use the ideas or exact wording of other writers without specific attribution.

Rule 10: Observe common courtesies of salutation in a business context: Use "Dear Jane/James" and close with something courteous, such as "Best regards," "Kind regards," "Thank you," or "Sincerely." Include your contact information at the end.

§ 6.5 REVISING, EDITING, AND PROOFREADING

As every experienced writer knows, the first draft is never good enough. Revising, editing, and proofreading are essential. Even a short letter should be reviewed for content, for clarity, for readability, for conciseness, and, finally, for errors and formatting. Longer, more complex documents, like memoranda, contracts, and other transactional documents, should be revised or rewritten several times. And for many writing projects, "several" revisions may not be enough.

Keep in mind that in this book we generally use the term revising to cover changes in the substantive analysis and structure. See Chapters One through Four regarding those topics. Editing refers to stylistic changes while proofreading is limited to hunting down typos and other glitches. For more about editing and proofreading, see Chapters Five and Eight through Ten.

Ideally, you will be able to construct a timeline that allows you to rest, revise, edit, proofread, and cite check your drafts. In a perfect world, someone else with "fresh eyes" would also read your last draft. Whenever possible, you should have someone else review it at the sentence level for readability, punctuation, grammar, and spelling. If your client can afford only one draft, then you must draft with extra care and review that draft conscientiously. When time pressure doesn't allow revising or polishing, someone else should review the work if that's possible. If you do have the luxury of time and multiple drafts, here's what we recommend.

Let your drafts rest. Put the work away for at least one day, or overnight, before major revisions or final editing. That lapse of time will allow you to return to the draft with greater detachment and make it easier for you to revise or edit your own work (always a difficult task).

If you have the option, consider revising and proofreading on a printed page, rather than exclusively on a computer screen. You may find it easier to keep the entire document in mind if you can flip through pages. And reading the document in a different format may help you to spot problems or errors.

When you revise, make sure that the document is complete, includes each required section, and says what you want it to say. Within longer sections, like the Statement of Facts or the Discussion, consider whether the large-scale organization is logical and whether you have imposed that structure consistently.

Review each paragraph to make sure that it begins with a topic or thesis sentence that clearly states the point that you prove in that paragraph. Consider whether each paragraph is unified around the topic or point articulated in the paragraph's first sentence. Check for clear transitions between paragraphs, paragraph blocks, and sections that will help keep your reader on track. Once you are satisfied with the document's content and structure, you are ready to edit.

For editing, review sentences for readability and precision. For troublesome sentences, use the simple method for editing described in Chapter Eight. After re-examining sentences, check for concise, parallel headings and subheadings. When writing on a computer or when dictating, it is especially important for you to see how paragraphs and sections look when printed. As part of the edit, read the whole document for uniform style and for consistency in wording and tone. Now you are ready to proofread.

When the document is revised and edited, your next step is to proofread to catch any typos, misspellings, or other glitches. Although typos and misspellings may provide comic relief to your reader, they do so at your expense. One lawyer learned just how expensive a typographical error could be after he signed and mailed a letter informing a prospective client that he would charge a "fat fee" (instead of a "flat fee").

All typographical errors and misspelled words are your responsibility, not the responsibility of a legal assistant or a "spell check" program. If you have difficulty spelling correctly, keep a list of words that you regularly misspell at your desk when you write. You might also have someone who spells well proofread your work.

Your final tasks are to check every quotation and every citation for accuracy and to then format those quotations and citations correctly. For more about quotations and citations, see Chapter Ten.

You have now completed the first part of Step Five, drafting advisory writing. The second part, drafting persuasive writing, is addressed in Chapter Seven. The same revision, editing, and proofreading skills discussed above apply to persuasive, or advocacy, writing, with the addition of strategies for rhetorical effects not needed or desired in advisory writing.

STEP 5

- Write first draft.
- Let that draft rest.
- Revise for organization and analytical content.
- Draft and revise again, as needed.

CHAPTER 7

ADVOCACY WRITING

§ 7.1 INTRODUCTION

This chapter addresses two forms of advocacy writing—litigation briefs and letters to opposing parties—and suggests techniques for presenting these documents persuasively. Every document a lawyer writes has a persuasive purpose. Even with a research memorandum, the writer seeks to persuade her reader that it is reliable and correct. While advocating for a particular person or policy, lawyers often must navigate between appropriate advocacy and an unfettered sales pitch.

§ 7.2 LEGAL BRIEFS

A. PURPOSE OF A LEGAL BRIEF

The purpose of a legal brief is to win your case or your motion. A winning brief will (1) demonstrate that your argument is either required or permitted by the law, (2) motivate the judge or clerk by showing that the result you seek is fair, (3) engage the reader with a succinct, precise, and compelling style, and (4) follow the conventions of legal writing unless there's a good reason to depart from them.

Three classical rhetorical appeals are at the foundation of persuading the legal reader: logos, or the rational and logical appeal of an argument, pathos, the emotional appeal of an argument, and ethos, the ethical appeal of an argument. You must attend to all three of these components to write a persuasive brief. Exactly how you execute the brief will depend on the audience for the brief, the purpose of the brief, and the general social context in which you write it.

B. PREPARATION FOR WRITING

1. Know the Rules

Brief writing for litigation is formal. The content, the format, the wording, and the writer's tone are all subject to conventions, discussed below. Before you start writing, read your course assignment or the rules of court to see what components are permitted or required in the brief, what format is required, and what the word or page limits are.

The trial-level brief for *Abrams v. Scott* in the Appendix is styled as a Memorandum of Points and Authorities as is typical of a trial brief addressed to California courts. It includes a Table of Contents, Introduction, Statement of Facts, Argument, and Conclusion. Appellate courts typically require other components, such as a Statement of Jurisdiction, a procedural history, and a Summary of the Argument. To ensure you include all required components, you might set up a document with the components of the brief on your computer before you start to draft.

2. Select Your Arguments

Start by reviewing the record of the case and your legal research. Follow the process outlined in

Chapters Two and Three to decide which facts in the record are significant and which legal arguments to advance. Then outline the Argument section of the brief.

Select a limited number of arguments. In general, judges and other specialists agree that too many arguments may detract from rather than enhance the persuasiveness of a brief. Argue the strongest points—perhaps only two or three—even though there are many attractive possibilities. If you cannot win on the strongest points, you should not expect to win on the weaker points. Of course, a case may be so complex that you must argue many points, for example, if you can only prove your case by demonstrating that you can win each of numerous elements.

Once you have identified your legal arguments, organize them. Write them as a series of contentions to assess whether some contentions must logically be addressed before others. If not, address your strongest point first.

3. Consider Your Theory of the Case

Your brief should establish a "theory of the case," that is, a theme or overall narrative to frame the issues in the case in a way that benefits your client. The theory of the case should be particularly evident in the introduction and the statement of facts. You should, however, weave it throughout your brief. The theory of the case should connect your argument about the law (the legal justification) with a theory for why you should win (the motivating theory). A theory of the case isn't just a sympathetic story—it should have a basis in the law.

To develop a theory of the case, consider the best story for your facts. Consider what kind of cultural "stock stories" might be told through your case. Your theory of the case may be the answer to the prompt: This is a case about . . .

- This is a case about corporate greed.
- This is a case about local control.
- This is a case about David and Goliath.

Think about how your client or others in your story may resemble characters in a myth or a fairy tale. These stories are deeply imbedded in our culture. They contain familiar concepts that may help you give shape to the facts that are good for you and help you explain away the facts that are bad for you.

The theory of the case should resonate with the law on a human level. If the facts aren't particularly sympathetic for your side, ask why the law is as it is. Does this issue raise delicate social questions that judicial bodies are less competent to decide? What is the law trying to accomplish? What interests does the law try to balance? How does my client's situation fit into the story of the law? Consider the real-world ramifications of your legal problem.

C. COMPONENTS OF A LEGAL BRIEF

1. Table of Contents and Point Headings

The Table of Contents lists the components of the brief and the point headings along with the corresponding page number where each component and point heading starts. A point heading is a concise, persuasive statement of a conclusion or reason that you want the court to accept. Point headings are used as the headings and subheadings within the Argument section of a brief. They are also included in the Table of Contents of the brief to summarize the parts of the Argument. Point headings have two main functions, one structural and one persuasive.

a. Example of Table of Contents

The defendant's brief in *Abrams v. Scott* includes these components and point headings:

INTRODUCTION

STATEMENT OF FACTS

ARGUMENT

A. No Jury Could Reasonably Find that the Plaintiff was Involuntarily Confined When the Complaint Alleges He Left the Conference Room When He Chose to and Fails to Allege that Anyone Took Physical Action to Prevent Him from Leaving.

B. No Jury Could Reasonably Find that the Plaintiff was Involuntarily Confined in the Unlocked Conference Room Because Mr. Scott's Alleged

Statements Are Insufficient to Show Unreasonable Duress.

CONCLUSION

b. Formatting Point Headings

Point headings and subheadings assert your main arguments, arranged in a logical order. Use outline numbering (I, II, III; A, B, C; 1, 2, 3) to help your reader understand the logical relationship of your arguments. Point headings enumerated with Roman numerals I, II, and III are typically used for dispositive arguments which, if accepted, would mean that your side would win on that basis alone. Subheadings set out the steps of logic or conclusions that prove your point heading. Generally, don't include a "1" if there's no "2." Include text under each heading. Single-space your heading, but skip a line between headings so your Table of Contents is readable.

c. Drafting Point Headings

The major point headings should each be stated in terms of the standard that the court will use to decide the question and should include the conclusion you want the court to reach and the supporting reason. If a point heading that includes these three parts would be too long, consider stating the supporting reason in a subheading.

Identify the conclusions that a court must accept in order to decide in your client's favor. Then identify reasons that support those conclusions.

Next, outline the necessary conclusions. Decide on an order that will, if logically possible, put your strongest arguments at the beginning. Use an order that keeps related parts of the argument together.

Once you have decided on the subject matter and order, write the point headings, using persuasive sentence structure and language. Keep in mind the following generally-accepted guidelines for how to persuasively assert your position in point headings:

If the point heading is purely on a question of law, include a policy argument or other rationale to express the reasoning that supports your conclusion.

If the point heading is about how the law should be applied to the facts of your client's situation, include one or more key facts specific to your case that relate to the legal issue.

Unacceptable generic description:

No jury could reasonably find that Plaintiff was involuntarily confined.

Use full sentences, not topical phrases.

Unacceptable topical heading:

Involuntary Confinement.

Use statements about your case, not abstract legal principles.

Unacceptable abstract heading:

A person is involuntarily confined only if he is physically restrained.

Use statements that demonstrate legal relevance.

Legal relevance not demonstrated:

Mr. Scott did not threaten Plaintiff with any serious consequence.

Finally, avoid long, complex statements.

Here is a point heading that demonstrates effective use of these guidelines:

No Jury Could Reasonably Find the Plaintiff was Involuntarily Confined When His Complaint Alleges He Left the Conference Room When He Chose and Fails to Allege that Anyone Took Physical Action to Prevent Him from Leaving.

d. Example of Point Headings from Opposing Briefs

With the above guidelines in mind, compare excerpts from the point headings taken from briefs filed before the United State Supreme Court in *Ewing v. California*, 538 U.S. 11 (2003).

1. *From Brief for Petitioner-Defendant Gary Ewing:*

I. THE CALIFORNIA "THREE STRIKES AND YOU'RE OUT" LAW

II. A SENTENCE OF LIFE IMPRISONMENT WITHOUT POSSIBILITY OF PAROLE FOR TWENTY-FIVE YEARS FOR SHOPLIFTING THREE GOLF CLUBS RAISES AN INFERENCE OF GROSS DISPROPORTIONALITY

A. The Gravity of the Offense

B. The Harshness of the Penalty

III. AN INTRAJURISDICTIONAL EVALUATION OF CALIFORNIA'S SENTENCING PROVISIONS

CONFIRMS THAT MR. EWING'S SENTENCE IS GROSSLY DISPROPORTIONATE TO THIS OFFENSE

IV. AN INTERJURISDICTIONAL EVALUATION OF MR. EWING'S SENTENCE FURTHER CONFIRMS ITS GROSS DISPROPORTIONALITY

A. No Life Sentence in Forty-Six Other Jurisdictions

B. Less Severe Sentences in the Remaining States

1. Louisiana

2. Oklahoma

3. Alabama

4. South Dakota

5. Vermont

6. Nevada

2. From Brief for the State of California:

A SENTENCE OF LIFE IMPRISONMENT WITH THE POSSIBILITY OF PAROLE, IMPOSED UPON A RECIDIVIST FOR A NEW FELONY CONVICTION, IS NOT "CRUEL AND UNUSUAL PUNISHMENT"

A. A punishment of imprisonment can violate the Eighth Amendment only if it is an "extreme sentence" that is "grossly disproportionate" to his criminal conduct.

B. Petitioner's sentence is not "grossly disproportionate" and therefore comports with the Eighth Amendment.

1. This Court previously has held comparable punishments for crimes that were not more serious than petitioner's.

2. The essential components of California's "Three Strikes" law ensure the proportionality of sentences imposed under it.

    a. Enhancement of sentences for recidivism is a longstanding and empirically-justified practice that warrants heightened judicial deference.

    b. Other essential facets of California's recidivist scheme provide guarantees of proportionality.

2. Table of Authorities

A Table of Authorities is a list of all authorities—cases, statutes, and regulations—cited in your brief. Most courts require a Table for briefs fifteen pages or longer. A Table of Authorities may be useful for shorter briefs to allow the judge or clerk to check your authorities against those of the opposing side. Consult the rules of the court you are addressing for formatting requirements of your Table of Authorities. Be sure to cite unfavorable authorities in your brief and include them in your table.

3. Questions Presented and Introductions

Most briefs contain one or more of the following components: a Question Presented (sometimes called an Issue Statement), an Introduction (sometimes called a Preliminary Statement), or a Summary of Argument. These components serve a common purpose: to focus your reader on the specific legal issue or issues addressed in your brief, in the context of the material facts of the dispute.

The Question Presented, Introduction, and Summary of Argument are introductory elements that condense the brief as a whole. They distill the arguments elaborated in the argument section of the brief. They may feel redundant to you, but your reader will appreciate being able to find a succinct summary of your argument in a predictable location in the document.

These components also make a strong first impression on the judge or clerk reading your brief. First impressions strongly influence how the reader will perceive your story. Once a person has a first impression, all other information may be viewed in light of that impression.

Because these components come at the beginning of the brief, they can also provide a favorable frame for your story. A framing device provides a context from which you tell your story. It can influence how your reader understands the facts. For example, a story about the increasing cost of gas may be "framed" positively by situating the story in the context of environmentalist's concerns about fossil fuel's effect on the environment or negatively by situating the story in the context of economic decline because of high energy prices.

a. Questions Presented

Questions Presented are more commonly used in appellate briefs in which the parties can focus on a small number of issues raised at the trial court. A Question Presented provides a quick picture of a case for a reader who knows nothing about it. The Question Presented should express your syllogism for why you win, that is, how the governing law applied to the material facts results in the holding that you hope the court adopts. Unlike the Questions Presented in an advisory memorandum, Questions Presented for a brief serve a persuasive function by providing a favorable picture of the case. Questions should therefore be written to serve that persuasive function—but without misleading or alienating the judges. That calls for skill and the touch of an artist.

A one-sentence Question Presented may be stated in either declarative form or question form ("The question is . . ." or "Whether . . ."). If the material facts cannot be stated very concisely, you may state the Question Presented in multiple sentences.

Questions Presented should be expressed in terms of the circumstances of the case without unnecessary detail. The statements should be short, concise, and persuasive. As discussed in Chapter Six for advisory writing, the questions should incorporate key facts rather than stating the legal question in abstract terms.

To write a persuasive Question, you must address an issue on which the outcome of the case depends and ask it in such a way that only one reasonable answer follows: yours. Select the facts carefully for their persuasive value. The question itself must be rhetorically structured so as to emphasize the most favorable facts. The conclusion that the court is to reach should be implicit. All this must be done without distorting either the law or the facts and without appearing to be argumentative. Here are examples of effective questions written from opposing viewpoints.

> *Petitioner's question*: Does petitioner's enhanced sentence for shoplifting three golf clubs—life imprisonment without possibility of parole for at least twenty-five years—violate the Eighth Amendment's prohibition against cruel and unusual punishments?
>
> *Respondent's question*: Does a sentence of life with the possibility of parole after twenty-five years for a felony recidivist convicted of grand theft amount to cruel and unusual punishment in violation of the Eighth Amendment?

Do not write a question that is argumentative, presuming to answer the question which you should be asking, such as this:

> Whether a sentence that violates the Eighth Amendment's prohibition against cruel and unusual punishments is unconstitutional.

Conclusory questions are also ineffective because they state the nature of the conclusion to be reached without giving a clue about the specific answer. For example, "The question is whether the defendant's sentence is unconstitutional."

b. Introductions

An Introduction is a relatively new idea in legal briefs, but it is an ancient concept. In classical rhetoric, an argument started with an "Exordium." The term "exordium" comes from the Latin term meaning "to urge forward." And indeed, the introduction should be a strong launching pad for your argument.

Think about your Introduction early, so that you can imbue the rest of your brief with the themes that you introduce here. Your first draft of your Introduction will not be the last draft. You will rewrite it as you go through your brief and particularly after you're done with your draft.

The Introduction should convey your theory of the case. It should marry the justifying rationales of your argument to the motivating ones. It should tell the basics of the dispute that brought the parties to the court to give the judge an overview.

Don't assume that the judge is familiar with your case even if this isn't the first motion before the same court. The introduction should introduce your reader to your argument, but you don't need to summarize all of your points in the argument section of the brief. Instead, tell your argument very concisely. Distill it down to a few short sentences for a short brief and a few short paragraphs for a brief that is longer than fifteen pages. Even if you will not include a Question Presented, try writing out the central syllogism of the brief, to help you focus on the legal issue that's at stake and the most material facts that are central to the controversy. Some say the introduction should be readable in 90 seconds.

Tell your best material facts first. Use actual facts, not general impressions or characterizations of facts. Tell your story with facts, using verbs and nouns rather than adjectives. Be concrete and specific. Tell clearly what you want the court to do. The end of the story should not be a secret.

c. *Summary of Argument*

Some courts require a Summary of Argument instead of an Introduction. Although the Summary of the Argument is placed before the argument in a brief, it should be written after the argument has been both written and revised. A Summary is often included in a brief that contains Questions Presented and answers the questions with reasoning that supports the answers.

The Summary should be a succinct, accurate, and clear condensation of the argument actually made in the body of the brief. It should not merely repeat the headings. Thus, the summary should be more than a mere assertion of your client's right to win the case. It should present the crux of the argument. It should weave together the strands of argument from the brief and identify the logical relationships between key points. Normally no authorities are discussed, although citations to one or two crucial cases may be included.

The paragraphs of the summary are set off with numerals or letters corresponding to divisions of the argument proper.

4. The Statement of the Facts

How the facts are stated may be more important than the argument of law itself. Judges frequently advise lawyers to spend more time writing the facts.

Some courts require a Statement of the Case, which is a Statement that includes both facts and procedural history. Try to avoid a lengthy summary of procedural steps before the human side of the case is introduced. First identify the parties (especially if your client might evoke sympathy). Summarize only those procedural steps that are material to the questions to be argued or necessary to an understanding of the case.

The judges initially know nothing about the case. They want to know what happened, when, where, and to whom. Do not deaden this desire to know with an overly detailed or dry recital.

Notice how the who, what, when, and where make this fact statement not only vivid, but also persuasive:

> On the morning of March 12, 2000, Petitioner Gary Ewing entered a golf pro shop in Los Angeles County, California. He asked the man who worked there several questions and then looked around the shop for about ten to fifteen minutes. He again approached the employee and purchased a token redeemable for golf balls on the driving range. He

> once more looked around the pro shop, this time in the area where golf clubs were displayed. He returned a third time to the employee, asking him where the driving range was. The employee directed him to an exit on one side of the pro shop.
>
> Instead of exiting through that door, however, Mr. Ewing left the shop through a door in the opposite direction, which led to the parking lot. The employee observed that Mr. Ewing was walking with a noticeable limp which he had not seen during their two earlier encounters. The employee called 911. When the police arrived, they discovered Mr. Ewing between two parked cars pulling three golf clubs from his pants leg. The police told him to put down the clubs, each of which retailed for $399. Mr. Ewing complied and was taken into custody without incident.
>
> . . .
>
> The trial court found the allegations of Mr. Ewing's 1994 felony convictions true and further found that the convictions qualified as strikes under the Three Strikes law. Mr. Ewing's prior strikes were three burglary convictions and a single robbery conviction that was related to one of the burglaries. The underlying conduct for these prior convictions all occurred within a single month in 1993 and was the subject of a single criminal proceeding. Two of the burglaries were non-violent, but qualified as "serious" crimes under the Three Strikes law. In the third burglary (also charged as a robbery), Mr. Ewing brandished, but did not use, a knife.

As illustrated in this fact statement, the facts must be stated to sound objective. For persuasive effect, the writer may arrange them, phrase them, and expand or condense treatment of particular events to emphasize favorable facts and to diminish unfavorable facts. In this statement, the fact that Mr. Ewing possessed a knife during one of the burglaries is mentioned, but not elaborated on or repeated. Similarly, the fact that he was previously convicted of four offenses that qualified as strikes is explained, but it is told in the context of other facts to minimize the significance of those offenses—that they all occurred "within a single month in 1993." The ordering of the facts, the choice of detail, and the vivid description of those details create an emotional response in the reader. As demonstrated in this Statement of Facts, the use of chronology, the placement within sentences and paragraphs of key facts, and the choice of verbs and nouns all assist in presenting the facts in a persuasive way.

Fact statements can be written persuasively by (1) selecting facts, (2) organization facts, and (3) presenting parties and issues with skillful word choices.

First, select the facts carefully to write a persuasive fact statement. You must, of course, include both favorable and unfavorable facts. Establish your credibility by distinguishing between disputed and undisputed facts and alleged and established facts. Include material facts, facts that give necessary context, and a limited number of substantively non-material details that add human interest or create the desired impression or context. But use of non-material details must be limited and subtle. Use visual details and direct quotes to arouse the reader's interest and draw the reader into the event.

Second, use a simple organizational pattern. The judges will assimilate the facts more readily if they are stated in chronological order or in clearly defined topical order. If the fact statement is long, use headings to help the reader understand and remember the facts. The facts that are stated first will have the most impact, followed by the facts stated at the end of a paragraph. Facts stated in the middle of a paragraph receive the least attention from a reader. Be aware of structural significance. You may suggest cause and effect by stating two facts in sequence.

Third, select words deliberately to precisely convey your meaning. The following suggestions should help you to set forth the facts clearly and favorably without distorting them.

Avoid using "plaintiff" and "defendant," particularly in describing your client, because it creates an impersonal tone and provides no specific factual information about the case. Instead, select designations that will be readily understood and also factually informative. For example, use "husband" and "wife" in a domestic relations case; use "employer" and "employee" or "worker" in a labor dispute. Or, once you describe your client with reference to the litigation or the nature of the case, refer to your client by name to humanize the client. Give special attention to distinctive designations in a case involving many parties.

Do not hide unfavorable facts, but do not highlight them either. For example, place such facts between statements of related favorable facts. Conclude with a fact or event favorable to your client's position, not with an unfavorable fact.

Use short sentences to increase readability. Use forceful verbs and nouns, chosen to characterize your client advantageously and to depict events favorably, but not so forceful that a fair-minded reader will lose faith in your credibility. Cases in which one party is always fair and right and the other party is always unfair and wrong are a rarity. Use adjectives sparingly and selectively; avoid adjectives that reflect bias, such as "reactionary" or "hysterical."

Avoid an obtrusive style: let the facts speak for themselves. Minimize adjectives or avoid them altogether. Do not editorialize or argue. Instead, rely on selection, juxtaposition, and careful word choice for persuasion.

Use diagrams or charts to present complicated facts, relationships, or chronology of events.

After writing the Argument section, review the fact statement. Add any significant facts that were omitted in the first draft. Omit any unnecessary facts that were included. If you are working with a record, be certain that you have supported fact statements by accurate references to the record in the form required by governing rules.

5. The Argument

a. General Writing Goals

If you have not already written a Question Presented, test your readiness to draft your argument by trying to state in one sentence the conclusion that you want the court to reach. Then consider your case from the perspective of a judge. Ask yourself what you would want to know first if you sat in a judge's chair. How would you want the law presented? As you draft, keep in mind that a judge reading your brief may be tired, may be reading your brief after reading others on different subjects, or may be able to devote only limited time to considering it.

Get to the point. Explain what your client wants and why. Tell the court what you want in the first page or two of the brief, not in the middle or at the end. Explain exactly what you want the court to do.

Be concise. Judges universally complain that briefs are too long. They complain that there is too much laborious, unapplied case analysis and too little effort to revise and condense. From the judge's point of view, shorter is better.

b. Organizing the Argument Section of Your Brief

Structure your brief from its beginning to its conclusion so that the judge will be able to scan it rapidly and understand your case and your argument quickly. Use headings to distinguish separate parts of your argument and clear thesis sentences so the judge can easily skim the brief to find a particular part of your argument. Judges are not always able to study each brief in detail.

Organize the large-scale structure of your brief by focusing on your key argument. In advisory writing you will usually explain the law fairly comprehensively. In the false imprisonment advisory memorandum, for example, the author analyzes each element of the cause of action. In the brief on the same topic, the author only discusses the elements that are in contention. Each element is phrased persuasively to assert the argument that the plaintiff's complaint has not stated a claim.

If you need to include background information about the law, start the Argument section of your brief with an umbrella section. Explain the standard of review, the general legal test of the legal issue that is the subject of your brief, and ancillary rules such as which party bears the burden of proof, to provide a legal context for your arguments. You may also want to include background information about the law to persuasively frame your argument. For example, telling about the purpose of a statute or just a bit of history of the law, or including a particularly apt quote from the cases, might open your reader up to your arguments.

If logically possible, make your strongest argument first. Keep your argument simple. Your case should make sense to the court in terms of everyday life. It should show the court how the people involved may be handled fairly and humanely within the structure of the law. One point—simply, directly, and persuasively argued—is sometimes all you need.

The small-scale structure of your brief should follow most of the organizational and analytical principles described in Chapter Six for advisory writing. As with advisory writing, your reader will expect the logical flow of the argument to be top-down, or deductive. In general, reason syllogistically to prove a conclusion deduced from premises that are proven or assumed to be true. The CRAC paradigm discussed in Chapter Six is syllogistic.

Because legal readers—including judges—are busy and impatient people, and do not want to wade through the law before getting to the point of your brief, tell the reader the conclusion that you want the judge to reach up front. Then explain the law and apply the facts of your case to the law. This mode of analysis attends to the needs of the audience of the brief—the busy lawyer or judge—to understand the determinative issues first.

When you write a brief, all of your choices are rhetorical, aimed at convincing a judge to adopt the position of your brief. Thus, when you describe the law, you will focus your discussion of the law to elaborate on the issues in your case. Indeed, a brief is about a concrete legal dispute, not about the law in the abstract. And that's a good thing, because reading about a concrete legal dispute is more interesting than reading about a legal abstraction.

You might modify these conventions for rhetorical purposes. After disciplining yourself to write a separate rule explanation and application, at some point you may find that you might "mix" rule and application a bit more in persuasive writing to get to the point of your argument more quickly. Or, if you think your reader will easily understand and adopt your explanation of the rule, and it needs no or little proof, you may be able to state the rule in a relatively cursory way.

c. *Crafting a Persuasive Rule*

In your brief, state the law in a way that favors your client's position. The explanation of the law should not sound the same for the different sides of a dispute. Emphasize the part of the rule that's more favorable to your client and minimize the parts that are unfavorable. Remember that string citations and multiple cases are rarely helpful and that long quotations from cases and other authorities may not be read.

You want the reader to see the law through the lens of your theory of the case. Develop your legal rule in a way that shows that the case law fits your theory. Without ignoring contrary authority, state the rule forcefully within the context of your narrative of the case.

Many a case has been won—or lost—because the judge found one theory of the purpose of the law more convincing than another. Even if a statute or case articulates a specific legal test, how that test should be implemented may depend on other factors. Three such factors that are worth considering are: (1) the purpose of the legislature in enacting the statute, (2) the problem that the law was meant to remedy, and (3) how the law might be seen differently given the changing nature of technology or society.

To shape the rule or legal test, you can use an analogy with relevant cases, as discussed in Chapter Two. Compare the facts of relevant and precedential cases to your facts, thus by analogy showing how the law is to be applied. Analogies give texture to the rule, helping the reader understand the law in a concrete way. For example, in the false imprisonment case we have used before, the facts can be used by analogy to show when "confinement" occurs:

> A plaintiff cannot be involuntarily confined if he is not "deprived of his or her freedom to leave a particular place." *Roberson v. Evangelical Orthodox Church*, 216 Cal. App. 3d 297, 303–04 (1989). The *Roberson* court affirmed summary judgment for the defendant on a false imprisonment claim because the plaintiff, who felt "trapped" when his minister ordered him to remain secluded in a cabin for a week, was not actually confined to the cabin. *Id.* at 304. Rather, the plaintiff had left the cabin to go for a drive, to take a walk, and even when out to dinner. *Id.* Absent extraordinary circumstances, a plaintiff may be involuntarily confined only when the facts show that she was "physically compelled" to remain in a particular place. *See Fermino*, 7 Cal. 4th at 707, 725, 724. In *Fermino*, the plaintiff's desire to leave a room, where she was being questioned about committing a theft at work, was overcome by the

physical actions of one of the defendant-employer's security guards. Immediately after the plaintiff "made a move toward the door," the security guard "slid in front of the door, threw up a hand and gestured for her to stop." *Id.* at 707.

d. Applying the Law to the Facts of Your Case

When you apply the law to the facts of your case, start with an assertion of your conclusion. Your explanation of the rule lays the groundwork to apply the law to the facts of your case. In the paragraph from the false imprisonment brief above, the precedent cases demonstrate what kind of confinement is enough to be false imprisonment. In the application paragraph, the brief writer can then compare those kinds of confinement with the facts of Artie Abram's case.

Ideally, your reader will reach your conclusion independently, based on the logic of your analogy. But to be sure, compare the facts of your case directly with the facts of the precedent cases. Use the same language for the rules—the words and phrases that you quoted from the precedent cases in the rule explanation section—in your application section. That way your application will feel fully integrated with the law.

e. Counter-Argument

You must address the other side's strongest arguments. You must "grasp the nettle," as Lord Denning famously expressed it. Even if the opposing side has not noticed its strongest possible argument, the court or law clerk may see it. A skillful use of persuasive strategies will allow you to emphasize the strengths of your case, without ignoring its weaknesses.

6. The Conclusion

The conclusion of your brief should concisely state what you want the court to do (such as grant or deny the motion), underscore your theory of the case, and, if the brief is longer than fifteen pages, summarize the major points of your brief. The basic arguments may then be succinctly presented as reasons for granting the requested relief. The relationship between multiple arguments should be identified, as in the following brief conclusion.

> The judgment for plaintiff should be reversed. Plaintiff did not have a valid contract or a business expectancy of the type protected against tortuous interference. In the alternative, the conduct of defendant, as a competitor, was privileged.

§ 7.3 WRITING TO PERSUADE

A. WRITING STYLE

Your writing should be lively and engaging. Lawyers are professional writers and should take the same care with our briefs as a journalist does with an article. We should strive to make our briefs as interesting to the reader as the *New York Times*.

Style matters. A judge will more readily agree with a brief that is well written. A fluid writing style, one with few hiccups and no need to re-read, can smoothly lead the reader to assent. Your brief should be written in the active voice using crisp verbs to keep the reader engaged. And it should be organized in a logical way with transitions between sentences and paragraphs. See Chapter Four and Appendix C for how to use transitions to help your reader see the connection between ideas.

B. CONTROLLING TONE

Tone is often overlooked by legal writers. It is never overlooked by readers. Any conspicuous tone interferes with reception of content by causing the reader to react first to the tone and only secondly to the subject matter. That is true whether the tone is informal, stuffy, pretentious, hyperbolic, bitter, casual, or uncertain.

Judges may react favorably or unfavorably to the substance of an argument according to the way its tone affects them. This is often a subconscious reaction, making it difficult for the reader to make allowance for an irritating tone.

The tone of your brief should be professional. The central characteristics of professional legal writing are that it be clear, succinct, and precisely correct. And for briefs, even more than for in-house memoranda, your writing should also be easy to read and engaging. The tone of your writing should be formal, without being stiff. Some legal writers use contractions in their writing, while others avoid them as being too informal. We use them here intentionally to create a more conversational tone. You should make a conscious decision whether or not to use them, primarily based on the expectations of your audience. Your syntax, or sentence structure, should not be so formal that it is stilted or difficult to parse. Choose simple words over complicated ones. Choose words with fewer syllables over longer one. Choose shorter sentences over ones with many clauses.

The most significant difference between a legal memorandum and a legal brief is the tone. You will argue forthrightly in a legal brief. The purpose of the brief is to argue for your client. You shouldn't be shy about stating your position.

Your writing must also be ethical. Your reader must trust that you are reporting the facts and the law fairly.

Most judges strive to be fair, yet they may also have ideological commitments or life experiences that influence their decision-making. If a judge's ideological commitments are in tension with the tenor of your argument, you have a bigger hurdle for your argument It's easier to reinforce someone's preconceptions than to change her mind. Thus, your tone may vary depending on how far a stretch your arguments are for the judge. If you think your judge will readily agree with your position, you might use a sharper tone. If you think the judge will not be inclined to find for your client, a more accommodating tone may help the reader understand your arguments without resisting them.

Your tone should reflect the high status of the court, as well as your position as an officer of the court. You should be deferential and, for that reason, not tell the court what it *should* do. The tone of your brief, however, should reflect your own awareness that your job is also an indispensable one in the system of justice.

Although it is sometimes difficult after a long battle, your tone should also be respectful of your opposing counsel and the opposing party. Blood feuds are boring and tedious. Judges do not want to mediate a personal debate. There may be times when you must point out that your opponent has misstated the record or the law, but do so in a matter-of-fact way, with courtesy and respect for opposing counsel and the court.

The following guidelines can help you control the tone of your briefs.

Establish an emphatic tone by directly asserting your points. Avoid prefacing your statements with phrases such as: "It appears to be the case that," "It can be argued," "It was clear to the court that," "It is conceivable that," and "One feature of which one should be aware." Do not, however, be aggressive. Do not tell the court what it must do or think.

Beware of humor unless you know your audience well. Attempted humor may annoy one or more judges of a court. However, judges, like all readers, appreciate the lightening, sometimes enlightening, effect of figures of speech, examples, and famous sayings—used sparingly. The following example of humor works because it grows directly out of the subject matter (legality of a search of defendant's person):

> When Officer McDonald patted down the Defendant, he discovered nothing but two lobster tails. Officer McDonald testified that he immediately recognized them as lobster tails and immediately knew that they were not weapons. Yet the search did not end with this discovery. Lobster tails are not contraband; there is no law against carrying concealed lobster tails with or without a sales receipt. Lobster tails are not inherently suspect. Nor do they become suspect because they are frozen or because they bear the label of the store that packaged them.

Do not make the case sound ridiculously easy or opposing counsel sound ridiculously blind. An arrogant or superior tone will not advance your case. For example, a sentence such as, "Cases cited by Plaintiff are inapposite and easily distinguishable," may offend the judicial reader who may find the plaintiff's cases difficult to distinguish. Sarcasm is never appropriate. Neither is an insulting or intemperate tone, however much opposing counsel deserves it.

Use "we" for yourself and your client, and use "counsel for appellant or respondent" for opposing counsel. Do not use "you" to refer to the court. Do not use "I" to refer to yourself.

C. CONSIDER THE PURPOSE OF YOUR DOCUMENT AND YOUR AUDIENCE

Vary your tone and develop your arguments to meet the needs of your audience. For example, an appellate brief focused on few arguments may contain multiple pages of in-depth analysis, permitting you to elaborate on the law and your arguments in greater depth than in a typical trial court brief. If you know the judge is familiar with the area of law, you may not need to explain the background law in as much detail as you would otherwise.

D. USING RHETORICAL DEVICES FOR PERSUASION

Rhetorical devices are means of achieving emphasis through special sentence structure, paragraph design, and wording.

The key to effective use of any rhetorical device is subtlety: the device must appear natural. It must not attract attention as a gimmick being used on the reader. The exception is the appeal to logic. That rhetorical appeal is more effective if it is obvious. Appeals to emotion, in contrast, will fail if obvious.

1. Achieving Emphasis with Sentence Structures

A. Place important words at the beginning and at the end of sentences. Use short sentences for special emphasis as in the following example.

> Whether surveillance is electronic, optical, or human is irrelevant where there is no reasonable expectation of privacy. While on a public street, the defendant had no such reasonable expectation.

In a conspicuous position, understatement is more effective than overstatement. The above example would be less effective if the words "clearly," "certainly," or "obviously" were added ("the defendant obviously had no such reasonable expectation").

B. Avoid beginning a sentence with an equivocation, such as, "it would seem to be" or "it may be that." Instead, write forcefully "it must follow that," or simply begin with the point itself and then state necessary qualifications.

C. Put subordinate thoughts in less emphatic positions. Compare this pair of sentences:

> The result is that enforcement of the rescission right is not uniform among the circuit courts. (The phrase "among circuit courts" receives undue emphasis.)
>
> The result is that enforcement of the rescission right among the circuit courts is not uniform. (The important words "result" and "is not uniform" receive the emphasis they deserve.)

D. Use active voice for forcefulness. See Chapter Eight for a discussion of active and passive voice.

E. Assert your position affirmatively. Even negative ideas can be expressed in positive, therefore more forceful, form.

> The approach of the English courts is somewhat uncertain and less clear-cut than that of the American courts.
>
> *Revised*: The approach of the American courts is more clearly defined than that of the English courts.

F. Use double negatives sparingly for understatement. The double negative, such as "not infrequently," has a respectable history as a rhetorical device for emphasis. Although it has fallen out of favor, it may still be employed on occasion as a means of understatement. For example, "not wholly unsuccessful" understates a lack of success, thus emphasizing it, as compared to its affirmative form "partially successful," which emphasizes a degree of success.

G. Use parallel constructions to draw attention to similar ideas.

> In *Cooper* the court considered damage to a number of motor cars caused by the negligence of a painting contractor. In *Runnels* the court considered damage to construction machinery caused by the negligence of the mechanic who repaired it.

H. Use parallel constructions for rhetorical effect. Similarity of structure in a pair or series of related words, phrases, or clauses will make them more memorable. ("He tried to make the law clear, precise, and equitable.") The principle of parallelism is that like things be phrased in like terms.

Variations of parallelism include:

1. Repetition of the same word or group of words at the beginning of successive clauses (anaphora): "They were common, though prohibited by law. They were common, though condemned by public opinion." This scheme establishes rhythm and produces a strong emotional effect.

2. Repetition of the same word or group of words at the ends of successive clauses (epistrophe): "To the good American many subjects are sacred: children are sacred, business is sacred, property is sacred." This scheme sets up a pronounced rhythm with special emphasis resulting from repetition of words and placement of words in the emphatic final position.

3. Repetition of last word of one clause at the beginning of the following clause (anadiplosis): "The crime was common; common be the pain." Or, a variation on this type of repetition from Chief Justice Louis D. Brandeis, "They believed liberty to be the secret of happiness and courage to be the secret of liberty."

4. Repetition of words, in successive clauses, in reverse grammatical order (antimetabole): "One should work to live, not live to work." Antimetabole gives the air of the neatly turned phrase.

5. Juxtaposition of contrasting ideas, often in parallel structure (antithesis): "Though argumentative, he was modest." The opposition in an antithesis can reside either in words or in ideas, or both.

2. Achieving Emphasis with Paragraphing

A. Use persuasive paragraph structure. In each section of a brief or in each paragraph, state your argument or position first—not your opponent's—and state it affirmatively. Then dispense with your opponent's argument. To make paragraphs affirmative: (i) State your argument or position first. (ii) Acknowledge contrary evidence, or state the opposing argument in the middle of the paragraph. (iii) Refute contrary evidence or opposing argument. (iv) Restate your argument as a conclusion.

One purpose of this structure is to put favorable arguments and facts in the most conspicuous place (the beginning and the end). The interior of a paragraph should contain less important elements. Both unfavorable facts and arguments must be included, of course, but they will be given less emphasis in the middle of a paragraph.

Another purpose of this structure is to give a balanced analysis of the issue, that is, to reflect fair consideration of both sides even if only one is fully developed in the paragraph.

Example of an unpersuasive paragraph structure:

Warwick v. Woodinville Company, 100 Wash. 200, 174 P. 15 (1920), however, represents an archaic view of "publication," and it may not be binding precedent today. More recent cases adopt the rule that to establish defamation when information is circulated among those with a "common interest" requires a showing of malice or bad faith. Applied here, if false medical information were circulated among supervisors evaluating an employee, a common interest in the information would probably be established. The complaining party would be required to show that the false statement was made with malice or in bad faith. See, e.g., *Sam v. Painter's Local Union*, 40 Wn.2d 800, 200 P.2d 754 (1955). Even though false medical information was circulated among Company personnel, who see the material in the course of their normal duties, the lack of evidence of bad faith distinguishes this case from *Warwick*.

In the above example, both unfavorable authority and an unfavorable fact appear in positions of emphasis. Recent authority and the present requirements for establishing defamation should be emphasized instead, as in the following revision.

Revised: Plaintiff has presented no evidence of malice or bad faith and therefore has not established that defamatory statements were made. A showing of malice or bad faith is necessary to establish defamation when allegedly false information is circulated among persons with a "common interest." *Sam v. Painter's Local Union*, 40 Wn.2d 800, 200 P.2d 754 (1955). Such "common interest" can be found in Defendant's circulation of medical information among supervisors evaluating an employee because the supervisors see the information in the course of their normal duties. Plaintiff's primary case, *Warwick v. Woodinville*

Company, 100 Wash. 200, 174 P. 15 (192), was decided before the court required evidence of malice or bad faith under these circumstances. Having failed to present evidence of malice or bad faith, Plaintiff has not satisfied current requirements for establishing defamation.

B. Use short paragraphs for emphasis. A short paragraph, like a short, climactic sentence, provides emphasis automatically. A one-sentence paragraph will provide extra emphasis, but only if used sparingly and skillfully. The following example illustrates effective use of a one-sentence paragraph.

Plaintiff's brief does not refer to the Plan itself. Rather, Plaintiff ignores the legal text and argues on the basis of a summary description of the Plan contained in a booklet, "Company Employee Retirement Plan." The booklet states that it is a summary and that "for a proper understanding of the Plan, the complete text should be read."

Construction of the Plan is controlled by its legal text, not by selective citations from a summary booklet.

3. Achieving Emphasis with Language

"Now, words in their proper order are the raw material of the law, and words have a magic of their own; they have color and sound and meaning and associations. But choice words in the right order have a more magical power still." —Birkett, *Law and Literature: The Equipment of the Lawyer*, 36 A.B.A.J. 891, 946 (1950) (Excerpted with permission from the American Bar Association Journal.)

A. Remember to consider word connotation. Words create impressions. The writer's task is to choose words that create the appropriate impressions for her persuasive purpose. While writing each word, keep your objective in mind: For example, are you trying to establish guilt, liability, a violation of constitutional rights?

Nouns: Nouns have negative or positive connotations; use them carefully and purposefully.

Positive	*Negative*
offender	criminal
control	coercion
debate	argument
reconstruction	fabrication
eminence	notoriety
adversary	enemy
rapid disassembly	explosion

Verbs: Verbs provide the most subtle, thus the most effective, coloration. Statements may be "affirmed" (implies trust), "asserted" (neutral), or "alleged" (implies doubt). The verb "sever," for example, makes a stronger impression than the verbs "cut" and "break."

Use active verbs, such as "conceal," "ignore," and "intend" rather than forms of the weak verb "to be" or its substitutes, "seem," "become," "exist," "appear," "arise," "relate to," "deal with," "involve," and "concern."

Adjectives: Use a minimum of these because they are less subtle than either nouns or verbs. Do not pile up similar adjectives like "inequitable and unconscionable." If an adjective is necessary, use only one and choose it carefully. As Voltaire remarked, the adjective is the enemy of the noun.

B. Use ornamental language cautiously. While neither lawyers nor their clients are willing to pay for literary skill for its own sake, one mark of an expert legal writer is the ability to use vivid examples, interesting similes, metaphors, or analogies. This ability grows out of a sensitivity to language, to how it sounds, and to what auditory and visual effects it has on the reader. It grows out of an awareness of human nature. Prose that delights us also instructs us more efficiently and effectively than writing that deadens our senses.

The ability to use figurative language skillfully develops over a lifetime of writing. The ability may, however, be cultivated by paying attention to the sensory dimension of words. Metaphors and similes should be fresh. Do not mix metaphors, for example, "We need this case like a horse needs a fifth wheel"; "when we come to that bridge, we will swim over it"; or "they built their argument on fuzzy ground." Clichés should be avoided unless "renovated" (for example, "no truer words were ever silenced").

C. Avoid unpersuasive words and ineffective rhetorical devices that may weaken the power of your arguments. Avoid using "clear" and "clearly" in a brief. These do not persuade the court that the case is clearly in your favor or even clear at all.

"Obvious" and "obviously" are similarly objectionable.

Avoid expressions of supposed candor, modesty, or any other attempts at personal expression, such as "frankly," "to be frank," "to be honest," "with all candor," "candidly," "I humbly disagree," "I do not pretend to be an expert."

Do not use words sarcastically or ironically to mean something other than their dictionary meaning. For example, in this sentence taken from a state supreme court brief, the word "remarkable" might boomerang on its author if the court agrees with the contention:

> Plaintiffs make the remarkable contention that the "well-established doctrine of restraint" is the appropriate rule.

Avoid words made trite by overuse. Both psychological terms and computer jargon have become trite and have a negative effect on many readers. The following words, among many others, have been degraded by imprecise use and overuse: actualize, appropriate, effectuate, duplicative, impact (as a noun or as a verb), implement (as verb), interface, input, meaningful dialogue, optimize, quality (as adjective), replicate, synchronization, update (as noun or verb), viable.

4. Using Classical Devices for Persuasion

The devices for persuasion have not changed since they were studied and described by the Greeks.

Three of the more important of these devices are discussed below.

A. Logical Appeal. Although the emotional and ethical appeal should never be ignored, the logical appeal is the most important and persuasive for the advocate. The logical appeal in legal writing is chiefly an appeal to precedent. Like cases are logically decided alike. The writer's task is to demonstrate the similarity or dissimilarity of decided cases with the client's case.

B. Emotional and Ethical Appeals. Remember that argumentative writing affects a reader's emotions and conveys an image of the author. Too often law students and lawyers aim only at a reader's logical mind and forget to consider the reader's emotions. After you have identified the result you want, identify the emotion or combination of emotions that will lead the reader to that result. Select the details of your case that will arouse that emotion: these should be subtly emphasized in your argument.

C. Ethical Appeal. Any writer is more persuasive if the reader respects her. This respect, traditionally called the ethical appeal, emerges from what is written as well as from how it is written. An image of honesty and straightforwardness should emerge, beginning with the fact statement. The writer should set forth the facts and all that follows in a well-balanced and reasonable way. The writer must not appear to be blinded by emotion. Nor should the writer be timid or apologetic. The best image for a brief writer is that of a strong but reasonable counselor, unafraid of taking a stand but not willing to exaggerate or contort the facts or law to make a point.

Brief writers inevitably find weak spots in their own cases. A good rule of thumb is to be critical of your case before the reader is. Acknowledge and then overcome obvious weaknesses through authority, policy, or reason. Account for weaknesses in your case before your reader discovers them. You will thus create an image of objectivity, while simultaneously making an appeal to the reason and logic of your reader.

Sophisticated brief-writers sometimes make educated allusions to historical events or people or repeat famous aphorisms and thus convey an image of urbanity and broadmindedness. A novice should avoid such risky flourishes. It is enough to establish an image of reasonableness by reflecting your understanding of both sides of a case, by conceding small points when necessary, and by acknowledging the possible validity of the opposing argument while undercutting it.

5. Avoiding Ineffective Emphasis

Mechanical contrivances like italics, underlining, boldface type, and exclamation marks should not normally be used for emphasis.

§ 7.4 WRITING ADVOCACY LETTERS

Lawyers often write advocacy letters to opposing clients or opposing counsel. All of the advice in

Chapter Six for writing advisory letters is relevant here.

If you are writing a letter to an opposing party, first find out if the client is represented by an attorney. If the party has a lawyer representing the party for this issue, you must contact the lawyer, not the party herself, unless the lawyer has given you permission to contact the client directly.

Just as when you're writing a brief, you must have the purpose of the letter in mind before you draft. Your purpose may be: to put the other side on notice about a problem; to entice the other party to cooperate; to settle a case; or to persuade the other party to settle a case.

All demand letters have multiple audiences. They may include:

- Opposing party or counsel (addressee)
- Your client
- Judge/Hearing Examiner
- Your supervising attorney

There is often a tension between your purpose in writing to one of them versus your purpose in writing to another.

Before you send the letter re-read it carefully, imagining that you are each of the audiences. Imagine yourself as a judge reading this letter at some point when negotiations have broken down. Does your letter make you seem reasonable? Consider the effect that your tone will have on the addressee. Will this tone serve the purpose you want?

The basics of writing an advocacy letter are much the same as with all legal writing. First, write clearly and directly. Tell who is writing the letter, you or client. Identify who the client is and what the client's relationship is to the Addressee. Tell what the client wants. Succinctly describe the facts, from your client's point of view. Consider whether or how to include sympathetic facts about how the problem has affected the life of your client. Integrate law and fact in a way that will likely induce the response you want. Remember that every side has a story. Write your client's story, without ignoring the other side of it. Conclude with a clear statement of the result or action that your client is seeking. The reader should know at the end of the letter exactly what your client wants and the precise and clear reasons that your client should have it.

You have now completed Steps One through Five for advocacy writing, as well as for advisory writing. You are ready to revise and edit your draft for clarity, precision, conciseness, and effectiveness. Chapters Eight, Nine and Ten will help you to polish your draft, as well as to proofread efficiently.

STEP 5

- Write first draft.
- Let that draft rest.
- Revise for organization and analytical content.
- Draft and revise again, as needed.

➤ ***Next Step, Chapter Eight.***

CHAPTER 8
SENTENCE DESIGN

§ 8.1 INTRODUCTION

The principles of clear, precise, and effective sentences construction are few and simple. First, whenever possible, begin a sentence with its subject. Second, place the verb close to the subject. Third, place the object close to the verb. Fourth, place modifiers next to things they modify. Finally, keep the sentence short, unless you have a rhetorical purpose for making it long.

§ 8.2 PRINCIPLES OF SENTENCE CONSTRUCTION

A. BEGIN SENTENCES WITH THE SUBJECT OR WITH OTHER SIGNIFICANT WORDS OR PHRASES

1. Open a Sentence with Its Subject

The reader expects the subject to come first. If it does not, then the reader must remember all the words that precede the subject until the subject appears. Non-legal professional writers place something before the subject in only 25 percent of their sentences. Legal writers do so 50 percent of the time. Try to limit the number of non-subject sentence openers that you use.

Example of a Confusing Non-subject Sentence Opener: Regarding the plaintiff's situation, it would be no clarification to state that the case previously discussed is not consistent with the plaintiff's case.

Revised: The plaintiff's situation is not clarified by stating that the previous case is inconsistent with plaintiff's case.

If you do begin a sentence with something other than its subject, use words or phrases that set the stage for the subject-verb unit to follow. Successful non-legal professional writers limit their non-subject sentence openers to adverbial phrases and clauses, that is, to words or phrases that establish time, place, cause, and condition. Readers easily identify adverbial ideas as stage setting information and easily remember such ideas until the subject appears. Help with identifying your subject may be found in the Micro-grammar in the Appendix.

2. Place Transitional Words Near the Subject

Readers expect to find transitional words somewhere in the first part of a sentence. Such words or phrases as "on the other hand" and "in a recent Supreme Court decision" may be used to open sentences or may be placed immediately after the subject. Although transitions are important, the subject of any sentence is generally more important. Thus, many writers prefer to place transitional elements after the subject. For example, rather than opening with "On the other hand, the proponents of the second view read the statute literally," you might more effectively place the subject first: "The proponents of the second view, on the other hand, read the statute literally." This places initial emphasis on the subject, "proponents," and final emphasis on the way in which the proponents read the statute, "literally."

3. Do Not Routinely Open Sentences with Full Citations

Avoid the habitual use of a full citation as a sentence opener. You should spare the reader from having to comprehend or skip over a full citation in order to arrive at the point of a sentence. Whenever possible, place a full citation at the end of a sentence, preferably in a separate citation sentence, as demonstrated below:

> *Awkward opening:* In *Kosters v. Seven-Up Co.,* 595 F.2d 347 (6th Cir. 1979), the court held that a franchiser was liable for breach of warranty to an ultimate consumer who was injured by a defective product.
>
> *Revised:* A franchiser has been held liable for breach of warranty to an ultimate consumer who was injured by a defective product. *Kosters v. Seven-Up Co.,* 595 F.2d 347 (6th Cir. 1979).

The separate sentence citation is permissible if the cited authority supports or contradicts the full statement in the preceding sentence. If the cited authority supports or contradicts only part of the statement in the sentence, the citation must follow that part of the sentence.

> A franchiser has been held liable to an ultimate consumer for breach of warranty, *Kosters v. Seven Up Co.,* 595 F.2d 347 (6th Cir. 1979), but a licensor of personal property has been held not liable on

warranty grounds, *Shaw v. Fairyland at Harvey's Inc.*, 26 App.Div.2d 576, 271 N.Y.S.2d 70 (1966).

If you wish to emphasize a case name or other authority for which the citation has not yet been given, then the case citation may begin the sentence. For example, "*Buckley v. Valeo,* 424 U.S. 1 (1976), is the leading case on federal regulation of campaign spending." Even where a case is being emphasized, however, the complete citation may be placed last to improve readability: "The leading case on federal regulation of campaign spending is *Buckley v. Valeo*, 424 U.S. 1 (1976)."

When deciding whether to place a full citation first or last, ask yourself if the reader will need that information before reading the subject-verb unit. If not, then the citation will be a visual obstacle for the reader.

Shortened citation forms do not create such an obstacle, for example, " 'Outrageous conduct,' 316 U.S. at 7, was the court's characterization of the law officer's treatment of the defendant." Shortened names of cases or other authorities may serve as helpful transitional elements. The shortened citation or case name may be placed first in the sentence, or it may be placed after the subject as follows:

> The Court in *Buckley* circumscribes federal regulation of campaign spending.

B. KEEP SUBJECT AND VERB CLOSE TOGETHER

Subject and verb should be kept as close together as possible. As English speakers, we understand the subject and verb only as a unit, that is, neither subject nor verb is fully processed until the other is discovered. Keep verbs and objects close together for the same reason. Help with identifying your verbs and objects may be found in the Micro-grammar in the Appendix.

If a subject and verb (or a verb and object) must be separated, then they should be separated by no more than seven words. This seemingly arbitrary rule requires an explanation. Our short-term memory accurate holds seven items, for example, telephone numbers, physical objects, such as cars or pedestrians in an intersection, decimal digits, and monosyllabic words. This mnemonic limit is sometimes referred to as the Magical Number Seven, Plus or Minus Two. Thus, for each group of seven words in a sentence, there must be "closure." That is, the words must form a self-enclosed unit, for example (i) a subject with modifiers ("the case on appeal"), (ii) phrases ("in other words"), and (iii) clauses ("that the court will recognize").

We read and remember in segments. Social security numbers and telephone numbers are segmented to help us remember them. In the same way, sentences must be segmented (have frequent closure) if the reader is to understand on first reading. In reality, lawyers and law students are compelled to read sentences containing segments of a dozen words or more. Each word in such a segment must be held individually in the short-term memory until the segment is closed. If closure is delayed too long, the reader forgets the initial words in the segment and so must reread.

Perhaps because lawyers have daily practice with long segments of words, they are accustomed to holding more than seven items in the short-term memory. Nevertheless, exceeding the Magical Number Seven impairs readability for lawyers as well as for lay readers. Longer gaps are not "wrong," of course; they may simply compel the reader to reread the sentence.

> *Subject and Verb Too Far Apart: Continuation* [*S*] of partnership upon retirement, death, or bankruptcy of a partner and *disposition of* [S_2] the partnership interests of the retiring, deceased, or bankrupt partner *should be* [V] subject to majority vote.

> *Revision that Keeps Subject and Verb Together: Continuation [S_1]* of partnership *should be* [V_1] subject to majority vote after any partner retires, dies, or suffers bankruptcy. At that time, *disposition of partnership interests* [S_s] *should* also *be* [V_s] subject to majority vote.

Subject and Verb may be moved closer together in various ways, as in these two additional revisions of the first sentence:

> 1. If a partner retires, dies, or suffers bankruptcy, *continuation* [S_1] of partnership *should be* [V_1] subject to majority vote.

2. After the retirement, death, or bankruptcy of a partner, *continuation* [S_1] of partnership *should be* [V_1] subject to majority vote.

C. USE SUBJECT-VERB-OBJECT PATTERN

Nearly all sentences should be written in the active voice, that is, following the Subject-Verb-Object pattern. This is the pattern most readily comprehended by English speakers. When the doer of an action is in the Subject position (and the receiver of an action is in the Object position), the sentence is active and thus most forceful: "Defendant's car hit the plaintiff's fence." When the doer of an action is moved to the Object position and the receiver of an action is moved to the Subject position (that is, Subject and Object are reversed), the sentence is passive and tends to lose forcefulness. "The plaintiff's fence was hit by the defendant's car."

When deciding whether to use active or passive voice, ask yourself, first, whether the reader needs to know the subject and, second, whether you want the reader to know the subject. If the answer to either question is affirmative, then use the active voice. If the answer is negative, use the passive.

In general, passive voice is more useful and customary in legal writing than in other forms of professional or technical prose. In persuasive forms of legal writing, passive voice provides a useful tool for shifting emphasis.

The passive voice is useful if you do not know the subject or if you wish to:

(i) emphasize what was done rather than who did it:

The defendant's car was crushed.

(ii) vary sentence structure:

The law clerk reviewed the record. The judge studied the record and the briefs. Afterward they agreed that *the record had been misread by* both counsel.

(iii) depersonalize tone by making acts anonymous:

The records were misplaced.

(iv) emphasize facts:

Drawers had been pulled out, clothes were strewn about the floor, even valuable jewelry had been scattered over the dresser top. These facts, found by the lower court, emphasize the reckless nature of the sheriff's search.

D. KEEP RELATED PARTS OF THE SENTENCE TOGETHER

1. Keep Modifiers Next to the Words They Modify

The most common result of not keeping related words together is the misplaced modifier. A misplaced modifier is a word, phrase, or clause that appears to modify the wrong thing. Modifiers should be placed next to the word or words that they modify. Misplaced modifiers can occur at any point in a sentence and often result in ambiguity.

Keep this general rule in mind: If a reader must reread a sentence in order to determine what modifies what, then the sentence is poorly constructed and should be rewritten. A charitable reader will be able to sort out most ambiguous modifiers. The legal writer cannot, however, rely on the charity of legal readers. If any two lawyers are asked the meaning of a sentence with an ambiguous modifier, they may give the same interpretation if they consider the sentence in the abstract. Their answers may differ, however, if they must consider the sentence from the viewpoints of clients with conflicting interests.

In a recent case, for example, a $55,000 judgment rested on the interpretation of an allegedly misplaced word. The disputed word, which cost the losing side $55,000, was "available": "The scour protection fill may be pit-run gravel available in natural position on shore at the project site or other suitable material acceptable to the engineer." The question was whether the fill "may be available" or whether pit-run gravel was available and might be used as fill. Depending on the drafter's intent, the sentence should have been written either of two ways:

> The pit-run gravel may be available in natural position.

> The pit-run gravel that is available may be used as fill.

2. Avoid Misplaced Modifiers at the Beginning of a Sentence

1. *Confusing:* By doing so, the security interest will not survive bankruptcy. (Who is "doing so"? Not the "security interest.")

Clear: If we do so, the security interest will not survive bankruptcy.

2. *Confusing:* As your lawyer, the dog must be leashed. (Who is acting as your lawyer? Not the dog.)

Clear: As your lawyer, I advise you to leash your dog.

3. Avoid Misplaced Modifiers in the Middle of a Sentence

Modifying words or phrases may "squint," that is, look both ways, in the middle of a sentence. Adverbs like "well," "only," "often," and "both" are particularly troublesome in mid-sentence.

1. A lawyer who can write *well* deserves her fee. (Does any lawyer who can write deserve her fee? Or do only those who write *well* deserve it?)

Revised by rephrasing: A lawyer who is a skilled writer deserves her fee.

2. A contractor who fails to complete construction on time often cannot be made to pay a penalty. (If a contractor fails often, then he cannot be made to pay? Or is it often the case that contractors who fail to complete construction on time cannot be made to pay?)

Revise by moving "often" or by substituting "cannot always be made to pay."

3. The decision favors *both* the arguments made in *Copra* and *Coldewey*. (Both arguments made in each case? One argument made in both cases? Two distinct arguments, one in each case? More than one argument made in each case?)

Clear: The decision favors the two arguments set forth in both *Copra and Coldewey.*

Clear: The decision favors the two arguments made in *Copra* as well as the single argument made in *Coldewey.*

4. Avoid Split Infinitives When Possible

Infinitives should be split only if ambiguity or awkwardness results from leaving them intact. For ease of comprehension, the two parts of the infinitive should be placed together. Standing alone, the word "to" can serve as other parts of speech.

Writers sometimes place modifiers inside an infinitive ("to *unduly* influence," "to *specifically* perform") to avoid such ambiguous sentences as these:

The court imposed new requirements *strictly to regulate* interstate sales of toxic sprays.

The court imposed new requirements *to regulate strictly* interstate sales of toxic sprays.

If the adverb "strictly" is not to modify either "imposed" (Meaning "imposed in a strict way") or "interstate" (Meaning "exclusively interstate"), then the infinitive "to regulate" must be split:

The court imposed new requirements *to strictly regulate* interstate sales of toxic sprays.

Sentences that require a split infinitive, like the above example, are relatively few. A simple revision will usually eliminate the potential ambiguity without the need for splitting the infinitive.

Unnecessarily Split Infinitive: Judicial discretion allows the court to *both fulfill* its role as parens patriae to the child and *to consider fully* the rights of the child.

Revised: Judicial discretion allows the court *both to fulfill* its role as parens patriae to the child and *to consider fully* the rights of the child.

5. Avoid Ambiguous Modifiers at the End of a Sentence

Avoid unwanted ambiguity stemming from ambiguous modifying words or phrases at the end.

1. *Confusing*: The court reviewed the 1965 Act in its dicta, changing the requirements for good faith bargaining. (Dicta changes? The Act changes? The Court changes?)

Clear: In its dicta, the Court reviewed the 1965 Act, which changes the requirements for good faith bargaining. (The Act changes.)

2. *Confusing*: The defendant had discussed the proposal to fill the drainage ditch with his partners.

Clear: The defendant had discussed with his partners the proposal to fill the drainage ditch.

3. *Confusing:* The defendant is accused of assaulting the plaintiff while he was delivering mail maliciously and with intent to do bodily harm.

Clear: The defendant is accused of assaulting the plaintiff maliciously and with intent to do bodily harm while the plaintiff was delivering mail.

E. END SENTENCES SWIFTLY AND EFFECTIVELY

As soon as you have completed a subject-verb unit, consider ending the sentence. Continue to write another subject-verb unit in the same sentence only if ideas are closely related or you have a rhetorical purpose in doing so.

If the ideas are closely related, identify the relationship and choose the right connecting word. The conjunction "and" is almost never the right connecting word because it has no specific substantive meaning. It functions like a plus in mathematics: it adds two things together without giving a reason.

If you find that you have connected two units of thought with the word "and," ask yourself why you want them in the same sentence. Be precise about the relationship of the two subject-verb units. In the example below, the reader is left to guess why the two ideas are combined with the word "and."

Unclear connection: She was an extremely wealthy woman, and he married her several months after meeting at the health club.

Alternate reasons for combining the units of thought:

1. She was an extremely wealthy woman, *therefore* he married her several months after meeting at the health club.

2. She was an extremely wealthy woman, *yet* he married her several months after meeting at the health club.

3. She was an extremely wealthy woman, *after* he married her several months after meeting at the health club.

Be precise about the substantive connection between two subject-verb units or separate them into simple sentences. Remember that readers prefer short sentences.

Generally, average sentence length is a useful measure of readability. Try to limit average sentence length to 20 words to assure ease of reading.

1. Put Significant Words or Phrases in the Final Position

The two "emphatic positions" in a sentence are the beginning and the end. Be certain that the words you place in these two emphatic positions deserve to be there.

Unemphatic: We recommend that the Company discuss with us further its plans for obtaining outside investment *in the future.*

Revised: We recommend that the Company discuss with us further its plans for obtaining *future outside investment.*

2. Avoid Prepositional Phrases in the Final Position

Final prepositional phrases are usually weak and sometimes ambiguous.

> *Rhetorically Weak and Ambiguous Series of Prepositions*: Also enclosed is a letter I prepared *in* response *to* a request *for* explanation *of* certain features *of* an individual employment contract *for* a plant supervisor.
>
> *Revised*: Also enclosed is a letter I prepared for a plant supervisor to explain certain features of an individual employment contract.
>
> *Or:* Also enclosed is a letter I prepared to explain certain features of a plant supervisor's individual employment contract.

§ 8.3 SENTENCE REVISION

A. A SIMPLE METHOD FOR REVISING TROUBLESOME SENTENCES

1. First, Lift Main Subject, Verb, and Object from the Sentence

Reread each unsatisfactory sentence quickly to find the subject, verb, and object, and "lift" them from the rest of the sentence. The following sentence, for example, needs revision:

> Having determined, as it has, that the protection of the public's interest in the shorelines, in water quality, in air quality, and in other subjects, requires compliance with a carefully drawn statutory scheme, the legislature is not entitled to single out one

specific activity or category of project for exception from the scheme in that its motive is clearly to sacrifice environmental protection to speeding up the licensing process.

Main Subject: "legislature"

Main Verb Phrase: "is not entitled to single out"

Objects: "one activity," "category"

If the key idea is "legislature is not entitled to single out one activity or category," then the revision should begin with that key idea. The idea should not be buried in the middle of the sentence, but should instead appear in a separate sentence.

Revised: The legislature is not entitled to single out one activity or category for exception from the statutory scheme. (The rest of the example is revised below.)

2. Second, Remove Imprecise Subject-Verb Combinations

Fuzzy sentences are often the result of an imprecise subject-verb combination. This imprecision, hidden by the rest of the sentence, becomes evident when the subject and verb are lifted from the rest of the sentence.

Initial subject and verb from above example:

[T]he *protection . . . requires* compliance.

This fuzzy notion, that "protection" can somehow "require" something, obscures the thought in the sentence. The subject, or the "who" in the sentence, should be the legislature: "the legislature requires compliance in order to protect the public's interest."

3. Third, Revise for Subject-Verb-Object Order

After you have isolated the subject and verb, consider moving the subject to the beginning of the sentence. This often means relocating an initial phrase or clause, such as the clause in (1) above: "Having determined, as it has, that the protection of the public's interest in the shorelines, in water quality, in air quality, and in other subjects, requires compliance with a carefully drawn statutory scheme." This 33-word introductory clause should be converted to a sentence of its own, again by first locating the subject(s) and verb(s) and then by revising:

> Legislature [S] has determined [V] (that) protection [S_2] requires [V_2] compliance [O_2].
>
> Revised: The legislature has determined that compliance with a carefully drawn statutory scheme is required for protection of the public's interest in the shorelines, in water quality, in air quality, and in other subjects.

Thus, the original long sentence has been revised by several simple procedures, into three shorter sentences:

> *Revised*: The legislature has determined that compliance with a carefully drawn statutory scheme is required for protection of the public's interest in the shorelines, in water quality, in air quality, and in other subjects. Having done so, the legislature is not

entitled to single out one activity or category for exception from the statutory scheme. The legislature's motive for making such exceptions is to speed up the licensing process at the expense of environmental protection.

B. SIMPLE TECHNIQUES FOR SHORTENING SENTENCES

1. Deconstruct Long Sentences

Long sentences may be broken into several shorter ones as demonstrated below by (i) eliminating unnecessary words, (ii) converting long sentences to simpler, shorter ones, and (iii) transferring parenthetical expressions to another sentence.

2. Eliminate Unnecessary Words

The legal writer must learn to distinguish between redundancy and helpful repetition of words or ideas. Do not, for example, eliminate structural clues, as described below in section 4.4 (E)(1). Do, however, eliminate such redundancies as "basic fundamentals" or "with lucid clarity."

Reread each word, and ask yourself, "Do I need this word? Will anything significant be lost if I take it out?" If you do this, you will begin to form the habit of writing concisely and precisely. Occasionally, words that could be left out improve the rhythm of a sentence or paragraph. Improved sound or rhythm is, however, no excuse for using flabby intensifiers like "very" and "pretty much."

When excess is removed, emphasis occurs naturally and rhythm is improved.

Avoid writing sentences beginning with an unnecessary "It . . . that" structure.

1. *Wordy*: It is the theory that lends itself . . .

Concise: The theory lends itself . . .

2. *Wordy*: It must be noted, however, that the authority . . .

Concise: Note, however, that the authority . . .

3. *Wordy*: It can be said with certainty, moreover, that a structural violation will be recognized by all courts.

Concise: Moreover, a structural violation will be recognized by all courts.

4. *Wordy*: Again, it should be emphasized that it is doubtful that a naked allegation of mismanagement of funds by the trustees would confer jurisdiction.

Concise: A naked allegation of mismanagement of funds by the trustees would probably not confer jurisdiction.

5. *Wordy*: It is unlikely that one who fails to make a case of wage discrimination under the Equal Pay Act would prevail with the same claim under Title VII.

Concise: One who fails to make a case of wage discrimination under the Equal Pay Act is not likely to prevail with the same claim under Title VII.

Also avoid sentences beginning with an "In that the" structure, and avoid internal clauses beginning with "in that." These are clumsy, difficult to read, and verbose.

Wordy: In that the witness is also an interested party, his testimony is suspect.

Concise: The whiteness's testimony is suspect because he is an interested party.

Or: Because he is an interested party, the witness's testimony is suspect.

3. Convert Long Compound Sentences to Shorter Sentences

Replace "and," "but," "or," "nor," and "for" with a period.

If he was not insured on reaching the age of 65, he does not become insured by reason of any insurable employment which he takes up later, and the special contributions which are payable under the Act only by his employer, in respect of such employment, do not give him any title to health insurance benefits or pension, and moreover a man is not at liberty to pay any contributions on his own account as a voluntary contributor for any period after his 65th birthday.

Revised: If he was not insured at age 65, he does not become insured by reason of any insurable employment that he takes up later. The special contributions that are payable under the Act only by his employer, in respect of such employment, do not give him any title to health insurance benefits or pension. Moreover, a man is not at liberty to pay any contributions on his own account as a voluntary contributor for any period after his 65th birthday.

4. Transfer Internal Clauses or Parenthetical Expressions to Another Sentence

Too Long: The district court in Maryland in a recent case stated that the EEOC's policy of sending right-to-sue letters immediately after the filing of the charge, *if the regional director ascertains that the charge cannot be investigated within 180 days*, was "inconsistent with an obvious congressional intent."

Revised: The EEOC's policy is to send right-to-sue letters immediately after the filing of the charge, *if the regional director ascertains that the charge cannot be investigated within 180 days*. The district court in a recent case stated that the policy was "inconsistent with an obvious congressional intent."

§ 8.4 TECHNIQUES TO ENHANCE READABILITY

A. USE SHORT AND MEDIUM-LENGTH SENTENCES

The best professional prose on complex or technical subjects averages 20 words per sentence. For legal writers, this average is slightly higher (20 to 25 words per sentence). Although a variety of sentence lengths is important to avoid monotony (which actually retards comprehension), even the longer sentences normally should not exceed 35 words.

To determine your average number of words per sentence, take a representative sample of your prose (at least 250 words) and count the words. Count as single words hyphenated words, abbreviations, numbers, and case names. Omit citation sentences from the count. In citations within a sentence, consider as single words the case name, the reported citation, and the date. Next count the number of sentences and divide for the average. If it is greater than 25, you should concentrate on writing shorter sentences.

Using the same writing sample, check for variety in sentence lengths. Sentences should vary from short to medium length, but not in a predictable order.

B. MAKE ONE POINT PER SENTENCE

Use simple sentences whenever possible. A simple sentence contains one unit of thought, that is, one subject and one verb, as discussed above. Readability is enhanced by keeping separate thoughts in separate sentences.

> *One Point Per Sentence*: This vesting ordinance should have been adopted last fall. There is no public opposition to it. On the contrary, there is unequivocal support for it on the basis of fundamental fairness. The commission approved it in concept ten months ago. There is no good reason for a further delay of its adoption.

> *One Point Per Sentence:* This is an action to foreclose a mechanic's lien. Judgment was entered for plaintiff. Defendant appeals.

C. WHEN POSSIBLE, MAKE SENTENCES AFFIRMATIVE, NOT NEGATIVE

We understand affirmative statements more quickly and easily than negative ones. In studies of the effects of language on the mind, researchers have found that affirmative statements are psychologically more linear than negative ones. With negative statements, we must first understand the affirmative sense, then negate it. This is analogous to understanding another language by first translating it into one's own. Avoid these nearly incomprehensible combinations: "not otherwise," "never unless," "none unless," "never otherwise," and so forth.

Note, however, that accuracy and precision in legal writing may require a negative statement. For example, "This case has no precedential value." An affirmative revision is possible, but would not be understood as readily by lawyers and judges.

Most negative statements can easily be made more readable, without losing accuracy, as shown in these examples:

Negative Sentence: The Plaintiff must not be prevented from bringing a suit.

Affirmative Revision: The Plaintiff must be allowed to bring a suit.

Confusing Negative Words or Ideas:

1. Contrary to opposing counsel's denial, the facts dispose of the primary defense.

Revised: The facts contradict the primary defense raised by counsel for the defendant.

2. Not only is there no evidence that Mr. Jones relied upon the booklet, but also, even if he had, it would not change the outcome of this case.

Revised: There is no evidence that Mr. Jones relied on the booklet. Even if he had done so, the outcome would remain the same.

D. USE PARALLELISM AND BALANCE IN SENTENCE STRUCTURES

Parallelism is similarity of structure, that is, repetition of like words in the same order. For example, "He came, he saw, he conquered." A reader will be better able to absorb new information if parallel structures are used because the structure will be "transparent." That is, only the meaning of the words themselves must be processed, not a new structure. Compare this nonparallel structure with the above version: "After he came, he looked and then conquered."

Parallel structure is particularly helpful in a sentence containing multiple subjects, verbs, or objects. Legal writers frequently use such compound structures, which tend to be confusing unless they are given parallel structure. If a compound structure must be used, keep word order and parts of speech the same when possible, for example, "We agreed *to exchange documents* and *to share expenses*."

Balanced structure refers to groupings of words which are of roughly the same length. Such structures need not be worded similarly. They need only "sound" rhythmical to the reader's ear. Rhythmic patterns within sentences, as well as a rhythmic variation of sentences within paragraphs, increase readability in two ways. First, rhythmic patterns allow the reader's mind to anticipate how much attention will be required for each syllable to come. This makes reading easier. In the same way, music in which sound patterns are rhythmic is easier to listen to than music in which every note comes as a surprise. When there is a discernible melody, we can prepare for what is to come. Thus we process what *does* come more quickly.

Effective use of parallelism and balance also lends emphasis and allows density (greater detail) without loss of readability.

Effective Use of Parallelism and Balance:

The conduct of the officers in *searching Mr. Smiley, seizing his property*, and *arresting him* is exactly the type of conduct the fourth amendment was designed to prevent.

"They believed that freedom to think as you will and to speak as you think are means indispensable to the discovery and spread of political truth." Justice Louis D. Brandeis.

Revision for Parallelism:

Without Parallelism: The Company should place on its stock certificates a disclaimer and should make a notation in its stock records.

Revised: The Company should place a disclaimer on its stock certificates and make a notation on its stock records.

E. PROVIDE EXTRA STRUCTURAL CLUES

1. Include Essential "That"

Use of the word "that" is frequently essential to the correct reading of a sentence. It is not an "extra" clue in these instances, but rather an essential structural clue. The italicized phrases or clauses in the following examples may be misread as discrete units. Without the essential structural clue, the reader may have to reread these sentences for initial comprehension.

1. The complainant has the burden of *proving the rates* violate the statute. (The reader wonders initially how the complainant will "prove rates.")

Revised: The complainant has the burden of proving *that* the rates violate the statute.

2. When a manufacturer advertises his product, *he knows his acts,* whether intended or not, may have consequences in another state. (The initial reading may be that a manufacturer "knows his acts," which is not the point.)

Revised: When a manufacturer advertises his products, he knows *that* his acts, whether intended or not, may have consequences in another state.

3. Accepting this construction of RCW 62A.9–311, the Defendants argue the security agreement must specifically provide the transfer of collateral is

a default. They point out neither the security agreement and note nor the U.C.C. define default.

Revised: Accepting this construction of RCW 62A.9–311, the Defendants argue *that* the security agreement must specifically provide *that* the transfer of collateral is a default. They point out *that* neither the security agreement and note nor the U.C.C. define default.

2. Repeat Some Structural Words to Improve Readability

Readability is often improved by repeating structural words, such as the prepositions "under" and "for" in the following example. Repeating such words may seem redundant, but it provides a structural clue that facilitates comprehension.

1. I am aware that the securities are not being registered under the federal Securities Act of 1933 or any state securities laws, pursuant to exemptions from registration.

Revised: I am aware that the securities are not being registered *under* the federal Securities Act of 1933 or *under* any state securities laws, pursuant to exemptions from registration.

2. We recommend that the Company discuss with us its plans for obtaining future outside investment and granting stock options.

Revised: We recommend that the Company discuss with us its plans *for* obtaining future outside investment and *for* granting stock options.

§ 8.5 USEFUL SENTENCE PATTERNS FOR LEGAL WRITING

A. BASIC SENTENCE TYPES

Of the three basic sentence types (simple, compound, and complex), simple and complex should dominate legal writing.

Most sentences should be simple in structure, that is, one subject-verb unit. Use an occasional four-to-six word sentence for emphasis. The simple sentence is the pattern best suited for expressing one idea at a time, something all legal writers should attempt to do.

Simple: Subject (*S*) + Verb(*V*)
(The boat leaks.)

If two ideas must be included in the same sentence, the complex sentence pattern may be more economical than the compound.

Complex:

(i) S + V, Subordinating Conjunction S + V

(The boat did not sink, even though it leaks.)

(ii) Subordinating Conjunction S + V, S + V

(Even though the boat leaks, it did not sink.)

Subordinating conjunctions include:

after	provided	wherever
although	since	where
as	so that	whether
as if	until	unless
because	when	
before	whenever	

Compound:

(i) S + V, Coordinating Conjunction S + V

(The boat did not sink, but it leaks.)

(ii) S + V; S + V

(The boat leaks; it did not sink.)

Coordinating conjunctions include:

and	for	or
but	nor	yet

(iii) S + V; Conjunctive Adverb, S + V

(The boat leaks; however, it did not sink.)

(iv) S, Conjunctive Adverb, V; S + V

(The boat, however, did not sink; it simply leaks.)

Conjunctive adverbs include:

also	likewise	still
besides	moreover	therefore
consequently	nevertheless	thus
henceforth	notwithstanding	yet
however	so	

The complex pattern is more efficient than the compound because it establishes a logical and a hierarchical relationship between two ideas. Because a subordinating conjunction subordinates one subject-verb unit to another, the relative importance of the two ideas in a complex sentence is automatically reflected by the sentence structure. Compare the relative importance of the two ideas (subject-verb units) in the following sentences:

1. *Compound Sentence Pattern:* The damages have exceeded the original estimates by 55%, and Mr. Brown is unable to settle this case.

Complex Sentence Pattern: Because the damages have exceeded the original estimates by 55%, Mr. Brown is unable to settle this case.

In the complex sentence, emphasis falls on Mr. Brown's inability to settle the case. In the compound sentence, the uninformative word "and" does nothing more than establish a loose connection, rather like a "plus" in addition. It carries no other information about the relationship between the clauses it joins.

2. *Compound:* The wage differential has existed since the initial hiring of the coaches, and it would be very difficult for the school district to assert seniority as the basis for that differential.

Complex: Since the wage differential existed when the coaches were initially hired, it would be very difficult for the school district to assert seniority as the basis for that differential.

B. USEFUL PATTERNS: "IF . . . THEN"

An "If . . . then" sentence pattern may be used to establish a condition, to describe a complex cause-and-effect situation, or to detail a sequence of events. This pattern permits complexity without a wide separation of subject and verb. Both the "if-clause" and the "then-clause" contain their own subject-verb units, making them easier for the reader to grasp. A "When . . . then" structure works identically, but has a slightly different meaning. The word "then" need not be included in the sentence, although it does assist the reader.

Ordinarily, use no more than two "if-clauses" in a sentence. A succession of "if-clauses" leading to a final "then-clause" will be hard to comprehend on one reading. You should indent and enumerate if more than two "if-clauses" are needed before a "then-clause" can follow.

1. *Confusing:* We will not discuss a settlement with you without the manager asking her bookkeeper to compile a final statement covering all construction costs and allowing Sam Perkins to look

at the books and satisfy himself that things were done properly.

Revised: If the manager will ask her bookkeeper to compile a final statement covering all construction costs and if Sam Perkins can look at the books and satisfy himself that things were done properly, then we will discuss a settlement.

2. *Confusing:* We ask that this be done and that the management problem be openly and honestly discussed in order that the matter be settled amicably and at the least possible expense.

Revised: If this is done and if the management problem is openly and honestly discussed, then the matter could be settled amicably at the lease possible expense.

In the first example, the second modifier "allowing" is too far from the noun it modifies ("manager") for rapid comprehension. The reader must reread the sentence. An "if . . . then" structure eliminates this problem. In the second example, the double object and the lengthy clause beginning "in order that" extend the sentence beyond the length comfortable for most readers.

C. USEFUL PATTERNS: STATING A RULE AND EXCEPTION

If a rule and an exception occur in the same sentence, the rule should be stated first. The reader will not understand the exception fully or remember it well without the rule already in mind. The best way to handle rules, exceptions, and conditions is to give each its own sentence, for example, "As a general rule . . . . An exception, however, is . . . ."

> The court has consistently recognized an absolute immunity for statements made in judicial proceedings. If a person has suffered special injury in such proceedings, however, the court has recognized an exception to that immunity by approving an action for malicious prosecution.

D. USEFUL PATTERNS: REVERSAL OF DIRECT OBJECT AND PREPOSITIONAL PHRASES

When the direct object is longer and more detailed than a prepositional phrase that modifies the verb, the prepositional phrase may be placed first after the verb. This gives the reader a better chance of remembering the verb while reading both the direct object and the prepositional phrase.

> *Confusing:* Cynthia Williams of Browning Associates transferred [V] the property [DO] that had been held in trust for twenty-five years as required by the trust document to George Berry [PP].

> *Clear:* Cynthia Williams of Browning Associates transferred [V] to George Berry [PP] the property [DO] that had been held in trust for twenty-five years, as required by the trust document.

E. USEFUL PATTERNS: PERIODIC SENTENCE

In the periodic sentence, the main thought is not completed until the end of the sentence, thus creating suspense and taking full advantage of the final emphatic position.

> 1. If the individual arrested is diagnosed as an alcoholic, early commitment for effective treatment, either on a voluntary or involuntary basis, is essential.
>
> 2. When you consider the chaos that ensued, it is remarkable that anyone—witnesses, victims, or defendant—can recall the details of the automobile collision.

To achieve its effect, the periodic sentence is often opened with "it" or "there" or "the fact that." These pronouns or other "place-fillers" stand in for the subject (itself reserved for a later or final position in the sentence). Although this sentence pattern can be effective if used sparingly, it is sometimes overused in legal writing, especially in argument. Use it with care and only for special emphasis.

§ 8.6 PRINCIPLES FOR AVOIDING AMBIGUOUS OR CONFUSING SENTENCES

A. AVOID THE "NOT . . . BECAUSE" SENTENCE PATTERN

If the word "not" comes before the word "because" in a sentence, the sentence may be ambiguous. It will frequently be hard to read, whether or not it is ambiguous. The reader may not know whether you mean "Not because of this, but rather because of that" or whether you mean "Not so, and for this reason."

1. *Confusing*: The fact that no mention of Defendant was made in the will does not preclude her because she is his legal heir. (Because she is his heir, lack of mention will not preclude her? Or does it preclude her not because she is his heir but rather because of something else?)

Clear: Because she is his legal heir, the absence of a mention of her in the will does not preclude her.

2. *Confusing*: The threshold requirement of a common core of tasks is not met because of the inherent differences between coaching baseball and coaching tennis. (Requirement is not met because of differences but rather because of something else? Or differences prevent the requirement from being met?)

Clear: Because there are inherent differences between coaching baseball and coaching tennis, the threshold requirement of a common core of tasks is not met.

B. AVOID AMBIGUOUS PREPOSITIONAL PHRASES

1. Introduction

Prepositional phrases present many challenges to the legal writer. They are easily misplaced and thus often misread. Ambiguities frequently result from strings of prepositional phrases inside a sentence and from prepositional phrases beginning with the word "with" at the end of a sentence.

2. Place Prepositional Phrases Next to What They Modify

Ambiguous: Plaintiff pleads that the letter was found to be insufficient in Paragraph IV of his complaint. (In Paragraph IV, the letter was insufficient?)

Precise: Plaintiff pleads, in Paragraph IV of his complaint, that the letter was found to be insufficient.

3. Avoid Strings of Prepositional Phrases

Multiple prepositional phrases may be ambiguous, especially at the end of a sentence. The following sentence, for example, may be read to mean two entirely different things:

Ambiguous: Seven debits to the account were made by the bank exercising its right to offset to pay toward or pay off personal loans by the bank to Charles Allen in the approximate sum of $125,500. (Were the seven debits in the sum of $125,500? Were the loans in the sum of $125,000?)

Precise: The bank made seven debits in the approximate sum of $125,500 to the account of Charles Allen, exercising its right to offset his personal loans.

4. Beware of Adjacent Prepositional Phrases

Ambiguous: They examined every figure in the account in defendant's handwriting. (Is the entire account in defendant's handwriting or just some of the figures?)

Precise: They examined every figure that defendant had written in the account.

5. Beware of "With" and "Without" Phrases in Final Position

These phrases are sometimes ambiguous at the end of a sentence. Substitute more precise words.

Ambiguous structure: Noun + Verb + Object + with + Noun

1. *Ambiguous*: Our client will finance the contract with expenses. (Client will finance using expenses?)

Precise: Our client will finance the contract and the expenses.

2. *Ambiguous*: The court found jurisdiction proper for a private complainant without offering any interpretation of the statute. (Did the complainant fail to offer any interpretation or did the court not offer any interpretation?)

Precise: Without interpreting the statute, the court found jurisdiction proper for a private complainant.

Or: Even without the private complainant's interpretation of the statute, the court found jurisdiction proper.

C. AVOID SENTENCES BEGINNING WITH RELATIVE PRONOUNS

Sentences beginning with "who," "which," or "that" will probably require rereading unless they are short.

1. *That* the group associated for the sole purpose of committing crimes constitutes a pattern of racketeering activity.

Revised: A pattern of racketeering is established because the group associated for the sole purpose of committing crimes.

2. *Which* decision the court will uphold is, given the balance of authority, impossible accurately to predict.

Revised: Because the decisions are of equal weight, it is impossible to predict which the court will uphold.

3. *Which expert* the opposing counsel uses as a witness will determine the cross-examination strategy we will adopt.

Revised: Our cross-examination strategy will depend on *which* expert opposing counsel uses as a witness.

To analyze the sentence structures and possible ambiguities in your own writing, see the Individual Writing Analysis in the Appendix.

You are now ready to finish revision and editing of your first draft. You have a detailed outline, based on legal analysis of the issues and on an application of the principles of both large-scale organization and small-scale organization. You have guidelines for making effective word choices and sentence structures. You know how to construct the type of document you need, whether it will be advisory or persuasive.

Regardless of the roughness of your first draft, let it rest a day or two, if you can. When you come back to it, you will see ways to revise for better organization and to refine analytical content. The process of revision will be iterative. With each substantive change, organization and analysis will shift in the direction of greater clarity and effectiveness.

STEP 6

- Edit revised draft for clarity, precision, conciseness, and effectiveness.

➤ ***Next Step, Chapter Nine.***

CHAPTER 9
PUNCTUATION AND GRAMMAR

§ 9.1 INTRODUCTION

Legal writers must have full command of punctuation and grammar. Punctuation tells the reader how to read a sentence or paragraph. Thus, the legal writer must punctuate precisely in order to control meaning. A misplaced comma, for example, can result in misreading by a judge, another lawyer, or a client.

The punctuation section in this chapter covers those rules most commonly needed in legal writing. The rules receiving greatest emphasis are those that prevent ambiguity and that save the reader from having to reread for comprehension.

Grammar refers to syntax, that is, to sentence structure. Grammar also refers to the operating principles of our language, for example, correct use of parts of speech. It is ungrammatical to say "The letter was signed by him and I," rather than by "him and me." For most native speakers, grammar is instinctive and understandable. The section below on grammar is intended to point out the most common grammatical errors in legal writing.

§ 9.2 PUNCTUATION

A. INTRODUCTION

The most common punctuation questions in legal writing are addressed here. For a complete review of punctuation, several standard guides are listed in the bibliography at the back. One handy reference is *The Elements of Style,* by William Strunk and E.B. White, which may be used with a few caveats. For technical writing, such as legal writing, a few of Strunk and White's rules of usage must be modified, as discussed below.

B. USE OF THE COMMA

1. Use a Compound Sentence Comma for Clarity

Use a comma to separate two independent clauses joined by "and," "but," "or," "for," "nor," or "yet." The comma precedes the conjunction.

Confusing: The plaintiff's car hit the road block and the defendant failed to stop. (The reader may at first think that the car hit the road block and the defendant. The appearance of "failed" sends the reader back to re-read the sentence.)

Clear: The plaintiff's car hit the road block, and the defendant failed to stop. (The comma signals a completed unit of thought. The reader is then prepared for a new subject in a new clause.)

2. Do Not Use a Comma with Compound Subjects, Verbs, and Objects

Legal writers use interior coordination frequently; that is, they use compound subjects, verbs, and objects, joined by coordinating conjunctions. These are often mispunctuated, as in the following examples.

1. *Incorrect division of a compound verb*: The Trust Fund suspended payments to plaintiff effective in April, and further determined that contributions received on his behalf should be refunded.

Correct: The Trust fund suspended payments to plaintiff effective in April and further determined that contributions received on his behalf should be refunded.

2. *Incorrect division of a compound object*: The appellants contend that the facts alleged by appellants were not sufficient to constitute duress, and that the case was controlled by *Ingebrigt v. Seattle Taxicab and Transfer Co.*

Correct: The appellants contend that the facts alleged by appellants were not sufficient to constitute duress and that the case was controlled by *Ingebrigt v. Seattle Taxicab and Transfer Co.*

3. Use Two Commas to Set Off Interruptions

Commas are used to enclose parenthetical, explanatory, or interruptive words, phrases, or clauses. These commas mark the boundaries of a phrase or clause. Thus, use two unless one is replaced by a period or other mark of punctuation.

1. A lawyer, with a stroke of the pen, can save an estate from bankruptcy.

2. The plaintiff's car hit the utility pole, according to witnesses, and thus caused a three-hour power outage.

3. Will you help us sort through the files, at your convenience, to find the missing deposition?

4. Use Commas for Nonrestrictive Phrases or Clauses

One essential use of the interrupting comma is to indicate nonrestriction, that is, a commenting word, phrase, or clause. Conversely, the absence of an interrupting comma indicates restriction, that is, a limiting word, phrase, or clause. For example, the interrupting commas in the following example tell us that there is only one defendant, not several: "The defendant, the Minamoto Corporation, requests dismissal of the charge." If there were more than one defendant, the commas would be omitted: "Defendant Minamoto Corporation requests dismissal of the charge."

A simple way to illustrate the difference between restriction and nonrestriction is by limiting or not limiting a category:

Category: tort

Restriction: a tort that involves a breach of contract

Nonrestriction (explanatory, not limiting); a tort, which ordinarily falls within the civil domain

5. Use a Comma with "Which" but Not with "That"

The use of "that" signals a limiting function; in other words, it introduces a restriction of the preceding word or phrase.

Restrictive: The judges will read the briefs that are well written. (Only the well-written briefs will be read.)

The use of "which" signals a non-defining function; in other words, it does not restrict the preceding word or phrase.

Nonrestrictive: The judges will read the briefs, which are well written. (All the briefs will be read, and all the briefs are well written.)

Many writers use "which" for both defining and non-defining clauses, adding a comma to try to make the distinction clear. A comma preceding a "which" clause is used to signal a non-defining function. A better practice is to use the word "that" to introduce a restrictive word or phrase.

6. Do Not Use a Comma to Separate a Long or Compound Subject from Its Verb

If the subject is so long that it needs a marker or boundary at the end, do not use the careless device of an incorrect comma. Rewrite or rephrase the sentence.

> *Confusing*: The dicta in recent Supreme Court opinions and the explicit recognition of that Court's authority by the lower courts, emphasize what was first developed in *Brown v. Waters*.

> *Clear*: (Omit the comma and rewrite) The dicta in recent Supreme Court opinions emphasizes what was first developed in *Brown v. Waters*. The lower courts' explicit recognition of the Court's authority has furthered that development.

7. Use an Introductory Comma to Set Off Introductory Words, Phrases, or Clauses

If the introductory element is short and no misreading is possible, the comma may be omitted, for example, "In 1975 the Corporation signed a collective bargaining agreement."

Examples that invite misreading:

1. *Confusing omission of comma:* To summarize the question is difficult.

Clear. To summarize, the question is difficult. Or: The question is difficult to summarize.

2. *Confusing:* Contrary to the holding in *Bracton v. Blackstone* at that time the practice of submitting documentary evidence to a jury was long established.

Clear: Contrary to the holding in *Bracton v. Blackstone,* at that time the practice of submitting documentary evidence to a jury was long established.

8. Use a Series Comma

Use a comma to mark each separate element in a series; that is, put a comma after each item and before the conjunction. (A, B, and C). The mandatory use of a series comma in legal writing varies from such sources as Strunk and White, which omits the final comma.

Confusing Omissions of Series Comma:

1. Both jobs require activities that are closely related, such as the teaching of sports skills, the supervision and coordination of practices and competitive activities.

Comma belongs after "practices" to avoid misunderstanding of what is supervised and coordinated: is it both practices and competitive activities or just practices?

Correct: Both jobs require activities that are closely related, such as the teaching of sports skills, the supervision and coordination of practices, and competitive activities.

2. Although blood alcohol levels depend on various factors, including body weight, amount and type of food in the stomach and time between drinking and testing, the primary factor is the amount of alcohol ingested.

If no comma follows "stomach," the reader does not know where the series ends.

Correct: Although blood alcohol levels depend on various factors, including body weight, amount and type of food in the stomach, and time between drinking and testing, the primary factor is the amount of alcohol ingested.

3. The witnesses included one representative from Washington, Oregon, Montana and Nevada and Utah.

One from Montana and Nevada and another from Utah? Or one from Montana and another from Nevada and Utah?

Correct: The witnesses included one representative from Washington, Oregon, Montana, and Nevada and Utah. *Or,* The witnesses included one representative from Washington, Oregon, Montana and Nevada, and Utah.

9. Use a Contrasting Comma for Emphasis

Use a comma to emphasize contrast or to add emphasis to a particular word, phrase, or clause.

Examples using a comma for emphasis:

He sold property in Washington, not in Oregon.

A narrow definition of "watercourse" has not been adopted, by any court, in Washington.

10. Use a Comma to Separate Dependent from Independent Clauses

If the dependent clause comes first, it should be separated from the independent clause by a comma. If the independent clause comes first, no comma is used if the dependent clause restricts the meaning of the independent clause.

1. If an employee objects to a medical examination, the case must be considered individually.

2. A case must be considered individually if an employee objects to a medical examination.

11. Do Not Use a Comma Before "Because"

Do not use a comma before "because" unless "because" introduces a nonrestrictive clause. That rarely happens.

Incorrect: This is contradictory to the common practice, because, according to that practice, the title of ownership will not be transferred to the buyer until payment is completed.

Correct: This is contradictory to the common practice because, according to that practice, the title of ownership will not be transferred to the buyer until payment is completed.

12. Use a Comma to Separate Some Adjectives

Coordinate adjectives are those that may be joined by "and": erratic, vague testimony ("erratic" and "vague" both modify "testimony").

Use no comma if the first adjective modifies the second adjective, that is, if "and" is not understood between them (thus, they are not coordinate):

"a good tasting dessert"

"illegal drug traffic"

"grey striped cat" (if the stripes are grey)

"grey, striped cat" (if the cat is grey and striped)

13. Use a Comma After Parenthetical Material

Use the comma after the parenthesis, not before.

Because the case was too old (1875), we omitted it.

14. Place a Comma Inside Quotation Marks

Both a comma and a period are always placed inside quotation marks.

He is not classified as an "employee."

He is not an "employee," nor is he a union member.

15. Use Commas with Numbers

Use a comma with dates, addresses, place names, statistics, measurements, and the like to increase readability.

January 18, 1980, (month and day, year,)

On January 18, 1,000 entries were received.

On 18 January 1980, we received your letter.

C. USE OF THE SEMICOLON

1. Use a Semicolon to Separate Two Sentences

Use a semicolon to separate two independent clauses if you have a good reason to keep them in the same sentence. Separate, shorter sentences are often more effective than a longer one stitched together with a semicolon.

(i) if joined without a connective:

It was 8:00 p.m.; the road was dry.

For greater emphasis, the semi-colon could be replaced with a period:

It was 8:00 p.m. The road was dry.

(ii) if joined with a conjunctive adverb, such as "however," "therefore," "moreover":

It was 8:00 p.m.; furthermore, the road was dry.

(iii) if joined with other transitional expressions, such as, "in brief," "on the other hand":

It was 8:00 p.m.; contrary to testimony, the road was dry.

Do not use a semicolon if one sentence is incomplete (*i.e.*, a fragment), as in these examples:

> 1. Because lawyers are expected to think and speak well, they are expected to write well; when in fact many of them don't.

Use a comma instead of a semicolon since what follows the semicolon is a fragment.

> *Correct:* Because lawyers are expected to think and speak well, they are expected to write well, when in fact many of them don't.

> 2. Mr. Gould replied that the NLRB would not discuss it; and would not need to.

The semicolon separates a compound verb and must be deleted.

> *Correct:* Mr. Gould replied that the NLRB would not discuss it and would not need to.

2. Use a Semicolon to Substitute for the Comma in a Complex Series

A semicolon should be substituted for a comma when internal punctuation obscures the main divisions of any series.

> The beneficiaries we must locate are Byron Kelley of Arcata, California; Shannon Squires of Victoria, British Columbia, Canada; Helen Driver, who has recently moved to San Antonio, Texas; and Eleanor Tremont of Oklahoma City, Oklahoma.

3. Place a Semicolon Outside Quotation Marks

The witness replied, "I don't know"; however, the record shows that she did know.

When a direct quotation ends in a semicolon or colon, the semicolon or colon may be dropped.

D. USE OF THE COLON

1. Use a Colon to Introduce a List or an Enumeration

A colon may be used instead of a comma to introduce a list or an enumeration. This helps the reader to distinguish between the description of the list and the list itself.

The plaintiff's legal position depends upon dicta from three decisions of the United States Supreme Court: *Anderson v. Shipowners, United Mine Workers v. Pennington*, and *Federal Maritime Commission v. Pacific Maritime Association*.

2. Use a Colon to Introduce an Example, Illustration, or Elaboration

Colons may be used to introduce an example, illustration, or elaboration, whether or not the words following the colon constitute a sentence fragment or an independent clause.

In *Anderson v. Shipowners*, the collective bargaining process was not used: a unilateral hiring procedure had already been set up by the Association.

In *Anderson v. Shipowners*, a different procedure was used instead of the collective bargaining process: a unilateral hiring procedure set up by the Association.

3. Use a Colon to Introduce Quotations or Formal Statements

The Court found that the activity was not permissible: "The shipowners have surrendered completely to the control of the Association, thus limiting the activities of both shipowners and seamen."

4. Use a Colon to Emphasize What Follows

A colon may provide more emphasis than other possible forms of punctuation, such as a semi-colon or comma:

Not only is the report itself hearsay, but most of it is second- and third-level hearsay: the statements of numerous persons are summarized, quoted, or otherwise relied upon.

When a complete sentence follows a colon, the capital letter at the beginning of the sentence is optional.

Examples, both correct:

1. Lay readers can be helpful in several ways: (1) they have not been "desensitized" to the obfuscation and convolutions of legal writing, and (2) they can identify the words, sentences, or ideas that will be difficult for non-lawyers to understand.

2. Lay readers can be helpful in several ways: (1) They have not been "desensitized" to the

obfuscation and convolutions of legal writing. (2) They can point out words, sentences, or ideas that will be difficult for non-lawyers to understand.

5. Place a Colon Outside Quotation Marks

This may seem counterintuitive since the colon is a part of the quotation. However, the conventional method of punctuating where a colon and quotation marks are together is to place the colon outside the quotation marks.

> No one has denied Plaintiff's statement that "mortgage instruments should be comprehensible": the court agrees, the defendant agrees, and the general public agrees.

E. USE OF PARENTHESES

1. Use Parentheses to Set Off Potentially Ambiguous Phrases

Sometimes parentheses are more reliable than commas for setting off phrases that are potentially ambiguous or that obscure the "main line" of the sentence.

> *Confusing*: Borrowers must be informed of limits on transfer or sale of their property other than with the Bank's consent before they are asked to sign a loan instrument. (Does the bank consent before they sign?)

> *Clear*: Borrowers must be informed of limits on transfer or sale of their property (other than with the Bank's consent) before they are asked to sign a loan instrument.

2. Use Parentheses to Enclose Interruptions

Explanations, digressions, and other interruptions to the main thought of the sentence may be set off with parentheses.

> The answer is "yes" and "no" (a lawyer-like response).

3. Use Correct Punctuation with Parentheses

If the parentheses occur at the end of a sentence, the end punctuation goes outside the last parenthesis. If the parentheses contain a full sentence, punctuation goes inside the last parenthesis.

> Law students must have writing exercises (as opposed to "search and destroy" missions in the library).

> Law students must have writing exercises. (They should do more than "search and destroy missions" in the library.)

4. Use Parentheses to Enclose Numbers and Letters Marking Divisions in the Main Text

> A deed of trust must: (1) be comprehensible to lay readers, (2) accurately reflect the requirements of the lender, and (3) clearly inform lay borrowers of their obligations.

F. USE OF THE HYPHEN

Use a hyphen with a compound adjective when necessary to prevent ambiguity, as in "first-class," "well-written," "well-timed," "year-long," "decision-making," "job-related." As shown in the examples below, the problem is that one word may be read as the wrong part of speech.

1. *Confusing*: The government financed research in the maritime industry is declining. (Is the research government-financed, or does the government finance research?)

With hyphen: The government-financed research in the maritime industry is declining.

2. *Confusing:* Furthermore, the state sponsored schools throughout this area provide the greatest portion of NCAA funds. (Are the schools state-sponsored or does the state sponsor schools?)

With hyphen: Furthermore, the state-sponsored schools throughout this area provide the greatest portions of NCAA funds.

3. *Confusing*: Watch for heavy vehicle traffic. (Heavy vehicles or heavy traffic?)

With hyphen: Watch for heavy-vehicle traffic. (Watch for heavy vehicles.)

Use a hyphen to form compounds with numbers:

Two-week trial

Thirty-five-year-old defendant

Five-year contract

G. USE OF A DASH

1. Use the Dash Sparingly

The dash is the least defined mark of punctuation. It suggests a connection rather than describing it. The dash has connotations of stream-of-consciousness thought and carries a conversational tone.

With those limitations in mind, the dash should be used sparingly in legal writing for one of the following purposes.

2. Use a Dash to Indicate a Break, Shift, or Interruption

A dash may be used sparingly to indicate a break, shift or interruption. For example, "dashes are forms of loose punctuation—useful in writing fiction—not generally favored in technical writing."

It may also be used strategically in an argument—for dramatic effect, as in these examples:

> When law graduates begin to practice law—which for most lawyers means writing every day under pressure—they should already know how to write well.

> When the defendant forgot what he was going to say—which happened often—the plaintiff's attorney had to repeat the question.

3. Use a Dash to Expand an Idea

Use of a dash to expand an idea is rhetorically effective when combined with repetition of a word or phrase.

> As a result of this accident, the plaintiff sustained severe and lasting injuries—so severe that his foot may require amputation.

Leave no space before, after, or between the two hyphens that make up a dash unless your style manual or software program dictates otherwise.

H. USE OF THE SLASH OR VIRGULE

The slash has become increasingly popular in legal writing, as a short cut. It is often misused to mean "and." It means "or." It indicates an "either-or" situation, that is, a choice of alternatives.

Do not use the slash for "and/or" if you mean both "and" and "or." It means one or the other, but not both. Do not use the slash for phrases like "public/private functions" if you mean both "public" and "private." It means "public" or "private," but not both. The better practice is to spell out alternatives, rather than using a slash as an ambiguous short cut.

Use a slash to indicate alternatives:

> The car is available with a white/brown exterior and a black/beige interior.
>
> The "will/shall" controversy is passé.

Use a slash to stand for "per" in abbreviation (40 mi./hr.).

Do not use a slash for dates, as in 10/12/15. Instead, write the date as October 12, 2015.

I. USE OF QUOTATION MARKS

Quotation marks follow after a period or a comma to indicate quoted material. ("Quotation."

"Quotation,") Quotation marks precede a semicolon or colon. ("Quotation"; "Quotation":)

Ordinarily, quotation marks are not required to enclose indented material unless indented material continues beyond one page. The indenting itself serves to punctuate the quotation. Note, however, that quotation marks are required for even indented quotations under some court rules.

Use a single quotation mark to indicate a quoted word or phrase within a quotation.

> As stated by the court, "Plaintiff's request for this relief is a 'red herring.' "

> Use quotation marks for defined terms in documents:

> This Agreement will terminate on January 1, 2017 ("Termination Date"), unless it is extended prior to that date.

J. USE OF THE APOSTROPHE

1. Use an Apostrophe to Reflect Possession

Add apostrophe plus "s" or apostrophe alone.

Woman's everyone's

Men's Justices'

If a singular word ends in "s" and if an " 's" would make it hard to pronounce, simply add an apostrophe. The apostrophe is usually added if the syllable is pronounced as in "goddess's," but not in "for goodness' sake."

To show joint or individual possession in a series of nouns or pronouns, use the apostrophe in the following manner:

> *Joint:* "Williams, Green, and Mucklestone's policy" (the policy of the group or firm)
>
> "Shannon, Forest, and Kassandra's property" (their joint property)
>
> *Individual*: "Shannon's, Forest's, and Kassandra's policies" (each has separate policy or policies)

Do not use an apostrophe for possessives of personal pronouns: his, hers, theirs, ours, yours, its, whose.

2. Use "Its" When You Need the Possessive Form of "It"

Perhaps the most frequent of all writing errors is the mistaken use of "its" for "it's" and vice versa. "Its" is a possessive, meaning "belonging to it." "It's" is the contraction of the two words "it is." Although common, this error gives the appearance of either sloppiness or ignorance. The argument section in an appellant's brief, for example, began with this sentence:

> There being no showing that the defendant exercised dominion or control over the alcohol in his car, it's mere presence in his unoccupied automobile was insufficient to establish his constructive possession of the alcohol.

The mispunctuation of "its" in this sentence may create an initial impression of carelessness that can affect the persuasiveness of the argument itself.

3. Use an Apostrophe to Indicate Omission of Letters

it's (it is)

they're (they are)

who's (who is)

Note, however, that use of contractions creates a casual tone. To maintain a consistent, business-like tone, write both words in full.

4. Use an Apostrophe for Certain Plurals

Use an apostrophe to make the possessive of plurals ending in "s."

First form the plural. If the plural ends in "s," add an apostrophe. If it does not, add " 's."

lawyers'	Johnsons'
witnesses'	mice's

Use " 's" to form plurals of words used as words, of letters used as letters, and of numbers:

1. How many "yea's" are there?
2. The "7's" in the receipt are blurred.
3. "Occur" has two "c's" but only one "r."

5. Use " 'S" with Gerunds but Not with Participles

Use " 's" with gerunds, which are verbs converted to nouns ending in "ing."

1. The judge's leaving the court provoked comment. (The gerund "leaving" is emphasized.)

Use no " 's" with participles, which are verbs converted to adjectives ending in "ing."

2. The judge leaving the court provoked comment. (The judge is emphasized. "Leaving" is a participle modifying the noun "judge.")

Decide which one to use according to what you want to emphasize, the word ending in "ing" or the noun preceding it.

3. The court's holding in *Patner* set an important precedent. (The holding is emphasized)

4. The court holding in *Patner* set an important precedent. (The court is emphasized.)

K. USE OF THE EXCLAMATION POINT

Unless an exclamation point occurs in a direct quotation, it should not be used by legal writers. It is rarely appropriate for professional or technical writing. As a mark of punctuation, it serves to intensify a statement as a whole, without providing additional information.

Writers tend to use exclamation points as a vague gesture to intensify or emphasize a point or idea. Rather than use a mechanical device, such as an exclamation point or underlining, select emphatic verbs and nouns.

L. USE OF BRACKETS

Brackets have the three following uses in legal writing.

Use brackets to comment within a direct quotation:

> "Provision for a joint and survivor annuity is required beginning on the date the employee reaches the earliest retirement age [*i.e.*, age 50] or ten years prior to normal retirement age [*i.e.*, 65 minus 10 = 55]."

Do not use brackets casually, however, to tailor quotations to fit your sentences. Design your sentences to fit grammatically and thematically with the quoted material.

Use brackets to indicate change of lower or upper case in the first letter of a direct quotation:

1. "[T]he site of the Company headquarters is the primary jurisdiction."
2. The booklet states that "[f]or a proper understanding of the Plan, the complete text should be read."

Use brackets to enclose a parenthetical expression inside parentheses:

> She fails to cite the only relevant section of ERISA (assuming that ERISA [section 205(b)] will govern).

M. USE OF ELLIPSIS POINTS

Three points signal omission of a word or words in a quotation. *"Give me liberty or . . . death."*

Do not begin a quotation with ellipsis points. Rather, use one of the following alternatives.

> 1. The Court held that the defendant "did not satisfy the conditions of the contract."
>
> 2. "[L]egal writers have a difficult audience: overworked judges."

Indicate omission of language from the end of a sentence by an ellipsis between the last word quoted and the final punctuation. In the following example, the fourth point is the sentence period.

> *Full sentence*: "A board of directors selected by vote of the shareholders shall have the authority to discharge for sufficient cause all certificated and uncertificated employees according to the bylaws of the corporation."
>
> *With Ellipsis*: A board of directors "shall . . . discharge for sufficient cause all certificated and uncertificated employees . . . ."

If a fully quoted sentence is followed by ellipsis, four periods are used. The first period is simply the normal sentence period. The remaining three periods are the usual ellipsis points.

> "Readability is always lessened by long sentences. . . . [L]ong paragraphs also tire the reader."

Ellipsis here means that words at the beginning of the second sentence have been omitted. If the capital "L" were not bracketed, omission of a full sentence would be indicated.

If one or more entire paragraphs are omitted, use four points and indent them. Then begin the next paragraph on the next line. If the first word in a second or subsequent paragraph is omitted, show the omission by indenting three points. If a quotation begins in mid-paragraph, simply begin at the indented margin without ellipsis.

When typing, leave a space before the first ellipsis point and after the last. If an ellipsis follows a complete sentence, however, then the sentence period is placed immediately after the last letter of the last word in the sentence. For example, "Readability is always lessened by long sentences. . . ."

N. PUNCTUATION OF CITATIONS

Citation sentences begin with capitals and end with periods. Citation clauses are set off from the rest of the text by a comma. Citations in a "string" are separated from one another by semi-colons. (See the "Blue Book," *A Uniform System of Citation,* for correct punctuation of introductory signals.)

O. USE OF ITALICS

Underlining is used in typewritten or handwritten work to show italics. Do not use underlining as a substitute for italics or as a form of emphasis in legal writing.

Use italics for foreign words and phrases unless they have been anglicized (*joie de vivre*, but not tortilla).

Use italics for the following Latin words and phrases, when used in legal writing:

qua	*quaere*
infra	*semble*
inter alia (alios)	
inter se (sese)	*sub nom.*
passim	*supra*

Most other Latin words and phrases commonly used in legal writing are presumed to have been incorporated into the language of the law, thus are not italicized.

Use italics for signals used to introduce citations of authority:

E.g.,	*But see*
Accord	*But cf.*
See	*See generally*
Cf.	*See also*
Compare . . .	*Contra*
With . . .	

"See" is not underlined if it is part of an introductory textual phrase:

For a discussion of the tortious interference rule, see *Restatement (Second) of Torts* § 766A and comments (1978).

Use italics for names of cases, books, periodical articles, newspapers, ships, and aircraft (when used in text, as the rule for use in footnotes may differ):

Spectre v. Bond, 107 F. Supp. 70 (D. Mass.1972)

New York Times

Princess Marguerite

Columbia

Use italics sparingly for words or phrases the writer wishes to emphasize. To emphasize words effectively, place them at the beginning or end of a sentence. Use word order rather than the mechanical device of italicizing. Underlining should not be used, even sparingly, for emphasis in legal writing.

Examples of italics used for emphasis:

1. We are not concerned with *opinions* but with *facts*.

More effective: Opinions are not our concern. We are concerned with facts.

2. Washington's strong public policy against punitive damages should *not* be subordinated to other state policies.

More effective: Washington's strong public policy against punitive damages should prevail over other, less significant state policies.

The most common use of underlining for emphasis is inside quotations, for example:

"Payment does not begin until Retirement Date; that date is the *later of* (1) date of entitlement or (2) month following 6-month absence for medical reasons." (emphasis added)

P. USE OF NUMERALS AND SECTION SYMBOLS

As a general rule, within the text of your writing, spell out the numbers zero to ninety-nine. In footnotes, spell out the numbers zero to nine. Use numerals for numbers over ninety-nine in text and for numbers over nine in footnotes.

Always spell out a number that begins a sentence.

Spell out round numbers like "thousand," "million," "hundred," if you wish. Simply be consistent.

If numbers over and under 100 occur in a series, use numerals for all. Items in a series containing only numbers under 100 should be spelled out.

Numerals should be used consistently for section numbers or other subdivision numbers, for percentages or dollar amounts, and for numbers containing a decimal point.

Leave one space between the section symbol (§) and the numeral: 18 U.S.C. § 2482.

Leave no space between the dollar sign and the numerals ($5.00) and the percentage sign and the numerals (7%).

If a symbol begins a sentence, write the word for the symbol out in full, for example, "Section 2482 was added in 1972." Do not begin a sentence with a symbol.

Do not use "th" as in "7th." Instead, write the date in full or write the word "seventh."

Use decimals instead of fractions or write out a fractional amount.

Q. PUNCTUATION OF STRUCTURED ENUMERATION

Introduce an enumerated series with a colon. If the elements of the series are incomplete sentences, use no initial capitalization and punctuate with semicolons or commas or omit punctuation.

Finally, if you are unable to find a solution to a punctuation problem in this *Nutshell* or in your handbook, make an educated guess and punctuate consistently in the same piece of writing.

§ 9.3 GRAMMAR

The basic components of English grammar are illustrated in a series of diagrams in Appendix B ("A Microgrammar").

A. SUBJECT-VERB AGREEMENT

Verbs agree in number and person with the subject. The key to assuring agreement is to find the true subject and to determine whether it is singular or plural.

1. Beware of Phrases Between Subject and Verb

Phrases coming between subject and verb do not affect the verb's form. Look for the true subject, especially where prepositional phrases come between subject and verb.

1. *One* of plaintiff's arguments *is* enough.

2. *Not one* of the witnesses *remembers* what happened.

3. *Principles of Medical Ethics*, published by the American Medical Association, *contains* provisions concerning confidential information.

2. Beware of Lengthy Subject Phrases or Clauses

Agreement problems often occur where lengthy subject phrases or clauses separate subjects and verbs.

1. *Incorrect*: Washington's interest-analysis approach to choice of law problems result in the following holdings.

Correct: Washington's interest-analysis approach to choice of law problems results in the following holdings.

2. *Incorrect*: The purpose for which a corporation may be organized under the current laws are "any lawful purpose or purposes, except for the purpose of banking."

Correct: The purpose for which a corporation may be organized under the current laws is "any lawful purpose or purposes, except for the purpose of banking."

3. *Incorrect*: The correct use of quotation marks, enumeration, and a few other technical devices are briefly covered below.

Correct: The correct use of quotation marks, enumeration, and a few other technical devices is briefly covered below.

3. Use a Plural Verb with Most Compound Subjects

1. A plumber and a pipefitter make more money than an English teacher.

2. Cars and one truck were trapped on the stranded ferry.

If the compound subject stands for a single unit, use a singular verb:

Finesse, Wrangle, and Pinch is a respectable firm.

If the compound subject consists of singular words joined by "or" or "nor," use a singular verb:

If oral ridicule or a written statement to a third person causes a person to be shunned or avoided, it may be defamatory.

Plural subjects joined by "or" or "nor" take plural verbs:

> If neither written statements to a third party nor instances of oral ridicule cause a person to be shunned or avoided, then they are not defamatory.

If a singular subject and a plural subject are joined by "or" or "nor," make the verb agree with the nearer one:

> If written statements to a third party or oral ridicule causes a person to be shunned or avoided, then there may be defamation.

4. Use Singular Verbs with Most Indefinite Pronouns and Collective Nouns

Singular verbs may be used with the following pronouns and nouns:

all	every	nobody
another	everybody	someone
anything	everyone	something
each	everything	such a
each one	many a	
either	neither	

A few of these may be singular or plural depending on intended meaning: all, any, none, some, each, group, audience, committee, crowd.

In conversation, plural pronouns are frequently used to refer to singular nouns or pronouns, for example, "Everyone wants to have their efforts praised." This commonly occurs when people try to avoid using the singular pronouns "his" or "her." Nevertheless, in formal writing, subject-verb agreement should be precise and accurate.

Mass nouns take a singular verb unless they clearly have a plural meaning.

aesthetics	logistics	politics
economics	news	

5. Make Forms of "To Be" and Linking Verbs Agree with the Subject

A linking verb agrees with the subject, not the complement:

1. The source of the funds [subject] is the property sale and the liquid assets [compound complement].

2. The property sale and the liquid assets [compound subject] are the source of the funds [complement].

When forms of "to be" or verbs of being follow "there," they agree with the complement or object that follows the verb:

1. There are dozens of unconvincing arguments.

2. There is no reason to try this case.

B. USE OF "WHO" AND "WHOM"

Use the pronoun "who" when it will serve as a subject. Use the pronoun "whom" when it will serve as an object. In writing, the distinction should be carefully observed. In conversation, many people use "who" instead of "whom" because "whom" sounds unnatural or too formal. Most English speakers continue, however, to use "whom" in conversation whenever it follows a preposition, sometimes correctly, as in "You know of whom I spoke" or "give it to whom you like" or incorrectly, as in "The letter was lost by whomever received it."

In a few instances, determining the function of a relative pronoun may be difficult. Whether a relative pronoun serves as a subject or as an object is determined by its use in its own clause, not by whether its antecedent serves as a subject or as an object. For example, in "We know the ones who pay the bills," the relative pronoun's antecedent is "ones," which is the object of "know." Rather than using "whom," which serves as an object, the writer must use "who" because "who" is the subject of its own clause ("who pays the bills"). The entire clause "who pays the bills" stands in apposition to "ones."

1. We know *who* you are. (With this potentially confusing structure, "who" appears to serve both subject and object functions. However, if you ask "*what* do we know," then the answer becomes clear: We know "who you are." "Who you are" is a clause in which "who" is the subject-form following the linking verb "are." The object of the sentence is the entire unit "who you are.")

But: We know of *whom* you speak.

2. Checks were made of applicants who the landlord felt might not have been "congenial" tenants. ("Who" is the subject of the clause "who might not have been.").

But: Checks were made of applicants about *whom* the landlord had doubts.

3. Ask *who* the judge will be. (Here "who" is the subject-form following the verb "will be." The case must agree on either side of a linking verb, that is, subject and subject complement must be in the same case. Since "judge" is the subject, "who" must be used instead of "whom.")

But: Whom shall we ask to determine who the judge will be?

4. Mr. Throgmorton has been described as an oyster of the old school, *whom* nobody can open. ("Whom" is the object of the verb "can open.")

But: Mr. Throgmorton, *who* has been described as an oyster of the old school, cannot be opened.

C. USE OF PERSONAL PRONOUNS

Whenever the first person pronoun replaces the subject, it must be "I." Whenever the first person pronoun replaces the object, it must be "me." Errors commonly occur when two or more pronouns are used together or when normal sentence order is inverted.

1. *Incorrect*: The trial was scheduled at the convenience of Ms. Buffum, Mr. Field, and I.

Correct: The trial was scheduled at the convenience of Ms. Buffum, Mr. Field, and me.

2. *Incorrect:* He thought the witness was me.

Correct: He thought the witness was I.

3. *Incorrect:* It is me.

Correct: It is I.

4. *Incorrect:* The court can read the record as well as us.

Correct: The court can read the record as well as we. (To decide, simply fill in the missing words "as well as we can.")

Whenever the third person singular pronoun replaces the subject, it must be "he" or "she."

Whenever the third person singular pronoun replaces the object, it must be "him" or "her."

1. *Incorrect:* This is her.

Correct: This is she. ("She" is the subject complement and must make sense on either side of "is," thus "she is she," not "her is she.")

2. *Incorrect:* It was him who argued.

Correct: It was *he* who argued.

3. *Incorrect:* It was them who requested the postponement.

Correct: It was *they* who requested the postponement.

4. *Incorrect:* Mr. Gann thought I to be her.

Correct: Mr. Gann thought her to be *me.* (To test this, reverse "me" and "her." "Thought *me* to be *her,*" not "thought *I* to be *her.*")

D. USE OF REFLEXIVE PRONOUNS

The reflexive pronouns are myself, yourself, ourselves, herself, himself, and themselves. Reflexive pronouns have two uses: to reflect back on an agent (the *witness* perjured *himself*) and to emphasize something already named *(I myself* wrote the brief).

Do not use reflexive pronouns instead of personal pronouns.

1. *Incorrect*: Ms. Blumhagen and *myself* took the depositions.

Correct: *Ms. Blumhagen and I* took the depositions.

2. *Incorrect*: The document was signed by Dr. Ross and *myself*.

Correct: The document was signed by Dr. Ross and *me.*

E. WHICH TO USE: "WHO," "WHICH," OR "THAT"

"**Who**" or "**whom**" is used to refer to a person.

He is the one *who* ran for office.

She is the judge of *whom* we spoke.

"**Which**" is used to refer to everything except a person.

The evidence, *which* he misplaced, would have resolved the case.

We had never seen golden pheasants, *which* are more brilliantly plumed than parrots.

"**That**" may be used to refer to either persons or things.

She is the representative *that* I mentioned.

We had never seen the golden pheasants *that* Mr. Clark raised.

F. PRONOUN REFERENCE

1. Avoid Pronoun Confusion by Using Proper Names or by Repeating the Antecedent

Meaning is more important here than elegant variation.

Confusing: The servant's liability stems from the duty owed to a third person under the law to conduct *himself* so as not to injure others.

Clear: the servant's liability stems from the duty owed to a third person under the law requiring the servant to act so as not to injure others.

2. Avoid the Indefinite Use of "It"

The use of "it" in legal writing causes more confusion than any other pronoun reference. Avoid "it" whenever possible.

Confusing: In this case, it is sought to carry forward, as it were, an anterior negligent omission of the defendants, though continuing, it is true, up to the time of the occurrence, and to assign to it the whole blame for the occurrence although by no effort of the defendants or of their servants could it at that stage have been prevented.

Clearer: In this case, plaintiff seeks to carry forward an anterior negligent omission of the defendants that continued up to the time of the injury and to assign to the omission the whole blame for the injury, although by no effort of the defendants or of their servants could the injury at that stage have been prevented.

Avoid phrases like "found it advisable." As Lewis Carroll demonstrates in *Alice in Wonderland*, this can be confusing:

"The patriotic archbishop of Canterbury found it advisable—"

"Found what?" said the Duck.

"Found it," the Mouse replied rather crossly: "Of course you know what 'it' means."

"I know what 'it' means well enough, when I find a thing," said the Duck. "It's generally a frog, or a worm. The question is, what did the archbishop find?"

G. USE OF SEX-LINKED PRONOUNS

Many readers object to the use of masculine pronouns to indicate both sexes. Writers, on the other hand, have difficulty replacing them. When you face this problem, first try to avoid using any pronoun. If this approach will not work in a particular situation, try to change a singular pronoun to a plural.

1. *With pronoun:* A taxpayer may obtain a refund from the IRS by amending her returns for 1976, 1977, and 1978.

Without pronoun: A taxpayer may obtain a refund from the IRS by amending returns for 1976, 1977, and 1978.

2. *With pronouns*: A witness may be able to complain of nuisance even though the chemical plant has a dust easement on his or her property.

With plural pronoun: Witnesses may be able to complain of nuisance even though the chemical plant has a dust easement on their property.

If a singular pronoun must be used, then alternate the use of "he" and "she." Although using "he or she," "his or hers," and "him or her" adds extra words and may be clumsy, it is also an acceptable alternative.

On printed forms, the use of "she/he" and "his/her" allows the individual user to cross out the inappropriate choice. The odd-looking "s/he" may save time in writing informal memoranda, but it should not appear in formal legal writing.

The third-person pronoun "one" may also be used to avoid the "he or she" problem. The pronoun "one," however, carries a formal tone, sometimes even a pompous tone, as in "One can hardly imagine oneself making such an argument." A few rare phrases are improved by replacing "man" with "one." The sentence "No man should trespass on another man's property" becomes "No one should trespass on another's property." Few opportunities of this kind, other than in statute drafting, are available to legal writers. Regardless of the solution found to the sex-linked pronoun dilemma, wording should be consistent within the same piece of work.

H. USE OF SUBJUNCTIVE MOOD

Although the subjunctive mood is disappearing from English, it still may be used to indicate a supposed, imagined, contingent, or nonfactual action or state.

> If her lawyer had succeeded, they would not now be bankrupt.
>
> If settlement were possible, I would agree to it.
>
> Whether the case be won or lost, we will get our fee.

Compare these forms of indicative and subjunctive:

Indicative	*Subjunctive*
I am; you are	If I be; If you be
I was; he was	If I were; If he were
I will be	If I should be
I will have been	If I should have been

§ 9.4 POSTSCRIPT TO PUNCTUATION AND GRAMMAR

Some of the most common punctuation and grammatical errors have been addressed in this chapter. As a professional writer, law students and lawyers should keep a more comprehensive guide at hand while writing. We have included several good guides in Appendix D, Selected References.

With the most common punctuation and grammatical questions answered, you are now ready to complete Step Six. In Step Six, you will have edited your draft, removed unneeded words, shortened sentences, and generally revised for clarity, precision, conciseness, and effectiveness.

After your draft is polished, you will be ready for the seventh and final step: proofreading. Chapter Ten will help you to proofread citations, quotations, and text, as well as to check appropriate format.

STEP 6

- Edit revised draft for clarity, precision, conciseness, and effectiveness.

➤ *Next Step, Chapter Ten.*

CHAPTER 10

FINAL STEPS: EDITING, PROOFREADING, FORMATTING CITATIONS AND QUOTATIONS

§ 10.1 INTRODUCTION

You have completed the polished draft of your document, so congratulations are almost in order. Your draft analyzes the pertinent legal issues thoroughly and logically. You have revised each required section so the draft says what you want it to say. But you aren't done yet. You still must take the final steps in the legal writing process: editing, proofreading, and formatting the citations and the quotations in your polished draft.

These final steps will produce a professional memorandum or brief that's ready to send to a senior lawyer, a client, a court, or opposing counsel. Your attention to detail will help you communicate effectively with your busy reader and inspire confidence in your expertise as a legal researcher, analyst, and writer.

Legal readers expect the details to be right. But sweating those details almost always takes more time than we think it will. With practice, you will learn to predict how much time to budget for finalizing your work. Getting every detail right is an elusive goal, and, like us, you will make a few mistakes. But combining a high level of effort with the best writing practices, including the ones we recommend here, will help you write clear, precise, and effective documents that will meet our profession's high standards.

§ 10.2 EDITING AND PROOFREADING

This section addresses the editing process. Keep in mind that we generally use the term editing to refer to stylistic changes while proofreading is limited to hunting down typos and other glitches. Revising covers changes in the substantive analysis and structure; see Chapters Two through Four regarding those topics. For additional advice about the substance of editing, see Chapters Five, Eight, and Nine that discuss language, sentence design, punctuation, and grammar.

A. REFINE YOUR EDITING PROCESS

You came to law school from another academic discipline with an existing set of writing skills, including the editing process you used to polish the essays in your successful application. Now you must elevate that process to satisfy your new and demanding audience. Your quest will begin almost immediately in your first-year legal writing class where, for pedagogical reasons, your teacher will often ask you to play the difficult role of self-editor. Ideally, when you practice law, a colleague will also have reviewed your documents and suggested edits before they are sent out to your ultimate audience. Meanwhile, here are some tips to help you find the editing process that will work best for you.

B. EDITING AND PROOFREADING TIPS

1. Edit and proofread every document, including emails and texts. This rule has no exceptions. Every email and document you write must be correct, clear, concise, and clean.

2. Budget time to edit and to edit again. While editing a short email may only take a few minutes, editing a research memorandum or a brief typically requires multiple editing sessions and hours of work, even for an experienced practitioner. Be attentive to how much time you need to edit and build that time into the timeline for each writing assignment.

3. Budget time between editing sessions. Factor in time to let the document rest before you begin an edit. Controlling the length of editing sessions and taking planned breaks both can help you ward off editing fatigue and solve problems more easily. A smart student suggested starting some editing sessions in the middle or toward the end of a document in order to put "fresh eyes" on more sections of the paper.

4. Identify and eliminate your "usual suspects." Your first-year writing class will introduce you to the best practices for writing clearly, precisely, and effectively about the law. You will continue to learn about those practices throughout your legal career. While some of your writing skills, habits, and strategies will transition smoothly to legal writing, like us, you may find that some won't make the cut. Run-on sentences and excessive use of hyphens or

exclamation marks are examples of the kinds of things that will need to change. With practice, you'll learn to identify the "usual suspects" in your own writing style and develop strategies to eliminate them. To discover your own patterns of writing and uncover habitual problems, see the Individual Writing Analysis provided in Appendix B.

5. Edit in layers. Many of us edit by trying to tackle a wide range of writing problems at the same time. We simultaneously try to revise a section's structure, fine-tune its legal analysis, hunt down extra words, tweak the parallelism in one sentence and the word choice in another, scan for typos, and format or reformat the citations.

We recommend that you control the twenty-first century instinct to multi-task. Break out revising, editing, and formatting tasks. Finish substantive revisions before you edit. Format citations and quotations after you edit. When you do edit, target an editing session on your "most wanted" usual suspects. For example, if you are wordy, limit an editing session to culling those pesky extra words.

6. Mix it up. Many, if not most, legal writers do most editing on a screen. Varying your approach can sharpen your focus when you are tired or confront an especially challenging section of your paper. If you stay on the computer, consider enlarging, or even temporarily changing, the font to give the screen a different look. Reading an awkward sentence or paragraph out loud can help you hear a better way to say what you want to say. Or try letting your computer read it to you. Switch to

editing on a hardcopy periodically. Experiment with editing tricky passages on a white board, or try the old fashioned way—pencil on a yellow pad.

7. Be ruthless. Editing, especially if it's your own prose, is hard. Really hard. But lawyers must perfect this skill, especially given the volume and velocity of electronic communication.

8. Slow yourself down when you edit or proofread. Give yourself time to catch mistakes and craft options for the more complicated edits.

9. Let technology help you proofread. Your computer's word processing tools can help you produce a correct, clean document. But those tools also can create a false sense of security, and even a little mischief, for example, from the auto-correct function.

a. *Hit the spell-checker early and often.* In addition to misspellings, this tool will catch repeated words. Set the spell-checker to review all the text, including headings and words IN ALL CAPS. Customize your spell-checker's dictionary to include terms, words, or names (including your clients' names) that are unusual or tricky to spell. For example, the doubled letters and the "s" at the end of the first word in this case name could easily generate errors: *Ebbetts Pass Forest Watch.* Finally, be sure to run the spell-checker through the final version of your document.

b. *Use the grammar check.* It won't catch everything, including missing articles like "a" and "the," but the grammar check can flag basic errors like subject-verb agreement or sentence fragments, as well as more complex problems like passive sentence structure. Some programs allow you to set this function to different levels of formality that you may want to vary depending on the document's audience or purpose. But take your computer's advice with a grain of salt. You may have a good reason not to follow a grammar convention, like avoiding the passive voice.

c. *Use find searches.* A find search is a great tool for eliminating or preventing mistakes. If a typo results in a correctly spelled word that's the wrong word, like "costumers" instead of "customers," the spell-checker won't save you. But when you spot a mistaken word, run a find search to locate any similar errors. Some words invite embarrassing mistakes. Running a preventative find search can help you make sure that you haven't inadvertently omitted that very important "l" in the word "public." Or the third "t" in statute.

d. *Customize electronic tools.* Reset your word processor's preferences and formatting defaults to conform to your document's requirements. For example, if a teacher or senior lawyer instructs you not to use contractions, set the grammar check preference to a level that will flag that informal language. If a court rule instructs you to use 12-point font, reset your word processing program's default so that it doesn't automatically shrink the font in footnotes. Default programming may also run afoul of the formatting rules in citation manuals. More about that later in § 10.3.

e. *Beware the auto-correct.* Although the auto-correct function often can help you, it also can cause mischief, as it did for an attorney whose computer software failed to recognize the Latin term *sua sponte* (meaning "on its own motion") and changed that term, several times, to "sea sponge" in an appellate brief. This cautionary tale about technology leads directly to our next editing tip.

10. Proofread a document's final version, preferably on a hard copy. While indispensable to a busy law student or practitioner, technology has limitations and shouldn't be the last step in your editing process. When you think your document is finished, take the final step of proofreading it yourself, from beginning to end, preferably on a hard copy. Here are a few questions we ask ourselves when we proofread:

- Does the document contain each required section?
- Is the document correctly and consistently formatted? (margins, line spacing, font size, indentations . . .)
- Is the pagination correct?
- Are any headings stranded at the bottom of a page without text that follows?
- Are there any misspellings, incorrect or missing words, typos, or other glitches?

11. Use customized checklists. Traditionally lawyers have used checklists to guide them in performing a variety of procedural and substantive tasks correctly. A customized checklist also can be a great way to make sure that you have covered all the analytical and stylistic bases for a writing assignment. A checklist can help you catch big mistakes, like leaving out a required section, and remind you to hunt down smaller ones, like grammar mistakes and misspellings. A sample checklist limited to writing style might include these questions:

- Have you broken up or simplified any long, complicated sentences?
- Have you used transitions to connect your sentences and ideas?
- Have you used the passive voice only when necessary?
- Have you used precise, specific language?
- Have you used concrete nouns, active verbs, and plain English?
- Have you avoided turning verbs into nouns or adjectives?
- Have you deleted every extra word?
- Have you deleted hyperbolic language?

These questions ask you to think about your stylistic choices at the sentence and word level. You should feel free to tailor this, or any, generic checklist to suit your purposes, including prioritizing your usual suspects.

§ 10.3 FORMATTING CITATIONS AND QUOTATIONS

This section generally addresses how to use and format citations and quotations, but these subjects are complex. For guidance about the details of formatting, consult the citation manual used in your law school or office, as well as any applicable court rules. Also note that we focus on the conventions used in practitioners' documents; the rules for academic documents may vary.

A. REMEMBER WHY WE CITE

Accurate attribution helps convince your reader that he or she can rely on you as a researcher, an analyst, and a writer. Your choice of citations helps convince your reader that the facts and the law are what you say they are. In addition to identifying the sources that support your statements about the facts and the law, citations also can give the reader important information about those sources. Correctly formatted citations help your reader find what you want her to find efficiently and show your attention to detail. Finally, accurate attribution helps you avoid plagiarism.

While citations to legal authorities get most of the attention, citations to the record are equally important. When you submit a brief or other document to a court, you must support any facts that you rely on with specific citations to the record in your case. In an in-house document, like a research memorandum, citations that support the facts also memorialize the work you have done reading and thinking about the record and may save you time (and your client money) in drafting related documents.

B. MAKE CITATIONS PART OF YOUR WRITING PROCESS

We recommend that you incorporate citations as you draft. But as you revise a document's text, you'll also change its citations. Those changes can determine the correct way to format the citations. Therefore, we also advise that you use abbreviated versions of citations as placeholders and wait to finalize their formatting until the late stages of the editing process. For cases, each placeholder should include a pincite to the page of case that you rely on. For example, this placeholder includes an abbreviated case name along with the pincite: *Ebbetts Pass* @ 958. Some legal writers bold or highlight these placeholders so they will be easier to spot when it's time to perfect the formatting. Depending on a document's length and complexity, finalizing the citations can take a very long time. With practice, you will learn how to budget for bluebooking.

C. FORMAT CITATIONS CORRECTLY

1. Choose a legal citation system. The first step in formatting citations is to figure out what set of citation and style rules to use. Many law school writing programs and journals have adopted either the *Bluebook* or the *ALWD Guide to Legal Citation.* First published ninety years ago and now in its 20th

edition, *The Bluebook* is compiled by student law review editors from Columbia, Harvard, the University of Pennsylvania, and Yale. “Bluebook” is sometimes used as a verb. In 2000, the Association of Legal Writing Directors published the *ALWD Guide* (pronounced either “all-wid” or “allwood”). Its fifth edition was published in 2014. Whichever style guide you choose, follow its conventions throughout your document. In addition to these general guides, many books, like this one, offer advice about citations and style.

Practitioners must also follow any applicable court rules. While many courts have adopted general guides like *The Bluebook* or *ALWD*, some states publish their own guides or supplement the general guides. For example, in California, court rules allow practitioners to format citations according to either *The Bluebook* or the state’s own *California Style Manual*. Finally, be alert for any formatting conventions used in your office.

The Bluebook and *ALWD* guides are both comprehensive and complicated, but even their rules and illustrations don’t cover every situation. If you can’t find clear guidance on a formatting issue, make a choice and apply that choice consistently throughout the document. The purposes of citation may help you to apply the rules, especially in gray areas. Citations identify the sources that support your statements about the facts and the law, give the reader information about those sources, and help the reader find what you want her to find as easily and quickly as possible.

Sometimes you may have a good reason to deliberately bend a formatting rule. For example, both *The Bluebook* and *ALWD* have detailed rules for abbreviating case names, particularly when a citation appears in a separate citation sentence (more about that below). While saving space is generally a good thing, an abbreviation can blur or even obscure a portion of a party's name with persuasive value. For example, which version of this party's name would be clearer to a judge who hadn't handled a case about California forestry issues before: Cal. Dep't of Forestry Fire Prot.? Or California Department of Forestry Fire Protection? If you represented the state, you might want to write out the department's full name in order to emphasize its purpose.

Finally, you should apply the major conventions of the style guide that you have chosen consistently.

2. Know the rules of citation. The newest *Bluebook* and *ALWD Guides* are 560 and 608 pages long, so we can't begin to cover the details here. Although the vast majority of legal research is now done electronically, the content of most legal citations still reflects the way legal research was done "back in the day"—in paper books. Furthermore, the rules in these guides aren't limited to legal citations. They also contain rules about how to style a document's text and how to cite to other materials like court records. With these caveats, some basics should help you think about the process for formatting documents.

a. *Formatting varies*. A citation's format will vary, depending on where it appears in your document. The first time you cite an authority you must use its "full" or "long-form" citation, but after that first full citation, you must choose among various abbreviated formats, sometimes called "short-forms." Picking the correct short-form depends on the citation's placement and context.

b. *Include pincites in most case citations*. You will write many, many case citations in school and in practice. These citations usually should include a reference to the page on which the cited quotation, paraphrase, or idea appears. This reference is called a "pincite" or "pinpoint citation." Here's an example of a full citation for the *Ebbetts Pass* case that includes a pincite.

> *Ebbetts Pass Forest Watch v. California Department of Forestry Fire Protection*, 43 Cal. 4th 936, 958 (2008).

Note that we have applied our "local rule" in formatting this citation, preferring the official California case reporter, California Reports, over two unofficial reporters. Case reporters collect judicial decisions chronologically. Originally, they were published only in book form. Official reporters typically are published by governments while unofficial reporters are published by commercial publishers.

In addition to the case name, the *Ebbetts Pass* citation tells a legal reader that the case can be found in volume 43 of the fourth edition of California Reports, beginning on page 936, and that a portion of the case on page 958 supports the writer's point. In addition to the year in which the case was decided, 2008, the citation also tells an experienced legal reader that the Supreme Court of California decided the case because California Reports only publishes cases from that court.

The *Ebbetts Pass* case is also available in two unofficial reporters: the California Reporter, which includes decisions from all of California's appellate courts, and the Pacific Reporter, which includes decisions from courts in fourteen states in addition to California. When decisions were only available in books, being able to find a case in more than one book was extremely helpful to researchers. Now, an electronic version of a case will include information that will allow you to write a citation using any or all of these three reporters.

After using the full citation in a practitioners' document, you may use a short-form endorsed by your citation manual. Note that each of these *Bluebook* short-forms is also a pinpoint citation.

Ebbetts Pass Forest Watch, 43 Cal. 4th at 958.

43 Cal. 4th at 958.

Id. at 958.

Generally, legal writers choose the shortest format that will not confuse their readers.

Noting pincites in outlines and drafts typically will save you time when you finalize your document's citations.

c. *Use signals and parentheticals correctly.* You can give your reader additional substantive or procedural information about a citation by using an introductory signal or a parenthetical. A signal can indicate that the authority provides support, contradiction, or background; it can also suggest a comparison. For example, if an authority supports a proposition but doesn't state that support directly, add a "see" signal to the citation.

> *See Ebbetts Pass Forest Watch v. California Department of Forestry Fire Protection*, 43 Cal. 4th 936, 958 (2008).

Like all full citations, this citation to *Ebbetts Pass* includes a parenthetical with the date of the decision. If the reporter doesn't clearly identify the deciding court, the date parenthetical typically must also include that information.

A second parenthetical could add information about the case's substance.

> *See Ebbetts Pass Forest Watch v. California Department of Forestry Fire Protection*, 43 Cal. 4th 936, 958 (2008) (declining to overturn Forestry Department's decision to approve three timber harvesting plans).

Legal writers also use parentheticals to convey information about an authority's weight. For example, if a citation relies on a dissent rather than a majority opinion, that information must be noted in a parenthetical. In the absence of such a parenthetical, the reader will correctly understand that *Ebbetts Pass* was a majority decision.

d. *Know where to place a citation.* The convention in practitioners' documents, including memoranda and briefs, is to either put citations in free-standing citation sentences or to embed them in text sentences. Because citations can clutter the text, we recommend putting longer or multiple citations in free-standing sentences that follow the text sentences that they support. Compare the citation placement in these two examples:

> In *Ebbetts Pass Forest Watch v. California Department of Forestry Fire Protection,* 43 Cal. 4th 936, 958 (2008), the California Supreme Court declined to overturn the California Department of Forestry's decision to approve three timber harvesting plans.
>
> In 2008 the California Supreme Court declined to overturn the Forestry Department's decision to approve three timber harvesting plans. *Ebbetts Pass Forest Watch v. California Department of Forestry Fire Protection*, 43 Cal. 4th 936, 958 (2008).

Moving the full citation into its own sentence makes the text sentence easier to read. However, embedded citations may be required when propositions in the text rely on different authorities. You may be able to lessen the impact of an embedded citation by using a short-form or by placing the longer citation at the end of the sentence.

Legal writing scholar Bryan A. Garner advocates switching to the approach used in academic writing, namely only incorporating the most important parts of a citation—like the case name, court, and date—in the text. The other details, like the reporter name, and the volume and page numbers, are placed in footnotes. For example:

> Recently in *Ebbetts Pass Forest Watch v. California Department of Forestry and Fire Protection*[fn], the California Supreme Court declined to overturn the Forestry Department's decision to approve three timber harvesting plans.
>
> Fn. 43 Cal. 4th 936, 958 (2008).

Mr. Garner argues that this approach improves legal prose while still giving readers convenient access to any citation details they choose to read. Supporters of the current convention counter that judges and other legal readers expect and want to find this information in the text and are adept at skipping over any details they don't want to read. Moreover, footnotes pull the reader's eyes out of the text, thereby decreasing its readability. At this time, most practitioners and courts still follow the convention of embedding citations in the text.

D. USE QUOTATIONS CORRECTLY

The golden rule for when to quote in legal writing is the same rule that governed the writing you did before law school. When you use language that is not your own, you must communicate that fact to your reader by putting that language in quotation marks and by supporting that quoted language with a citation. For practitioners' documents, including memoranda and briefs, the golden rule applies to language in the full range of legal materials, including cases, statutes, regulations, and secondary sources like law review articles. In using case law, this rule is not limited to the court's legal analysis. It also applies to the court's statements about the procedural history and facts.

1. Exception to the Golden Rule

In practitioners' documents, once you have quoted key legal language and supported that language with an appropriate citation, then you typically may incorporate that language into the analysis or argument without repeating either the quotation marks or the citation. However, you may choose to quote that language again or to repeat its citation. Adding quotation marks can remind the reader that the language is not your own, and adding a citation can remind the reader that the language came from a potentially controlling case. Follow the practice in your law school or legal office.

2. Quoting Directly

In addition to when you must quote, also consider when you should quote. Especially in your first year of law school, you may only feel comfortable using a legal authority when you quote it directly. In explaining pertinent legal rules, you will be tempted to string together a series of quotations, joined by a few words or phrases of your own, or to use lengthy block quotations. Resist that temptation and use direct quotations when they serve an important purpose. Ask yourself the following questions:

- Does the quotation state key legal language that articulates an important part of the legal rule?
- Is the quoted language particularly memorable or elegant?
- Is all of the quoted language relevant to your analysis or argument?
- Could you accurately paraphrase some or all of the quotation?

3. Paraphrasing

As you become more accustomed to working with legal materials, you will become more confident about paraphrasing. Remember that you also must support paraphrases with appropriate citations. An effective paraphrase must be more than merely rearranging a few words or adding a few of your own words. If you only make cosmetic changes, quote instead and follow the rules in the style guide you are using. *The Bluebook* and *ALWD Guide* both contain detailed rules about how to alter quotations.

4. Block Quotations

The legal style guides also have rules about how to format block quotations of 50 or more words. We recommend that you avoid block quotations unless you have a specific need to use one. Block quotations tend to make our busy readers work harder. Our goal is to do exactly the opposite. We want to make even complex points easy for our reader to understand.

5. Ideas from Secondary Sources

Unlike other academic writing, legal writers may use ideas about the law, and even arguments, suggested by secondary sources without attribution. Legal ideas and arguments are considered to be in the public domain, as distinct from direct statements by an authority, which must always be directly attributed. However, even if quotation is not needed, if the source has persuasive value, we may want to credit those ideas. When the law is unsettled and you are advocating a new rule or applying a rule to a new situation, citing secondary, persuasive authorities may be the best practice. Similarly, if a treatise or other secondary source is well respected in a field of law or in a jurisdiction, the best practice also may be to cite that authority even if doing so isn't required.

§ 10.4 A NOTE ABOUT WRITING SAMPLES

Law students typically must provide a sample of their legal writing when they apply for jobs in both the public and private sectors of our profession.

Your busy legal reader may only read a few pages of your writing sample and may not be familiar with its legal issues. But that legal reader will pay attention to the details and will still spot typos, misspelled words, grammar mistakes, and inconsistent formatting in the text or in the citations. Therefore, you must be hyper-vigilant about the document's style and format so that you and your paper both make a good impression. Here are a few tips.

1. The paper must be "squeaky clean," with no grammatical, punctuation, or mechanical errors. Ask another person to read it for you. Read it out loud. Make the first few pages reflect your best written work.

2. The paper must be consistently styled and formatted. That advice extends to all components of the document, including the style of the text and citations.

3. Consider being conservative about style. Although legal writing conventions have traditionally been conservative, some of those conventions, like avoiding contractions or the first person, may be changing. If you aren't sure who your audience will be, consider defaulting to the traditional, and more formal, stylistic conventions in your writing sample. For example, choose "are not" over "aren't," and avoid the first person "I" or "we" and the second person, "you."

§ 10.5 CONCLUSION

You have now completed the Seven Steps we outlined for a clear, precise, and effective legal document. You have achieved your stated goal. You have addressed the appropriate audience. You have gathered the necessary facts and analyzed the relevant law. You have applied the law to the facts to reach logical conclusions. After outlining and organizing your analysis, you have written an objective or persuasive legal document that is clear and precise.

Finally, you have revised with an eye to brevity, clarity, and readability; edited to improve word choice, sentence structure, and overall effectiveness; and proofread to catch errors and ensure that your finished document is polished and meets all judicial or other requirements. Congratulations for meeting the exacting standards of our profession for legal analysis and writing.

STEP 7

- Check citations, quotations, and document format.
- Proofread.
- Proofread a hard copy of your final draft.

APPENDIX A

SAMPLE LEGAL MATERIALS AND DOCUMENTS

I. AUTHORS' NOTE

This appendix includes an appellate decision and various sample documents developed for a hypothetical about the tort of false imprisonment. The documents include a case brief, a detailed outline of a research memorandum's discussion section, a research memorandum, and a persuasive brief for a trial court that is styled as a "memorandum of points and authorities." Our version of *Wilson v. Houston Funeral Home* has been edited for pedagogical purposes, as have some of the cases cited in the sample documents. Case citations in these documents are formatted according to *The Bluebook's* style rules for practitioners and also apply our "local rule" that requires official reporters for California cases.

The proper format for research memoranda may vary, so be sure to follow the conventions used at your law school or legal office. Like research memoranda, the proper format for trial briefs, or memoranda of points and authorities, also will vary. If you are writing a brief, or any pleading to file with a court, you always must check the specific rules that apply in that court, including any rules about formatting.

II. WRITING A FORMAL CASE BRIEF

A formal case brief typically includes these elements: (1) case name and citation; (2) procedural history; (3) facts; (4) issues; (5) holdings; (6) rules; and (7) reasoning. You may add your own notes and observations. Include page numbers to avoid duplicating your efforts at a later stage.

(1) **Case Name and Citation.** Include the name of the case and its complete official citation.

(2) **Procedural History.** Describe the nature of the legal controversy, for example: "claim for false imprisonment." Also described the parties. You can identify the parties by their roles in the trial court, such as "Plaintiff" or "Defendant," or by using their roles on appeal, such as "Appellant" or Appellee." However, referring to the parties by their substantive roles, such as "widow" or "funeral home director" may create a clearer and more memorable picture of the dispute. Describe what happened in the lower courts: "The trial court sustained the demurrer without leave to amend, and Plaintiffs appealed." This section may be combined with the facts section. The procedural details of the cases you will read can be complex, but try to keep this

section short unless procedural rules are at issue in the decision or in your case.

(3) **Facts.** Summarize the case's key facts. Include facts that describe the parties' dispute and are critical to the court's decision.

(4) **Issues.** State the questions that the court decided in order to resolve the parties' dispute. Typically written as an objective question or statement, a legal issue combines a principle of law with key case facts. You can craft an issue broadly or narrowly, depending on the facts that you include. However, you should include enough facts to make the issue specific to the case you are briefing.

(5) **Rules of Law.** You may note any rules that the court applied to decide the case (sometimes called "inherited rules") either in a separate section here or in the reasoning section below. You may also include any legal principles coming out of the case (sometimes called "processed rules").

(6) **Holdings.** Describe the court's answers to the legal issues before it. Like an issue, a holding combines a principle of law with material facts. Often a holding can be written by turning the issue into a statement. In a case brief, a holding may be reduced to "yes" or "no" if the issue is

written narrowly. A holding should be objective and can be written broadly or narrowly. You may choose to include the court's disposition or result in this section, such as "judgment of dismissal reversed." Sometimes the disposition is referred to as a "procedural holding."

(7) **Reasoning (also called Rationale).** Summarize and break down the court's reasons for its holdings so that you can review the decision critically. The court's analysis may be based on statutes, mandatory or persuasive case law, administrative regulations, legal principles or tests, analogies from other areas of the law, claims of fairness and justice, pragmatism, logical reasoning, intuition, morals, or other policy considerations. Identify dicta in the court's reasoning. Concurrences or dissents may be listed here or in a separate section.

(8) **Your Own Notes and Observations (optional).** If appropriate or requested, add your own notes and observations. What do you think was really going on? Was anything missing from the court's explanation of its reasoning? Was the court's reasoning persuasive? Why or why not? Is the case good for your client? How would the rule in this case be applied to the case you are analyzing?

III. APPELLATE OPINION: *Wilson v. Houston Funeral Home*

Wilson v. Houston Funeral Home, 42 Cal. App. 4th 1124 (1996)

Plaintiffs are the wife, daughter, and sister of Melvin Wilson, deceased. Defendants are the Houston Funeral Home and its director, Willie Houston (sometimes referred to collectively as Houston).

Facts and Proceedings Below

Construed in the light most favorable to the plaintiffs, *Westinghouse Electric Corp. v. Newman & Holtzinger*, 39 Cal. App. 4th 1149, 1199 (1995), the second amended complaint alleges as follows. Melvin Wilson died on September 18, 1991. Two days later plaintiffs, Wilson's widow and daughter, entered into a contract with Houston Funeral Home under which Houston agreed to handle the funeral and burial services.

At the time the parties entered into the contract, Ms. Wilson showed Houston an insurance policy for Mr. Wilson and a $5,000 check from a mortgage loan broker. She was informed Houston thought funeral and burial arrangements could be paid for out of the insurance policy. It was agreed Ms. Wilson would retain the $5,000 check and, should the need arise for Ms. Wilson to cash the check to pay for Houston's services, Houston would so inform

Ms. Wilson and wait for payment until the check had cleared the bank.

On the day following the funeral, plaintiffs gathered at Ms. Wilson's home to wait for Houston's limousine to take them to the burial service in Riverside. When the limousine arrived, the plaintiffs got in, believing they were going to Riverside for the burial service. The limousine, however, drove past the mortuary without stopping to join the hearse carrying the body. Plaintiffs asked the driver where they were going and he replied, "Willie Houston wants to see you." At this point plaintiffs became fearful and frightened because, despite their insistence that they be taken to the mortuary, the driver refused to stop or turn around.

The limousine arrived at a bank where plaintiffs were met by Willie Houston. Mr. Houston asked Ms. Wilson if she had the check with her. She told him she did. Mr. Houston then shouted at Ms. Wilson: "Give me the check!" Ms. Wilson gave Mr. Houston the check, and he told her to accompany him into the bank. Once in the bank, Mr. Houston went from teller to teller trying to persuade one to cash the check. When none would do so, Mr. Houston shouted in a voice loud enough to be heard by plaintiffs and the bank employees: "I want my money and I want it now! Ain't nobody going nowhere until I get paid." This statement caused plaintiffs to fear they might never be taken to the cemetery or allowed to bury the decedent. Plaintiffs were detained at the bank, unable to leave, for 45 minutes to an hour while Willie Houston tried to cash Ms. Wilson's check.

Finally, a bank employee agreed to allow Mr. Houston to cash or deposit the check if he purchased a cashier's check payable to Ms. Wilson for the amount in excess of the burial charges he claimed were due. Prior to this incident at the bank, plaintiffs had never been told they had to negotiate the check or make any payment to Houston.

Burial services were eventually held that day for Mr. Wilson.

Plaintiffs filed their original complaint in this action on September 23, 1993. Houston demurred to the complaint on the ground it failed to state a cause of action. The trial court sustained the demurrer without leave to amend and ordered the action dismissed. Plaintiffs filed a timely appeal from the judgment of dismissal.

Discussion

For purposes of this appeal we accept as true the properly pled factual allegations of the complaint. *Thompson v. County of Alameda,* 27 Cal. 3d 741, 746 (1980).

False imprisonment is a willful and wrongful interference with the freedom of movement of another against his will. *See* Cal. Penal Code § 236 (West 1996); *Parrott v. Bank of America*, 97 Cal. App. 2d 14, 22 (1950). "Any exercise of force, or express or implied threat of force, by which in fact the other person is deprived of his liberty or is compelled to remain where he does not wish to remain, or go where he does not wish to go, is false imprisonment." *People v. Agnew,* 16 Cal. 2d 655, 659–60 (1940).

Plaintiffs allege they entered the limousine believing they were being driven to Riverside for Mr. Wilson's burial services. Instead, they were driven against their will and over their protests to Willie Houston's bank. From these facts a jury could find the plaintiffs were deprived of their liberty and compelled by force to go where they did not wish to go.

The complaint further alleges once plaintiffs arrived at the bank they were compelled to remain there against their will. The complaint quotes Willie Houston as shouting, "I want my money and I want it now! Ain't nobody going nowhere until I get paid." The restraint necessary for false imprisonment may be effectuated by any form of "unreasonable duress" for any "appreciable time, however short." *Fermino v. Fedco, Inc.*, 7 Cal. 4th 701, 715 (1994). Willie Houston's statement that no one was going anywhere until he got paid could reasonably have been interpreted by plaintiffs to mean there would be no burial service until he received the payment he was demanding. Under these circumstances the plaintiffs could not have simply walked out of the bank and hailed a taxi to take them home. To do so would have been to abandon the remains of their loved one to an uncertain fate at the hands of Houston. A reasonable jury could find from the circumstances that the plaintiffs remained at the bank under duress. A jury could also find a period of 45 minutes to an hour was a sufficiently long detention to constitute false imprisonment. *Cf. Alterauge v. Los Angeles Turf Club*, 97 Cal. App. 2d 735, 736 (1950) (holding fifteen minutes was an unreasonable amount of time to detain plaintiff when no facts showed he had done anything unlawful on racetrack's grounds). Finally, even if Willie Houston believed in good faith he was entitled to plaintiffs' $5,000 check, the provocation, motive and good faith of the defendant are irrelevant to pleading a cause of action for false imprisonment. *Collins v. Owens*, 77 Cal. App. 2d 713, 716 (1947).

Disposition

The judgment of dismissal is reversed.

IV. SAMPLE CASE BRIEF: *Wilson v. Houston Funeral Home*

Wilson v. Houston Funeral Home, 42 Cal. App. 4th 1124 (1996)

Procedural History

The Plaintiffs, a widow and two family members, filed a complaint. The Defendants, a funeral home and its director, demurred because the complaint did not state a cause of action. The trial court sustained the Defendants' demurrer without leave to amend and dismissed the case. The Plaintiffs appealed.

Facts

Decedent's (Mr. Wilson's) widow and daughter contracted with Houston Funeral Home to have Houston handle the funeral and burial services. Houston agreed to accept payment for its services from an insurance policy for Mr. Wilson. The widow also showed Houston a $5,000 check from a mortgage loan broker. Although the parties agreed the widow would keep the check, they also agreed that if circumstances changed and required the widow to cash the check to pay for Houston's services, Houston would tell her and wait to be paid until the check had cleared at the bank. @1129

On the day after the funeral, a Houston employee picked up the Plaintiffs in Houston's limousine. The Plaintiffs, who thought that they were to be taken to the burial, got in the car. But the driver, on the funeral home director's orders, drove past the mortuary and took the Plaintiffs to a bank, where Mr. Houston was waiting for them. @1130 He yelled at the Plaintiffs to give him a check, saying "[a]in't nobody going nowhere until I get paid." The Plaintiffs were at the bank for 45 minutes to an hour, until the bank finally cashed the check. Houston had never asked to be paid before this incident. @1131

Issues

Can the Plaintiffs, the widow, daughter, and sister of a man who had recently died, state a claim for false imprisonment against a funeral home, for (1) having them picked up in a car and then driving them to a bank instead of to the mortuary where the burial was to have taken place, or for (2) keeping them at the bank for 45 minutes while the funeral home director tried to cash a check?

Rules of Law ("Inherited Rules")

- The court accepts as true properly pled facts in the complaint. @1133
- False imprisonment is "a willful and wrongful interference with the freedom of movement of another against his will." @1134
- "Any exercise of force or implied threat of force, by which the other person is deprived of liberty or is compelled to remain where he does not wish to remain, or go where he does not wish to go, is false imprisonment." @1134

- False imprisonment "may be effectuated by any form of 'unreasonable duress' for any 'appreciable time, however short.' " @1135
- 15 minutes can be an "appreciable" length of time and sufficient for false imprisonment. @1135
- "Provocation, motive and good faith of the defendant are irrelevant to pleading a cause of action for false imprisonment." @1136

Holdings

(1) Options for Issue 1

a. Narrow: Yes. The Plaintiffs were sufficiently compelled by force and deprived of their liberty to state a claim for false imprisonment when, against their will and over their protests, the Defendants' employee drove the Plaintiffs to a bank instead of to the burial service of their loved one.

b. Broad: Yes. The Plaintiffs were sufficiently compelled by force and deprived of their liberty to state a claim for false imprisonment when they were driven to a location where they did not intend to go despite their protests.

(2) Options for Issue 2

a. Narrow: Yes. The Plaintiffs can state a claim for false imprisonment when they were held at the bank for 45 minutes by a funeral home director who demanded payment and threatened not to bury their loved one until the director was paid.

b. Broad: Yes. The Plaintiffs can state a claim for false imprisonment when they were held for a period of time by the Defendant who threatened not to perform critical professional services as promised until the Plaintiffs paid him.

Disposition

The judgment of dismissal is reversed, thus reinstating the Plaintiffs' lawsuit.

Reasoning

Unreasonable duress does not need to be a physical confinement or an implied threat of physical force. @1135 The Plaintiffs were compelled to stay at the bank against their will because they may have felt, with good reason, that the Defendant would not bury their loved one unless they paid him immediately. @1135 They couldn't have just walked out of the bank because "to do so would have been to abandon the remains of their loved one to an uncertain fate at the hands of Houston." @1135

Notes for Artie Abrams' Case

Artie's case is less egregious than Wilson's case, but both of them were subject to "unreasonable duress" for "an appreciable length of time." The widow and relatives' duress from not knowing whether their husband and father would be buried, and worrying that they would not be present for the burial, surpasses the duress that Artie experienced. But Artie is a juvenile, and he would have felt compelled to stay in the room, particularly with Dwight standing outside of the room. It's less clear that the ten minutes that Artie was made to stay in the room is an "appreciable" length of time.

V. OUTLINE FORMAT FOR RESEARCH MEMORANDUM'S DISCUSSION SECTION

I. Umbrella Paragraph or Section, which may include:

  A. Legal Rules (Broad → Narrow)

  B. Analytical Framework

  C. Roadmap

  D. Thesis Statement (Optional)

II. Heading for First Issue or Sub-Issue (using CRAC paradigm)

  A. Conclusion

  B. Rule statement, explanation, illustration, proven with citations to authorities

  C. Application—Arguments and Counterarguments

  D. Conclusion

III. Analysis of Second Issue or Sub-Issue

Repeat

Authors' Notes

The legal rules included in the umbrella paragraph or section typically apply broadly to the Discussion's analysis.

If a heading is a topic rather than a conclusion, the first sentence of text will typically state your conclusion. But if the heading states the conclusion, some writers move directly to stating the rule in the first text sentence. Another option is to write the heading and the first text sentence so that they work together to state a more specific conclusion. For example, the heading could state a broad conclusion, like "A jury could find that Scott intended to confine Abrams." Then the first text sentence could briefly explain "why" you reached the conclusion stated in the heading.

This outline format can be adapted to suit your particular problem. For example, you may be asked to analyze several issues each of which also has sub-issues.

An example follows of a detailed outline for a discussion section. The sample memorandum that comes next illustrates how you might flesh out your outline.

VI. SAMPLE DETAILED MEMORANDUM OUTLINE, *Abrams v. Scott*

Umbrella Paragraph (stating rules applying throughout Discussion's false imprisonment analysis)

1. False imprisonment is both a crime and tort, defined identically. *Fermino* @ 715.

2. False imprisonment is "the unlawful violation of the personal liberty of another." Cal. Pen. Code § 236.

3. Tort's four elements: (1) defendant's intent to confine, (2) whether defendant exerted such unreasonable duress as to involuntarily confine plaintiff, (3) "for an appreciable length of time," and (4) "without lawful privilege." *Fermino* @ 715.

   Authors' note. The four elements in this rule provide an analytical framework and a roadmap for the Discussion because each element is analyzed in the stated order.

4. Whether confinement is lawful generally is a question of fact. *Fermino* @ 723 n. 8.

A. Defendant's intent to confine [first element; begin each element with a heading]

   1. Rule

      a. A plaintiff must show a defendant intended to confine but not to cause harm. *Fermino* @ 715. In *Fermino* a "personnel manager summoned . . . [plaintiff] to a windowless room and . . . interrogated her concerning . . . alleged theft" from the defendant's store. *Fermino* @ 715.

b. Defendant's belief that the plaintiffs owed him money was not a defense. *Wilson* @ 1136.

2. Application. Like the summons by the defendant's manager in *Fermino*, Scott ordered Schrute to "escort this young man to the conference room" and also told Abrams "you will come out when you decide to give me a discount on the pizza."

3. Conclusion. Abrams can easily show that Scott intended to confine him.

B. Plaintiff's involuntary confinement [second element]

1. Rule

a. Confinement is "[a]ny exercise of force, or express or implied threat of force, by which in fact the other person is deprived of his liberty." *Wilson* @ 1134.

b. In the absence of physical compulsion, courts look to whether the plaintiff was subject to such duress as would overcome his or her free will. *See Wilson* @ 1135. In

Wilson, the funeral home director did not physically confine plaintiffs in the bank, but he essentially threatened not to bury their loved one, thereby causing plaintiffs unreasonable duress. *Wilson* @ 1135.

c. The restraint necessary to show false imprisonment "may be effectuated . . . by any form . . . of 'unreasonable duress.'" *Fermino* @ 715. In *Fermino*, plaintiff-employee was "physically compelled" to remain in a room where her employer interrogated her about theft of money. *Fermino* @ 707. The security guard prevented her from leaving. *Fermino* @ 707.

d. No confinement takes place if the plaintiff is not "deprived of his or her freedom to leave a particular place." *Roberson* @ 303. For example, no confinement took place when the plaintiff was not actually confined to the cabin. *Roberson* @ 304.

2. Application

a. Analogy to *Fermino*: Schrute is like the security guard in *Fermino* because Schrute would be as frightening to a 16-year-old as a security guard would be to an adult.

b. Analogy to *Wilson*: Scott could counterargue that the consequences of Abrams' failure to comply with Scott's order are not as dire as the consequences in *Wilson*. But Abrams could have lost his delivery driver job if he had not collected payment for the pizzas, and Scott screamed and ranted at him.

c. To let the litigation proceed, a court does not need to find that Abrams was subject to undue duress as a certainty, only that a jury could reasonably find that he was subject to undue duress.

3. Conclusion. A jury could find that Abrams was subject to unreasonable duress that overcame his free will to leave the conference room.

C. Confinement for an appreciable length of time [third element]

1. Rule

a. Defendant only must confine the plaintiff for "any appreciable time, however short." *Wilson* @ 1135 (finding forty-five minutes to an hour was long enough). *See also Fermino* @ 706–07, the plaintiff alleged that she was confined "for more than an hour."

b. Even fifteen minutes can be sufficient. *See Wilson* @ 1135.

2. Application. Ten minutes is less than the times in the precedent cases. But *Wilson* suggests that even a very short time could satisfy this element, especially at an early stage of the litigation.

3. Conclusion. A jury could find that Abrams' ten-minute confinement was for an appreciable time.

D. Absence of defendant's lawful privilege [fourth element]

1. Rule

a. Employer's Privilege. All employers have a right to make reasonable attempts to investigate employee theft, but employers must be reasonable and cannot deprive an employee of liberty either through force or "other coercive" strategy. *Fermino* @ 717, 721–22.

b. Merchant's Privilege. Merchants with probable cause to believe someone is about to injure their property may detain that person for a reasonable time and in a reasonable manner. But if the merchant's purpose is to secure a confession, the detention is unreasonable. See reasoning in *Fermino* @ 716.

c. Religious Privilege. Protected religious speech cannot be a basis for tort liability. *Roberson* @ 305.

2. Application. Unlike the plaintiff in *Fermino*, Abrams is not Scott's employee. Similarly, Scott is not a merchant, nor is religion at issue.

3. Conclusion. No lawful privilege would negate Abrams' claim for false imprisonment.

VII. SAMPLE RESEARCH MEMORANDUM, *Abrams v. Scott*

MEMORANDUM

To: Jeanne Merino, Supervising Attorney

From: Sarah Student

Date: September 12, 2016

Re: Artie Abrams v. Michael Scott

Question Presented

Artie Abrams is a sixteen-year-old who works part time delivering pizza. A company manager ordered pizzas from Artie's employer. When Artie would not accept coupons for the pizzas, the manager refused to pay and asked another employee to escort Artie to an office, where he was held for ten minutes. Does Artie have a claim, under California law, for false imprisonment?

Brief Answer

Yes. The manager intentionally violated Artie's personal liberty. No recognized, lawful privilege would excuse that behavior. Even though Artie was not physically constrained, a jury could reasonably find that the sixteen-year-old was intimidated by the older office employees and thus was confined involuntarily. A jury could also find that ten minutes was an "appreciable period of time."

Statement of Facts

Artie, a sixteen-year-old Scranton High School junior, works at Pizza by Alfredo, delivering pizzas on the weekends and after school. On October 15, 2015 he delivered sixteen pizzas to the Scranton, California branch office of Dunder Mifflin, a paper and office-supplies distributor that services small businesses. Dunder Mifflin has since been acquired by Sabre, Inc., a Florida-based electronics company. The branch manager of Dunder Mifflin, Michael Scott, ordered the pizzas to celebrate the launch of the company's new website. When Artie delivered the pizzas, however, Scott refused to pay the $64.00 tab for the food, insisting that Artie honor a two-for-one coupon. Scott claimed he informed Pizza by Alfredo about his coupon at the time he ordered the pizzas, and that the person who took his order agreed to honor the coupon.

Artie refused to accept $32.00 as payment for the pizzas, explaining to Scott that the coupons were only good for purchases of two pizzas. But when he threatened to leave and take the pizzas with him, Michael Scott ordered an employee, Dwight Schrute, to "escort this young man to the conference room." He also warned Artie that "you will come out when you decide to give me a discount on the pizza." Scott then screamed "this young man needs to learn that's not how to treat people." Schrute took Artie and the pizzas to a windowless conference room, closed—but did not lock—the door, then stood, with arms across his chest, in front of the door. At no time did Schrute, Scott, or any other Dunder Mifflin employee touch Artie, though Scott did touch the pizza boxes. Nor did any employee tell Artie that he could not leave the room. Artie left the conference room ten minutes later. Scott then paid Artie for the pizzas, including a two-dollar tip.

Discussion

A court would probably find that Artie has a claim for false imprisonment against Michael Scott. False imprisonment is both a crime and a tort, *Fermino v. Fedco*, 7 Cal. 4th 701, 715 (1994), and is defined as "the unlawful violation of the personal liberty of another," Cal. Penal Code § 236. The tort "consists of the 'nonconsensual, intentional confinement of a person, without lawful privilege, for an appreciable length of time, however short.' " *Fermino*, 7 Cal. 4th at 715 (citation omitted). Consequently, to determine whether one can make a claim for false imprisonment, courts consider the intent of the defendant, whether the defendant exerted such unreasonable duress as to involuntarily confine the plaintiff, the length of confinement, and whether any lawful privilege might excuse the defendant of false imprisonment. *Id.* Because whether a confinement is unlawful is generally a question of fact, *see Fermino*, 7 Cal. 4th at 717 n.1, courts allow a claim to proceed beyond the pleading stage if a jury could reasonably find that the plaintiff was falsely imprisoned, *Wilson v. Houston Funeral Home*, 42 Cal. App. 4th 1124, 1135 (1996).

Artie can likely make a claim for false imprisonment against Michael Scott. A jury would have reason to find that Scott intended to involuntarily confine Artie for an appreciable length of time and that no lawful privilege applies in these circumstances.

A. A Jury Could Find that Scott Intended to Confine Artie

A jury could reasonably find that Scott intended to confine Artie. A plaintiff must demonstrate that the defendant intended to confine the plaintiff. *Fermino*, 7 Cal. 4th at 715. For example, in *Fermino* a "personnel manager summoned . . . [plaintiff] to a windowless room and . . . interrogated her concerning . . . alleged theft" from the defendant's store. *Id.* But a plaintiff need not show that the defendant intended to cause harm. *Id.* at 715 ("false imprisonments often appear to arise from initially legitimate motives"). *See also Wilson*, 42 Cal. App. 4th at 1135 (citation omitted) ("the provocation, motive and good faith of the defendant are irrelevant to pleading a cause of action for false imprisonment"). Thus, in *Wilson* the defendant's belief that plaintiffs owed him money was not a defense to plaintiffs' claim that he held plaintiffs in a bank until they were able to cash a check. *Id.*

As in *Fermino*, Scott's intent to confine may be demonstrated by his words and directions to others. Scott ordered Schrute to "escort this young man to the conference room." His warning to Artie that "you will come out when you decide to give me a discount on the pizza," may be construed as an intent to confine Artie in the windowless room. Moreover, like the defendant's belief in *Wilson*, Scott's belief that he was entitled to a discount would not be a defense. Therefore, Artie can easily show that Scott had the requisite intent.

B. A Jury Could Find that Artie was Involuntarily Confined

Even though Scott did not physically constrain Artie, a jury could reasonably find Scott confined Artie against his will. Confinement may be found in "[a]ny exercise of force, or express or implied threat of force, by which in fact the other person is deprived of his liberty or is compelled to remain where he does not wish to remain, or go where he does not wish to go." *Wilson*, 42 Cal. App. 4th at 1134 (quoting *People v. Agnew*, 16 Cal. 2d 655, 659–60 (1940)). In *Fermino* the court accepted the plaintiff's characterization that she was "physically compelled" to remain in a windowless room where her employer interrogated her about an alleged theft of money. 7 Cal. 4th at 712. In that case, the employee's desire to leave was overcome by plaintiff's actions; when she attempted to leave the room, one of the defendant's security guards "slid in front of the door, threw up a hand and gestured for her to stop." *Id.* On the other hand, no "involuntary confinement" occurs if the plaintiff is not "deprived of his or her freedom to leave a particular place." *Roberson v. Evangelical Orthodox Church*, 216 Cal. App. 3d 297, 303 (1989). Thus, summary judgment was affirmed in *Roberson* because the plaintiff, who felt "trapped" when his minister ordered him to remain secluded in a cabin for a week, was not actually confined to the cabin—he went on a drive, left the motel, took a walk, and even went out to dinner. *Id.* at 304.

Although "[t]he restraint necessary for false imprisonment may be effectuated by any form of 'unreasonable duress,'" *Fermino,* 7 Cal. 4th at 712, in the absence of physical compulsion the plaintiff must be subject to such duress as would reasonably overcome his or her free will. *See Roberson,* 216 Cal. App. 3d at 304 (quoting *Parrott v. Bank of America*, 97 Cal. App. 2d 14, 22 (1950)) ("false imprisonment can be accomplished by threats that 'interfere with the freedom of movement of another against his will.'") In *Wilson*, for example, a funeral home director ordered the company's limousine driver to take the widow and daughter of a deceased man to a bank, instead of taking them to the deceased man's burial service. *Id.* at 1131. When the plaintiffs were at the bank, the director shouted at the widow to pay him a $5,000 check, saying "[a]in't nobody going nowhere until I get paid." *Id.* The court held that the plaintiffs had stated a cause of action for false imprisonment based on both the drive to the bank, in which the plaintiffs were physically confined against their will, and their stay at the bank. *Id.* at 1135. The court reasoned that a jury could find the plaintiffs remained at the bank under unreasonable duress because walking out of the bank would have been to "abandon the remains of their loved one to an uncertain fate." *Id.*

A jury could reasonably find Artie was subject to unreasonable duress so as to overcome his free will to leave the office. Like the employee in *Fermino*,

Artie was escorted to a windowless room and ordered to remain there. In *Fermino*, defendant's security guards prevented the employee from leaving. Similarly, Dwight Schrute stood guard outside the office, with his arms folded across his chest. The duress from having a security officer guard the door in *Fermino* is greater than in Artie's case, in which a mere officer worker stood at the door. Additionally, the consequence of Artie's failure to obey Scott's order—leaving the office without collecting payment for the pizzas—was not as dire as the consequence in *Wilson*—risking the burial of their loved one. But a jury also would consider Artie's age in deciding whether Schrute's display of authority combined with Scott's threats not to pay for the pizza exerted unreasonable duress on Artie, a sixteen-year-old high school student, leaving Artie sufficiently fearful of Scott to remain in the office. Therefore, a jury could find that Artie was involuntarily confined.

C. A Jury Could Find that Ten Minutes was an Appreciable Length of Time

A jury could find that Artie had been confined for long enough to state a claim for false imprisonment. The defendant must have confined the plaintiff for "any appreciable time, however short." *Wilson*, 42 Cal. App. 4th at 1135. In *Wilson* the court held that a jury could find that forty-five minutes to an hour was long enough to establish false imprisonment. *Id.* Even fifteen minutes can be an "appreciable length of time." *See id.* (citations omitted). Although Artie's confinement was a few minutes shorter, a jury could decide that ten minutes was an "appreciable" period of time, especially in light of Artie's age.

D. Scott had No Lawful Privilege to Confine Artie

The law of false imprisonment recognizes privileges that excuse liability in discrete situations, none of which is presented here. These privileges include: (1) an employer's privilege to make reasonable attempts to investigate employee theft, *Fermino*, 7 Cal. 4th at 717, 721–22; (2) a merchant's privilege to detain a person, for a reasonable time and in a reasonable manner, when the merchant has probable cause to believe that person is about to injure the merchant's property, *id.* at 716; and (3) a religious privilege broadly protecting all religious speech from tort liability, *Roberson*, 216 Cal. App. 3d at 305. Scott is neither an employer nor a merchant, nor is religion an issue in this case.

VIII. SAMPLE TRIAL BRIEF, *Abrams v. Scott*

Beth McLellan
McLellan Alvarez LLP
1850 Beresford Avenue
Beresford, California 94000

SUPERIOR COURT OF CALIFORNIA
COUNTY OF SILICON VALLEY

ARTIE ABRAMS,

Plaintiff,

v. Case No.: CIV161616

MICHAEL SCOTT,

Defendant.

DEFENDANT'S MEMORANDUM OF POINTS AND AUTHORITIES IN SUPPORT OF DEMURRER TO PLAINTIFF'S COMPLAINT

INTRODUCTION

The Plaintiff, Artie Abrams, has not alleged sufficient facts to show that he was involuntarily confined, which is a required element of a viable cause of action for false imprisonment under California law. First, the alleged facts show that the Plaintiff was actually able to walk out of the unlocked conference room immediately after he chose to do so, and that no person, including the Defendant, took any physical action to prevent the Plaintiff from leaving the room. Second, the Plaintiff has not alleged facts to show duress that could have reasonably overcome his free will to leave the unlocked room whenever he chose to do so. Allowing Plaintiff's case to proceed will encourage other meritless false imprisonment claims. Both the Defendant and the California taxpayers should be protected from the unjustified costs of dealing with such frivolous lawsuits. Therefore, the Defendant's demurrer should be sustained without leave to amend.

STATEMENT OF FACTS

On September 1, 2016, the Plaintiff filed a complaint against Michael Scott. (Compl.) The complaint alleges a single cause of action for false imprisonment. (*Id.*) Artie Abrams ("Plaintiff") is a senior in high school who works part-time delivering pizzas for Pizza by Alfredo. (Compl., ¶ 1.) Mr. Scott works as a branch manager of a paper and office-supplies distributor in its office in Scranton, California ("the Office"). (*Id.* ¶ 3.) On October 15, 2015, Mr. Scott ordered sixteen pizzas from Pizza by

Alfredo to celebrate the launch of the company's new website. (*Id.* ¶ 3.) The Plaintiff brought the pizzas to the Office, where the parties disagreed about whether the bill for $64.00 could be partially paid for with current coupons issued by Pizza by Alfredo, as well as cash. (*Id.*) The Plaintiff refused to accept the coupons and threatened to take the pizzas and leave. (*Id.*)

The Plaintiff's complaint alleges that Mr. Scott "ordered an employee, Dwight Schrute, to 'escort this young man to the conference room,' and warned the Plaintiff that 'you will come out when you decide to give me a discount on the pizza.' " (*Id.* ¶ 4.) Mr. Scott "then screamed 'this young man needs to learn that's not how to treat people.' " Mr. Schrute walked with the Plaintiff, who had the pizzas, to the conference room and closed—but did not lock—its door. (*Id.* ¶ 4.) Mr. Schrute waited in front of the conference room door. (*Id.*) Ten minutes later, the Plaintiff walked out of the conference room. Before the Plaintiff left the Office, Mr. Scott paid the Plaintiff for the pizzas, and gave him a $2.00 tip. (*Id.* ¶ 5).

The complaint does not allege that Mr. Scott, or Mr. Schrute, or anyone else in the Office on October 15th, at any time, touched the Plaintiff. (Compl.) The complaint does allege that Mr. Scott touched the pizza boxes. (*Id.* ¶ 4.) Nor does the complaint allege that Mr. Scott, or Mr. Schrute, or anyone else in the Office told the Plaintiff that he could not leave the conference room or the Office. (Compl.)

ARGUMENT

A defendant may object by filing a demurrer if a complaint "does not state facts sufficient to constitute a cause of action." Cal. Civ. Proc. Code § 430.10 (e) (West 2016). "A ruling on a general demurrer is . . . a method of deciding the merits of a cause of action on assumed facts without a trial." *McKenney v. Purepace Pharm. Co.*, 167 Cal. App. 4th 72, 76 (2008) (quoting *Linder v. Thrifty Oil Co.,* 23 Cal. 4th 429, 437, n. 4 (2000)). A court must "assume the truth of all well-pleaded factual allegations of the complaint . . . ." *Id.* at 78 (quoting *Kearney v. Salomon Smith Barney, Inc.*, 39 Cal. 4th 95, 101 (2006)). A court should sustain a defendant's demurrer if the plaintiff fails to allege sufficient facts to support "any essential element of a particular cause of action . . . ." *See Rakestraw v. Cal. Physicians' Serv.*, 81 Cal. App. 4th 39, 43 (2000).

Involuntary confinement is an essential element of a cause of action for false imprisonment. *See Fermino v. Fedco*, 7 Cal. 4th 701, 715 (1994) (explaining tort "consists of the 'nonconsensual, intentional confinement of a person, without lawful privilege, for an appreciable length of time, however short.' "). To sufficiently plead confinement, a complaint must allege facts to show some "exercise of force, or express or implied threat of force" that "deprived [the plaintiff] of his liberty or . . . compelled [him] to remain where he . . . [did] not wish to remain, or go where he [did] not wish to go." *See Wilson v. Houston Funeral Home*, 42 Cal. App.

4th 1124, 1134 (1996) (quoting *People v. Agnew*, 16 Cal. 2d 655, 659–60 (1940)). A court will only allow a false imprisonment claim to proceed beyond the pleading stage if a jury could reasonably find that the plaintiff was falsely imprisoned. *See id.* at 1135.

Mr. Scott's demurrer should be sustained. Assuming the facts in the complaint are true, no jury could reasonably find that the Plaintiff was involuntarily confined in the unlocked conference room.

A. No jury could reasonably find that the Plaintiff was involuntarily confined when his complaint alleges he left the unlocked conference room when he chose and fails to allege that anyone took any physical action to prevent him from leaving.

A plaintiff cannot be involuntarily confined if he is not "deprived of his or her freedom to leave a particular place." *Roberson v. Evangelical Orthodox Church*, 216 Cal. App. 3d 297, 303, 304 (1989). The *Roberson* court affirmed summary judgment for the defendant on a false imprisonment claim because the plaintiff, who felt "trapped" when his minister ordered him to remain secluded in a cabin for a week, was not actually confined to the cabin. *Id.* at 304. Rather, the plaintiff had left the cabin to go for a drive and to take a walk, and even went out to dinner. *Id.* Absent extraordinary circumstances, a plaintiff may be involuntarily confined only when the facts show that she was "physically compelled" to remain in a particular place. *See Fermino*, 7 Cal.

4th at 707, 715, 724. In *Fermino*, the plaintiff's desire to leave a room, where she was being questioned about committing a theft at work, was overcome by the physical actions of one of the defendant-employer's security guards. Immediately after the plaintiff "made a move toward the door," the employer's security guard "slid in front of the door, threw up a hand and gestured for her to stop." *Id.* at 707.

The Plaintiff has not alleged any facts to show that he was actually confined in the conference room. Nor has the Plaintiff alleged that Mr. Schrute, Mr. Scott, or anyone else, took any physical action to prevent him from leaving the unlocked room when he chose to do so. Like the plaintiff in *Roberson*, the Plaintiff in this case was not actually confined in the unlocked conference room because as soon as he tried to leave, he could and he did. The complaint merely alleges that the Plaintiff left the conference room after ten minutes and that Mr. Scott paid the Plaintiff for the pizzas, giving the Plaintiff a small tip before he left the premises. Moreover, unlike the employee in *Fermino*, this complaint does not allege any facts to show that the Plaintiff was physically compelled to remain in the unlocked conference room. The complaint only alleges that an office worker, Mr. Schrute, stood outside the door. Unlike the allegations about the security guard in *Fermino*, the allegations in this complaint do not say that Mr. Schrute made any physical move or gesture that prevented the Plaintiff from walking out of the conference room.

Therefore, the allegations in the Plaintiff's complaint could not reasonably support a finding that the Plaintiff was actually confined or physically compelled to remain in the unlocked conference room.

B. No jury could reasonably find that the Plaintiff was involuntarily confined in the unlocked conference room because Mr. Scott's alleged statements are insufficient to show unreasonable duress.

Duress can constitute "[t]he restraint necessary for false imprisonment," but only if the duress is "unreasonable." *Fermino,* 7 Cal. 4th at 715. In the absence of physical compulsion, the plaintiff must allege facts to show duress that would reasonably overcome his or her free will. *See Roberson,* 216 Cal. App. 3d at 304 (quoting *Parrott v. Bank of America,* 97 Cal. App. 2d 14, 22 (1950)) ("[F]alse imprisonment can be accomplished by threats that 'interfere with the freedom of movement of another against his will.' "). In *Wilson*, for example, a funeral home director ordered his limousine driver to take the widow and daughter of a deceased man to a bank, instead of to the deceased man's burial service. *Id.* at 1130. When the plaintiffs were at the bank, the owner shouted at the widow to pay him with a $5,000 check, saying "[a]in't nobody going nowhere until I get paid." *Id.* The court held that the plaintiffs had stated a cause of action for false imprisonment based both on the drive to the bank, in which they were physically confined, and the stay in the bank, in which the plaintiffs were not physically confined. *Id.* at 1134–35. The plaintiffs' stay in the bank supported their claim because a jury could find that the plaintiffs only remained at the bank under unreasonable duress. *Id.* at 1135. In particular, walking out of the bank would have been to "abandon the remains of . . . [the plaintiffs'] loved one to an uncertain fate." *Id.*

No jury could find that the Plaintiff's allegations support a finding of unreasonable duress because Mr. Scott's statements did not suggest that any serious consequence would follow if the Plaintiff did not do what Mr. Scott wanted him to do. Unlike *Wilson*, in which not complying with the defendant's order to pay could have jeopardized burying a family member, the only consequence of Mr. Scott's demand for a discount, and better treatment as a customer, was that the Plaintiff might have had to leave without collecting payment for the pizzas. Although the Plaintiff was a high school junior, the complaint does not allege that the Plaintiff was in any way fearful or even bothered by Mr. Scott's statements. The Plaintiff merely walked with Mr. Schrute to the conference room, as requested, and then walked out of the room ten minutes later after he decided to leave.

Plaintiff has failed to allege facts showing physical compulsion. Similarly, the complaint's allegations fail to show duress that could have reasonably overcome the Plaintiff's will to leave the unlocked conference room when he chose to do so.

CONCLUSION

The Plaintiff's complaint does not allege sufficient facts to show he was involuntarily confined in the unlocked conference room, which is an essential element of a cause of action for false imprisonment. Therefore, this Court should sustain the Defendant's demurrer without leave to amend.

Respectfully submitted,

____

Beth McLellan
Attorney for Defendant Michael Scott

APPENDIX B

INDIVIDUAL WRITING ANALYSIS AND MICROGRAMMAR

I. INDIVIDUAL WRITING ANALYSIS

This Individual Writing Analysis is designed to identify your writing habits based on a 500-word writing sample. For the exercise to work, you must choose a typical sample, not an unusually well-crafted one or an unusually poor one. Ideally, the writing sample will be from the discussion section of a legal memorandum or the analysis section of a brief. To begin, select a 500-word writing sample (roughly two typed pages) that reflects your normal, substantive writing style. Use a worksheet to record your analysis. A sample worksheet is shown below. This method of analyzing an individual writing style was developed to help practicing attorneys improve their writing.

The goal of this analysis is to identify writing habits. We often write automatically, using the same sentence structures and favorite forms of punctuation. Becoming aware of these habitual choices is the first step to greater control over clarity, precision, and effectiveness in your writing.

Step One: Count the number of sentences and the total number of words.

See Chapter 8, page 199–200, for instructions for counting words. Divide the number of words by the number of sentences in order to find the average number of words per sentence. Record this average on your worksheet. Count the number of sentences containing 35 or more words. Count the number of sentences containing six or fewer words.

As discussed in Chapter 8, the average sentence length for legal writing should be 20–25 words per sentence. This is longer than the recommended sentence length for general expository writing because legal writing is inherently more detailed than non-technical forms of writing.

If your average sentence length is longer than 25 words per sentence, then you should practice the techniques for shortening sentences discussed in Chapter 8.

If more than 25% of your sentences contain 35 or more words, then you need to focus on sentence division, as described in Chapter 8. If you have no sentences with six or fewer words, then you should try using this technique for adding emphasis and increasing readability.

Step Two: Identify and count the types of sentences in your sample. For samples of each type of sentence, see Chapter 8. The grammatical diagrams in this Appendix may also be helpful. Your worksheet should show the number and percentage of:

(1) simple sentences (one subject, one predicate)

(2) compound sentences (two or more sets of subjects and predicates joined by a coordinating conjunction)

(3) complex sentences (at least one subordinate clause in addition to a subject and predicate)

(4) sentences containing compound subjects, verbs, or objects (these may be compound or complex sentences)

Although there are no fixed guidelines for the percentages of types of sentences, at least 50% of your sentences should be simple in structure. The rest should primarily be complex, with few using the compound structure. A compound sentence can usually be converted to two simple sentences to enhance clarity and increase readability.

If you find that more than half of your sentences contain compound subjects, verbs, or objects, you should experiment with pairs of the appropriate subjects and verbs in separate sentences.

Step Three: Identify the structural pattern or "voice" of your sentences. Count the number of sentences written in the active and passive voice:

(1) Subject-Verb-Object pattern (active voice)

(2) Object-Verb-Subject (stated or implied) pattern (passive voice)

For each use of passive voice, identify the actor or agent. Determine the reason for removing or subordinating the actor or agent. For a review of active and passive voice, see Chapter 8.

Step Four: For each sentence, count the number of words that separate the Subject and the Verb. Divide by the number of sentences to find the averages. Count the number of sentences in which the Subject and Verb are separated by 7 or more words. Repeat these counts and calculations for Verbs and Objects.

For readability, no more than 7 to 10 words should separate the key parts of speech in a sentence, that is, the subject and verb (or predicate) and the verb and object. For further discussion, see Chapter 8.

Step Five: Count the number of sentences containing negative statements. Count any double negative structures, for example, "not without reason." Determine the percentage of sentences containing one or more negative statements or structures. Whenever possible, write in positive terms. Avoid double negatives, which slow your reader's comprehension and may be misread.

Step Six: Chart the sequence of sentences to check rhythm and variety. List the sentence lengths in the order that they appear. Look to see if the lengths are varied.

Step Seven: Count and identify the number and type of sentence "openers," that is, phrases that precede the true subject of the sentence. Transitional words, such as "however" or "therefore," do not count as non-sentence openers. Identify the types of non-subject sentence openers. Divide the total number of non-subject sentence openers by the number of sentences to find the percentage. Ideally, for maximum readability, 75% of sentences should open with the subject. Thus, the percentage of non-subject openers should not exceed 25%. Very short and simple opening prepositional phrases, such as "In the preceding appeal," do not lessen readability significantly unless they are used frequently.

If non-subject openers exceed 25%, then identify the type of openers that are used instead of subjects:

(1) prepositional phrases as openers

(2) adverbial phrases as openers

(3) adjectival phrases as openers

(4) other parts of speech used as openers

Step Eight: Check all modifying phrases by locating the noun or verb that they modify. For example, check these prepositional phrases from the writing sample below: "stored by carriers in the course of providing services to subscribers." Does the phrase "in the course of providing services" modify the word next to it, "carriers"? Are "carriers" the ones who would provide services? If not, then the modifier is misplaced and could create ambiguity. In this example, the carriers are providing services, so the modifier is correctly placed. Note any modifiers in your own writing sample that could be misread to modify more than one word or phrase. See Chapter 8 for more examples.

Step Nine: Paragraph Analysis:

(1) Count the number of paragraphs.

(2) Count the number of words in each paragraph.

(3) List the numbers of words per paragraph in the order that the paragraphs occur to check for variety of paragraph length.

(4) Calculate the average number of words per paragraph. If the average number of words per paragraph exceeds 150, you should find ways of shortening some paragraphs.

(5) Identify the reason for each paragraph break: logical division, rhetorical effect, or visual effect. If you have no rhetorical or visual paragraph breaks, try using them for emphasis.

(6) Identify the topic sentences in each paragraph. Count the number of paragraphs that begin with the topic sentence. Ninety percent of your paragraphs should begin with the topic sentence. For those paragraphs that do not open with the topic, identify the reason for delaying it. Is the reason sufficient given the reader's expectation and need to know the topic immediately?

(7) Evaluate the first and last sentences of each paragraph. Do they deserve to be in positions of greatest emphasis?

(8) Underline transitional words and phrases. Are there enough transitions to move

the reader smoothly from sentence to sentence and from idea to idea? Are the appropriate transitional words used? For additional transitional words, see Chapter 4.

Step Ten: Punctuation:

(1) Count the number of interruptions resulting from sets of commas, sets of parenthesis, sets of brackets, and sets of dashes. Calculate the average number of interruptions per sentence. For greatest readability, this percentage should be kept below 50%.

(2) Notice any mark of punctuation that recurs. Do you tend to use semicolons to separate units of thought? Could you use periods and transitional words instead? Do you tend to use dashes to slow the reader down? Would more careful word choice accomplish the same goal more effectively?

Step Eleven: Language:

(1) Count the number of verbs that denote action ("transitive" verbs like "run") and the number of times that forms of "to be" occur. Writing with specific active verbs rather than forms of "to be" will strengthen and clarify your writing. At least two-thirds of your verbs should be active verbs.

(2) Count the number of adjectives and adverbs. Calculate the number of adjectives and adverbs per sentence. If you have more

than 100%, experiment with deleting them. Use stronger verbs and nouns to avoid the tendency to add unneeded modifiers. Adjectives and adverbs sometimes weaken the nouns and verbs that they modify; thus removing them can strengthen a sentence.

Step Twelve: Wordiness and Redundancy:

As an exercise, strike through 100 words in your writing sample. Eliminate each word that is not essential. Eliminate all redundancy, even if it serves a rhetorical purpose. The point of this exercise is to identify your individual tendencies to wordiness. Print out your 400-word writing sample and ask someone to compare it with the original. Which is easier to read? Which communicates more clearly? How much substance has been lost? Does it matter?

WRITING SAMPLE AND EXAMPLE OF ANALYSIS:

The following example is the introduction and summary of argument from a reply brief for a federal appeals court. The petitioners are replying to an opposition brief filed by the respondents to their appeal. The paragraph numbers have been added for use in the writing analysis that follows.

Paragraph 1

The opening brief of petitioner and intervenors (collectively, "petitioners") demonstrated that the FCC's construction of Section 222, which addresses customer proprietary network information ("CPNI"), is unreasonable and arbitrary in several fundamental respects: it contradicts Congress' intent in enacting Section 222; represents a sudden and unwarranted departure from prior Commission policy; and is utterly unprecedented among federal laws. In light of the serious constitutional issues raised by the FCC's interpretation of Section 222, the FCC was bound to construe the statute to avoid those constitutional questions. *E.g., Edward J. DeBartolo Corp. v. Florida Gulf Coast Council,* 485 U.S. 568, 575 (1988). Indeed, the FCC's very efforts to brush off these grave constitutional issues warrants vacating the CPNI rules, because that failure "to give adequate consideration" to constitutional objections to agency action is "the very paradigm of arbitrary and capricious administrative action." *Meredith Corp. v. FCC,* 809 F.2d 863, 865 (D.C. Cir. 1987).

Paragraph 2

The FCC and its supporting intervenors (collectively, "respondents") mischaracterize the nature of CPNI and distort what is at issue in this case. CPNI is generated, gathered, organized, maintained, and stored by carriers in the course of providing services to subscribers. After a customer requests particular services, the carrier generates a record of the services. Respondents further confuse the issues of (i) CPNI in the hands of a carrier that has an existing relationship with a customer with (ii) third-party disclosure of CPNI to unrelated, unaffiliated entities that do not have any existing relationship with the customer. Respondents' privacy argument focuses on third-party disclosure and is therefore irrelevant here.

Paragraph 3

Respondents also claim that CPNI "belongs to" customers. That, too, is erroneous. Although consumers undoubtedly have certain expectations regarding carriers' use of CPNI—which the record demonstrates petitioners have always respected—CPNI is owned by carriers. Respondents' contrary view is a radical one that, were this Court to embrace it, would turn well-settled property law on its head and would profoundly upset the property rights of mail-order catalogs, credit card companies, and practically any other firm that, as part of its routine business operations, maintains individually identifiably customer information.

Paragraph 4

Finally, respondents misstate the applicable First and Fifth Amendment principles. They insist that the CPNI rules do not by their express terms dictate what carriers can and cannot say. However, they ignore the direct choking impact of the FCC's rules on intra-corporate communications and also ignore the Supreme Court's repeated teaching that the first amendment is concerned with the practical effect of a regulation on speech. Here, the practical effect of the FCC's rules on carrier-customer communication is devastating.

Paragraph 5

With respect to the Fifth Amendment, respondents' argument hinges on the mistaken premise that carriers have no reasonable, invest-backed expectation in owning or using CPNI. The CPNI rules should be vacated.

DISCUSSION OF EXAMPLE:

Using the twelve steps of the individual writing analysis, this writing sample can be clarified, its readability can be improved, and it can become more persuasive.

Step One: The average sentence length is 25 words per sentence. This is at the long end of the spectrum for readability. Shorter sentences will improve this sample. Equally important are the five sentences longer than 35 words. At about 27%, this number of very long sentences slows the reader. The first sentence contains 57 words. This presents an immediate obstacle to a judge or any other reader. The first sentence in a brief, or any legal writing, should not present an obstacle or readability challenge for the reader. The five very long sentences in the sample can be broken into shorter ones for ease of comprehension. There are two extremely short sentences, both six words or less. These are each used effectively for emphasis. Adding one or two more might be added, but overuse will reduce the rhetorical effect.

Step Two: There are eight simple sentences, which is just under one-half of the total of 18 sentences. There are seven compound sentences, or 44%. This is too many. It is also where improvement will be easiest. Separating the units of thought into separate sentences will speed up the reading process and clarify the units of thought. The three complex sentences bring good variety and a welcome break from the over-long sentences that surround them.

Step Three: The voice is almost entirely active. Only two sentences contain passive voice. One is the last sentence in which it is an effective deferential device for addressing the court.

Step Four: Most of the sentences contain subjects and verbs close together. This is not the source of the readability problems for the most part. In the overlong sentences, it is the verbs and objects that are separated by too many words. This often happens within compound sentence structures.

Step Five: There are no troubling double negatives or confusing negative statements.

Step Six: Overall, the variety and rhythm of sentence lengths could be improved. In the first paragraph, there are only three sentences, creating a clogged, dense effect. The second paragraph contains one complex sentence in the middle of compound sentences. Breaking the compound sentences into simple ones will speed up reading and provide variety. The third paragraph begins with two short simple sentences. Notice how much easier it is to read than the first two paragraphs. Even though longer complex and compound sentences follow, they are tolerable because of the short simple sentences that introduce the topic of the paragraph. The fourth paragraph again starts with a short simple sentence. The compound sentence that follows is relatively readable because it is introduced by a simple one. The paragraph ends with another short simple sentence, which makes its point effectively and is easy to comprehend. The fifth paragraph makes good use of two sentences of different lengths, the last one being only six words. This is an effective rhetorical device.

Step Seven: Only 22% of the sentences open with words other than the subject or subject phrase. There are a few long opening prepositional phrases, but since most sentences begin with the subject, this is not a focus for revision.

Step Eight: The modifiers in the writing sample are tightly structured to avoid ambiguity. There are a number of prepositional phrases that could be confusing, but the syntax is such that the meaning is clear.

Step Nine: The average number of words per paragraph is 90, with generally good variety in paragraph length. The paragraph breaks are logical. They are based on the arguments: the first paragraph states the arguments of the petitioners; the second, third, and fourth paragraphs state the arguments of the respondents; and the fifth paragraph states the conclusion of the petitioners. The last paragraph is rhetorically and visually effective for the same reason that the last sentence is effective: it is very short in contrast to what has come before.

The positions of emphasis in each of the five paragraphs are well used. None of the highly visual space at the beginning and end of paragraphs is wasted on unimportant phrases or clauses. Although the first paragraph ends with a citation, it is offered as the governing precedent for the case at hand.

The transitions used between the paragraphs are simple, but make clear connections. Paragraph three is tied to paragraph two by "also." Paragraph four is tied to the preceding three paragraphs by "Finally." And paragraph five is tied to the whole by "With respect to the Fifth Amendment."

Step Ten: The chief punctuation issue is with sets of commas and series of semi-colons. This type of punctuation is used to separate units of thought in the overlong compound sentences. By breaking these into simple sentences, the punctuation will be simplified.

Step Eleven: Over two-thirds of the verbs are active. Adjectives and adverbs are not overused on the whole. The word "very" is a throw-away adjective in paragraph one, as are "indeed" and "in the light of." The word "very" almost never adds emphasis as intended.

Step Twelve: To shorten this sample, the overlong compound sentences have been broken into simple sentences. Compound subjects, verbs, and objects have been separated into simple sentences containing one unit of thought wherever possible. This sample does not contain many redundant words or phrases, thus the main focus for revision is on shortening and simplifying sentences for readability.

REVISION OF EXAMPLE:

The opening brief of petitioner and intervenors (collectively, "petitioners") demonstrated that the FCC's construction of Section 222 is unreasonable and arbitrary in several fundamental respects. The FCC's construction of Section 222 addresses customer proprietary network information ("CPNI"). In so doing, it contradicts Congress' intent in enacting Section 222. The FCC's construction represents a sudden and unwarranted departure from prior Commission policy. It is utterly unprecedented among federal laws. Moreover, serious constitutional issues are raised by the FCC's interpretation of Section 222. The FCC was bound to construe the statute to avoid those constitutional questions. *E.g., Edward J. DeBartolo Corp. v. Florida Gulf Coast Council,* 485 U.S. 568, 575 (1988). The FCC's efforts to brush off these constitutional issues warrants vacating the CPNI rules. A vacation of these rules is warranted because, as this Court has previously held, the FCC's failure "to give adequate consideration" to constitutional objections to agency action is "the very paradigm of arbitrary and capricious administrative action." *Meredith Corp. v. FCC,* 809 F.2d 863, 865 (D.C. Cir. 1987).

The FCC and its supporting intervenors (collectively, "respondents") mischaracterize the nature of CPNI. They distort what is at issue is this case. CPNI is generated, gathered, organized, maintained, and stored by carriers in the course of providing services to subscribers. After a customer requests particular services, the carrier generates a record of the services. Respondents further confuse the issues of (i) CPNI in the hands of a carrier that has an existing relationship with a customer with (ii) third-party disclosure of CPNI to unrelated, unaffiliated entities that do not have any existing relationship with the customer. Respondents' privacy argument focuses on third-party disclosure. That argument is therefore irrelevant here.

Respondents also claim that CPNI "belongs to" customers. That, too, is erroneous. Consumers undoubtedly have certain expectations regarding carriers' use of CPNI. The record demonstrates that petitioners have always respected those expectations. However, CPNI is owned by carriers. Respondents' contrary view is a radical one. If this Court were to embrace it, well-settled property law would be turned on its head. It would profoundly upset the property rights of mail-order catalogs, credit card companies, and practically any other firm that, as part of its routine business operations, maintains individually identifiably customer information.

Finally, respondents misstate the applicable First and Fifth Amendment principles. They insist that the CPNI rules do not dictate what carriers can and cannot say. However, they ignore the direct choking impact of the FCC's rules on intra-corporate communications. They also ignore the Supreme Court's repeated teaching that the first amendment is concerned with the practical effect of a regulation on speech. Here, the practical effect of the FCC's rules on carrier-customer communication is devastating.

With respect to the Fifth Amendment, respondents' argument hinges on the mistaken premise that carriers have no reasonable, invest-backed expectation in owning or using CPNI. The CPNI rules should be vacated.

COMMENTS ON REVISION:

Notice the persuasive effect of shorter sentences in the third paragraph. The third sentence in that paragraph has been broken into two shorter ones by replacing the relative pronoun "which" with the noun "record."

Before: Although consumers undoubtedly have certain expectations regarding carriers' use of CPNI—*which* the record demonstrates petitioners have always respected—CPNI is owned by carriers.

After: Consumers undoubtedly have certain expectations regarding carriers' use of CPNI. *The record* demonstrates that petitioners have always respected those expectations. However, CPNI is owned by carriers.

"Record" then becomes the subject of an important sentence. The idea that the petitioners have always respected the consumers is worth stating in its own sentence, rather than being tucked inside a long, convoluted complex sentence. Similarly, the point that CPNI is owned by carriers deserves its own emphatic short sentence. The radical nature of the contrary view is also more emphatic if stated in a simple, short sentence. The next sentence provides variety in length and sentence type, as does the longer sentence to follow. Because of the series of short, simple sentences that open the paragraph, the reader is more willing to tackle the last, longer sentence.

The most important goal of the revision of this writing sample is to keep the reader engaged, fully comprehending, and focused on the points that are most important to the writer.

II. WRITING ANALYSIS WORKSHEET

1. Total number of sentences ___

   Total Number of words ___

   Average words per sentence ___

   Number of sentences with 35 words or more ___

   Number of sentences with 6 words or fewer ___

2. Number of simple sentences ___

   % of simple sentences ___

   Number of compound sentences ___

   % of compound sentences ___

   Number of complex sentences ___

   % of complex sentences ___

   Number of sentences with compound subjects, verbs, or objects ___

3. Number of sentences in Active Voice ___

   Number of sentences in Passive Voice ___

   % of sentences in Active Voice ___

   % of sentences in Passive Voice ___

Reasons for use of Passive voice: _______

4. Number of words separating subjects and verbs ___

Average number of separating words per sentence ___

Number of sentences with more than 7 words separating the subject and verb ___

Number of words separating verbs and objects ___

Average number of separating words per sentence ___

Number of sentences with more than 7 words separating the verb and object ___

5. Number of sentences with negative statements ___

% of sentences with negative statements ___

6. List sentence lengths in the order they occur.

Check for variety of sentence length.

7. Number of sentences that open with their subject ___

Number of sentences that do not open with their subject ___

% of sentences that open with their subject ___

Number and % of prepositional phrases used to open sentences _______

Number and % of adverbial or adjectival phrases used to open sentences _______

Number and % of other parts of speech used to open sentences _______

8. List any dangling or ambiguous modifiers (see Chapter 8).

9. Count the number of paragraphs ___

Calculate the average number of words per paragraph ___

Count the number of words in each paragraph separately, then list the numbers in the order that the paragraphs occur to check for variety of paragraph length.

10. Identify the reason for each paragraph break (see Chapter 4).

Number and % of logical breaks _______

Number and % of rhetorical breaks _______

Number and % of visual breaks _______

11. Identify the topic sentence in each paragraph.

Number and % of paragraphs beginning with topic sentence _______

Reasons for placing topic sentences in the middle or at the end:

12. Check the first and last sentences of each paragraph. Are these positions of emphasis used effectively?

13. Locate all transitional words and phrases. Do they provide logical links between all sentences and paragraphs?

14. Count the number of sentence interruptions caused by commas, parentheses, brackets, dashes, or internal citations ___.

Calculate the average number of interruptions per sentence ___

15. Number and % of semi-colons per sentence _______

Number and % of dashes per sentence _______

Number and % of any other frequently used punctuation mark per sentence _______

16. Number and % of active verbs per sentence _______

    Number and % of forms of "to be" per sentence _______

17. Number and adjectives per sentence _______

    Number and adverbs per sentence _______

    Note: if the percentages are 50% or greater, try reducing your use of adjectives and adverbs.

18. Omit 100 words in your writing sample. Print the shorter version. Which version is clearer? Which is easier to read? Ask a friend to compare the two versions.

III. A MICROGRAMMAR

Diagrams for grammatical analysis are visual aids to understanding sentence structure. The following diagrams reflect a conventional method of "mapping" parts of speech. Reviewing these diagrams should assist writers in identifying the true Subject, Verb, and Object in their sentences. Only with a clear understanding of Subjects, Verbs, and Objects and how they interrelate can a writer produce clear and direct sentences.

A MICROGRAMMAR

1. Simple Sentence

   a. Subject and Predicate:

      i. Cars disappear.

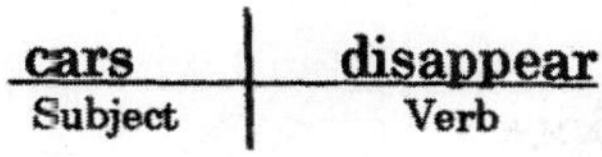

ii. Court decided.

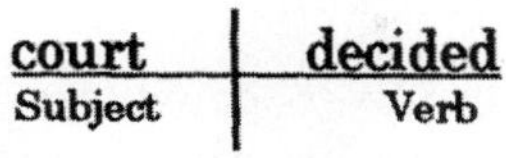

b. Subject and Predicate with Adverb and Adjective:

i. Race cars disappear swiftly

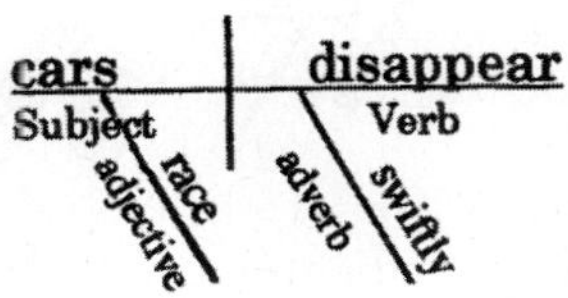

ii. Trial court decided carefully

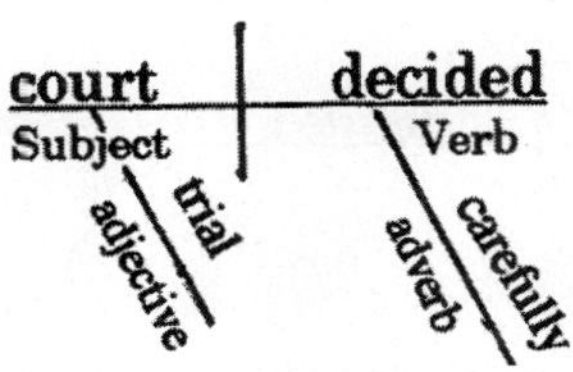

c. Subject and Predicate with Prepositional Phrases:

i. An antique car from Bellingham will win the race with a record time.

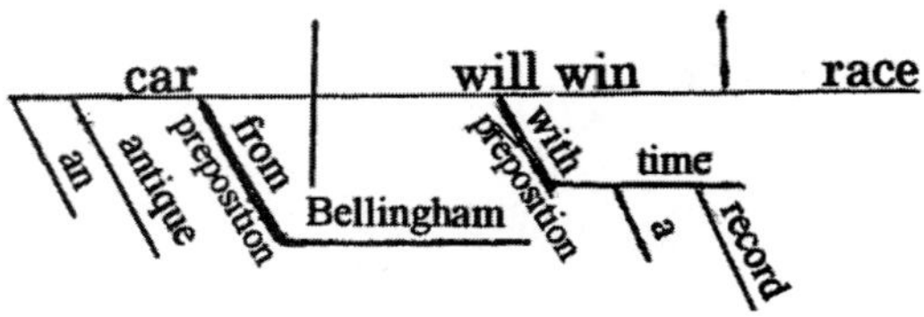

ii. The lower court in a similar case decided directly from the bench.

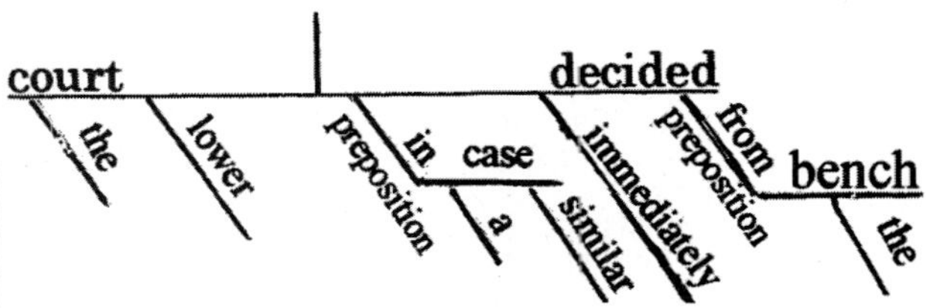

d. Subject, Predicate, Object, and Subjective Complement:

i. Court decided the case

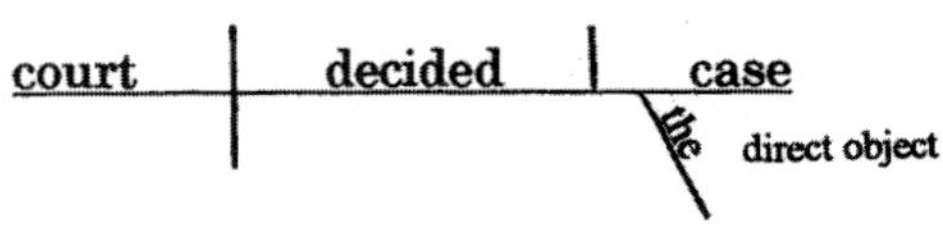

ii. Race cars are expensive

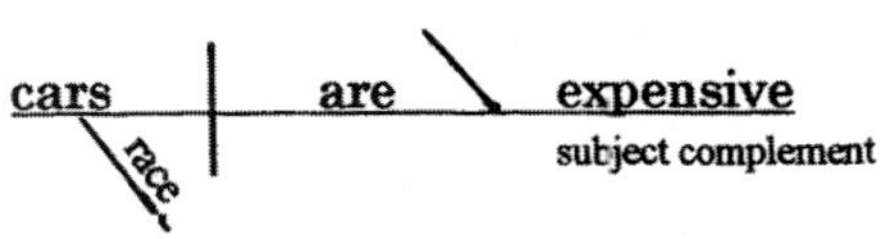

e. Compound Subject, Verb, Object

i. The Plaintiff and the Defendant settled the case

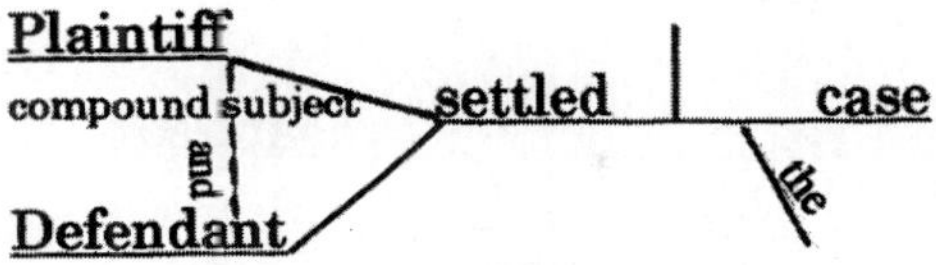

ii. The Plaintiff filed a stipulation and moved to dismiss the case.

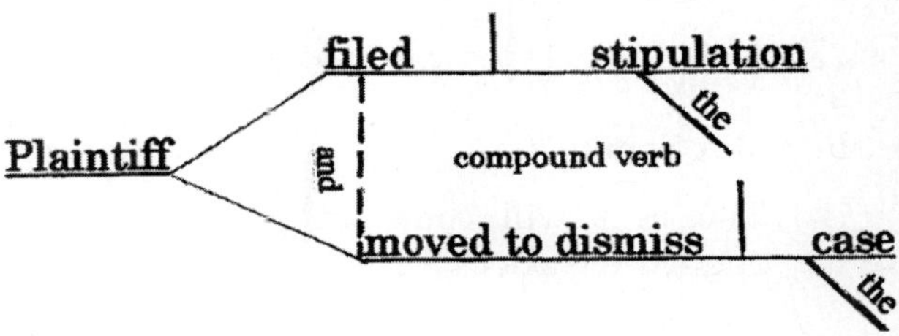

iii. The Plaintiff brought a claim for damages and a separate claim for injunctive relief.

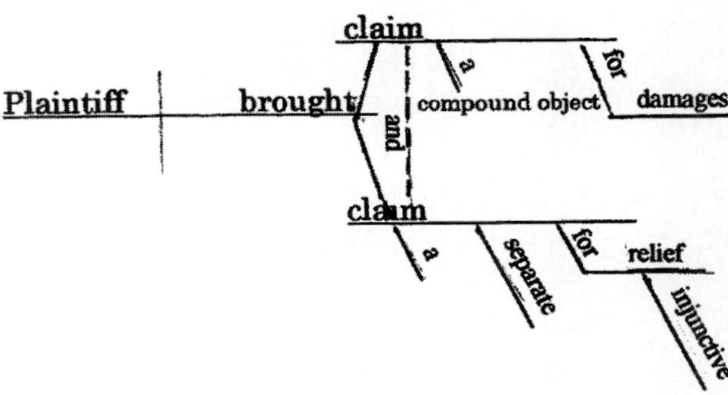

2. Compound Sentence

Race cars disappear, and flags fly.

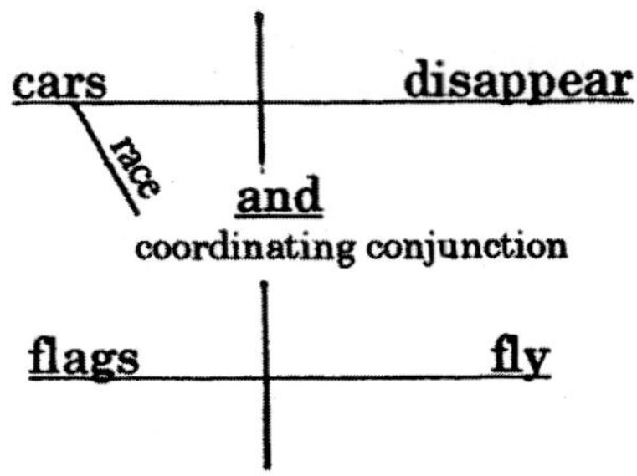

3. Complex Sentence

i. The race will continue unless the rain ruins the track.

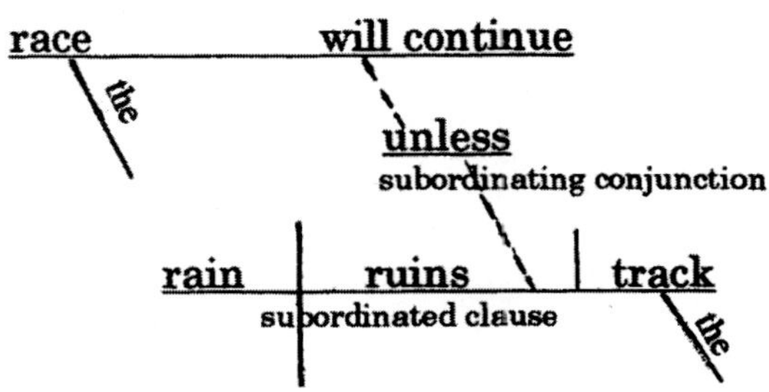

ii. Until the motion is heard, the court will not rule.

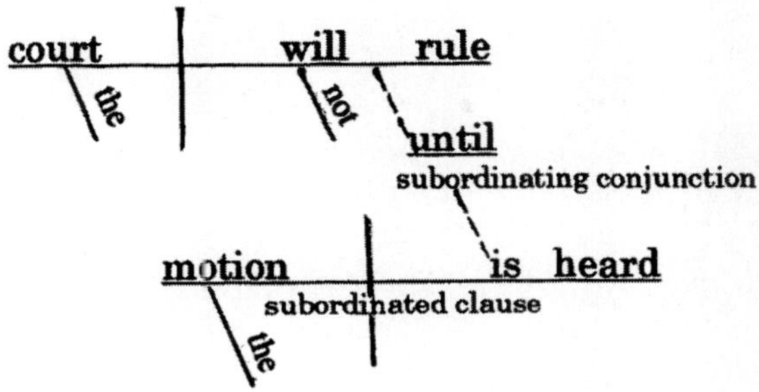

APPENDIX C

GLOSSARY OF WORDS COMMONLY MISUSED IN LEGAL WRITING

Every legal writer should regularly consult a standard usage text. This glossary is not intended as a substitute. Rather, it is intended as a law-oriented supplement to standard references such as those cited in the Selected References at the end of this *Nutshell*.

above, as in the *above* theory. Usage experts acknowledge this use of *above* with a noun to be permissible but prefer reversed order (theory *above*) by analogy to other indicators of place (*e.g., below*). Use of *above* with a verb is more precise (*e.g., above*-mentioned theory, theory summarized *above*) because what has been done *above* is identified. All of these usages are to be preferred to *aforesaid* in legal prose.

abstruse, obtuse. *Abstruse* is an adjective meaning "hard to understand." *Obtuse* is an adjective meaning "dull, insensitive in perception or imagination, slow to understand." A lawyer's reasoning may be *abstruse* because the lawyer is *obtuse*.

accuse, accused, as in *The plaintiffs were accused of conspiracy to defraud creditors.*

1. The preposition *of* is correct.

2. Use of *accuse* in relation to a civil fault is incorrect. In non-legal usage *accuse* means "to

charge with a fault or an offense." In legal usage it has been limited to charging a crime.

adverse, averse. *Adverse* is an adjective meaning "against, opposed, harmful, or unfavorable," as in *adverse to the plaintiff's position. Averse* is an adjective meaning "unwilling, reluctant, or set against," with connotations of distaste or repugnance, as in *Law students are sometimes averse to rigorous writing exercises.*

affect, effect.

1. As nouns. *Effect* is probably the word you want to use. It means "result or accomplishment." *Affect* (*af 'fect*—accent on the first syllable) is a psychological term that you will probably have few occasions to use in legal writing. It refers to an outward emotional appearance.

2. As verbs. Confusion of the two words commonly occurs in their use as verbs. *Effect* means "to bring about, to accomplish." *Affect* (accent on the last syllable) means "to influence."

allege, allegation.

1. *Allege* is spelled without a "d" before the "g."

2. *Allege* means "to declare or assert without proof." Do not use it when you mean contend or argue in the sense of giving reasons for or against something.

alternate, alternative.

1. *Alternate* as an adjective means "by turns." The derived adverb has the same meaning, as in

Defendant's two lawyers sought to question witnesses alternately.

Alternative as an adjective means "offering a choice between two or more possibilities." The derived adverb has the same meaning: *Appellant's counsel argued alternative theories—that there was no contract and that if there was, it was breached by the defendant. Or, she argued that there was no contract and, alternatively, that if there was a contract, it was breached by the defendant.*

2. *Alternative* as a noun also means "a choice between two or more incompatible possibilities," as in *There is no* [not *no other*] *alternative* or in *The only alternative is settlement or trial* (that is, the only choice is the choice between settlement or trial). The noun also has a secondary meaning, that is, one of the several incompatible possibilities to be chosen, as in these sentences: *The settlement alternative is unattractive. The only alternatives are settlement and trial.*

3. Do not use the adjective *alternative* as a synonym *for new, other*, or *revised.*

among, between. *Among* is precisely used to express a relation of more than two persons: *among the four parties. Between* ("by-twain") is precisely used to express a relation of two persons: *between the two parties.* Therefore, the common contractual language *among and between parties A, B, and C* is not a redundancy. It means: among A, B, and C; between A and B, B and C, and A and C. From its first use, however, *between* has extended to more than two things in some situations and is the only word for expressing the relation of a physical thing to many surrounding things, as *in the property between the three rivers.*

and/or. Avoid this confusing usage. *And/or* may be interpreted as (i) both *and* and *or,* (ii) either *and* or *or* but not both. In other expressions, the slash stands for the words "or" or "per." Therefore, *and/or* should carry the second meaning (ii). Because its usage is erratic, however, legal writers should state what is intended: *fined or imprisoned or both* rather than *fined and/or imprisoned.*

anticipate, expect. These words should not be used synonymously. Use *expect* to mean "to look for as likely to occur" or "to look for as necessary or proper," as in *We expect the judge to grant a continuance.* Use *anticipate* to mean "to forestall, to take steps beforehand, to use or enjoy in advance, to do something before someone else," as in *Opposing counsel anticipated our strategy and moved for a continuance.*

appeal. To *appeal* (verb) means "to seek review of a decision in a legal action as a matter of right." If review is not available as of right, but only within a court's discretion, then one *applies for a writ* (*e.g.*, of certiorari).

appellee, appellant. See **parties in litigation**.

argue, contend, maintain. Courts do not *contend, maintain, or argue.* Counsel *contend* and *argue.* Courts *hold, decide, reason, state, suggest, imply, conclude.*

as. Do not use the conjunction *as* when you mean "since," "because," "when," or "while." Its broad and vague meanings can create confusion. For example, *As a potential work stoppage threatened to block the opening of school, the arbitrators revised the wording of the contract.* Does *as* mean "when," "because," or "while"?

as if, like. Do not use *like* in place of *as if*: *The judge proceeded as if* [not *like]* *counsel had raised no objection.*

as, like. *As*, as a conjunction, is used to introduce a clause (a verb must follow *as*): *Students must learn to think as lawyers do. Like*, as a preposition, is used for comparisons: *Students must learn to think like lawyers.*

as such, as in *The court limited the decision to subsequent cases; as such, the decision does not affect our case. Such* is here used as a pronoun. It should therefore have a referent. Its use seems most justified when a comparison is to be made, for example, *It was a prospective decision; as such it does not affect our case. As an indication of the court's attitude, however, it is significant.*

assume, assumption. *Assume* means "to accept as granted that something is true or accurate." Do not use the word or its derivatives when you mean "conclude," that is, to accept something on the basis of reasoning.

attorney, counsel, counselor, lawyer. The distinctions have been explained as follows: *Lawyer* is a general term, designating one who practices law. *Attorney* refers to one who has been designated to transact business for another (that is, a lawyer who has a client). A *counsel* is one who gives legal advice. *Counselor* means the same thing as *counsel*; it is most commonly used in court as a term of address. See also **counsel, counselor**.

based on, as in *Based on this decision, our client may be held liable for a breach of contract*. This use of *based on* is common but incorrect. In the example, *based on* modifies *our client*, thus suggesting that *our client was based on this decision*. To correct the example, substitute *given* for *based on*. (Note also the use of *breach* as a noun. Purists would object to the expression *for breaching the contract*, although dictionaries now bless the use of *breach* as a verb.)

basic, basically. Basic means "fundamental." The derived adverb, *basically*, should not be used as an introductory word without any clear meaning, as in these sentences: *Basically, I am reluctant to recommend that we go to trial. Basically, the statute is not clearly drafted.*

basis, as in *on the basis of*. Single prepositions or other more precise phrases can often be substituted for this wordy phrase, *e.g.*, substitute *under* in *It is nowhere stated that entitlement on the basis of section 416(h)(7)(A) must be full entitlement.* Substitute *by* in *Our client will be judged on the basis of the new standard.* Substitute *on* in *The case was presented to the court on the basis of certified questions.*

between. See **among, between**.

blatant. *Blatant* means "noisy, clamorous, obtrusive." It is often used when *flagrant* is intended as in this sentence: *This result is in blatant conflict with the purpose of the Act.* Even the correct use of *flagrant*, meaning "gross, openly evil," is usually overstatement or over-argument in legal prose.

breach, as a verb. See **based on**.

by, as in *by January 15.* The phrase is ambiguous. Does it mean *before* January 15 or *on or before* January 15? Say which one you mean.

case.

1. *Case* signifies, among other things, a dispute regularly and properly before a court for resolution. Do not personify *case,* as in *The Sutton case so held.* Rather, write *In the Sutton case, the court so held.* Do not write *This case presented itself to the court on certified questions.* Rather, write *This case was presented to the court on certified questions.*

2. Do not use *where* with *case* when you mean *in which* or *wherein*: *The most significant case is United Labor, where the court so held.* Instead, use *in which the court so held.*

3. Do not use *case* when you mean *court* or *opinion*. See **court 4**.

4. *Case* may also refer to a dispute or other matter not yet before a court for resolution. Because the word can be used in the two different senses, it should be used with clear modifiers to avoid confusion. For example, if you use *this case* in a law

office memorandum, it may not be clear whether you are referring to a decided *case* that you have just cited or to the client's *case* about which the memorandum is written. If you use *this case* in a brief, it might be taken as a reference to a decided *case* previously cited or to the *case* in which the argument is being presented. Here are some frequently used forms of reference that avoid such confusion. For decided cases: use an abbreviated part of the case title (for example, *Brinkly*) or use *that case* or *the cited case*. For your client's case: *The case before this court* or *our case*. *Case at hand* and *instant case* are also commonly used, but may seem formal in tone.

5. In a more general sense, *case* is used for a situation, a set of circumstances, an instance, an example, and other less clearly defined referents. It has been imbedded in trite phrases that have, at best, no meaning, or at worst, an ambiguous meaning, *e.g., in the case of, in any case*. When tempted to use a phrase containing *case*, consider (a) whether the phrase is necessary, and (b) if it is, whether a more precise word can be substituted for *case*.

citation, cite.

1. In legal writing, indications of authorities are called *citations*, not *references*.

2. *Cite* is a verb. It should not be used in place of *citation*, as in *The plaintiff's citations* [not *cites*] *are inaccurate*.

claim. This word has a special meaning under federal civil procedure rule 8(a), relating to *claims for relief*. More generally, it also means "to assert or demand a right or title to something." Unfortunately, it is commonly used incorrectly for *allege, state, declare, argue, argument, or conclude*. One student managed to squeeze most of these different meanings into one paragraph: *One claim*[1] *that could be made is that the Commission does not have the power to impose a sanction. Plaintiff could also claim*[2] *that the action cannot lie since the complaint does not claim*[3] *any arrest or seizure of property and special injury, which the Washington court has held is necessary in any claim*[4] *for malicious prosecution. Translations:* [1]*argument,* [2]*argue,* [3]*allege or aver and* [4]*claim.* The fourth and final use is the only correct one in the special sense of civil procedure. Here is another misuse: *The court claimed that the minority position was erroneous. Claimed* should be *concluded* or some other verb. See **argue, contend, maintain**.

compare to, compare with. We *compare* one case *with* another (examine similarities and differences) but *compare* a cliché *to* a comfortable old shoe (liken one thing to another).

compose, comprise. *Compose* means "to make up" or "to constitute." *Comprise* means "to be composed of" or "to consist of." *The American Digest System comprises nine units and a current supplement* (or *is composed of*). *Nine units and a current supplement compose the American Digest System* (or *are comprised in*).

conclusions of law. See **find, finding**.

conform. A contract may *conform* to law or be *in conformity with law*. Goods may *conform to* description or be *in conformity with* description.

construction, interpretation. These words are commonly used interchangeably to refer to the process of determining the meaning of contracts and statutes. A useful distinction has been suggested, however, in *3 Corbin on Contracts 9* (1960): "[T]he word *interpretation* is commonly used with respect to language itself—to the symbols, the words and acts of expression . . . By 'interpretation of the language' we determine what ideas that language induces in other persons. By 'construction of the contract' . . . we determine its legal operation—its effect upon the action of courts and administrative officials."

contain. Search for a more precise verb if you are tempted to say something like this: *The Rosenberg opinion contains several relevant factors that should be developed in our case. (identifies? suggests? summarizes?)*

contend. See **argue, contend, maintain**.

continual, continuous. *Continual* means "frequently or closely repeated." *Continuous* means "without interruption."

contract. One is a party *to*, not *of*, a contract. But, does one *enter* or *enter into* a contract? The latter seems to be the correct usage (though the former occasionally appears in otherwise carefully written court opinions).

counsel, counselor. Note the correct spelling for the words used to describe one who gives legal advice. Note also that *counsel* is the correct form for both singular and plural. See also **attorney, counsel, counselor, lawyer.**

court.

1. A court with more than one judge is an entity (*it*), not a collection of individuals (*they*). If the judges are not unanimous in deciding a case, then you may refer to *the majority of the court* and the *dissenting* (or *concurring*) *judges* or to *dissenters*. You may also refer to the majority's decision as the decision of *the court* (or *the Court* if you are referring to the United States Supreme Court). If you are reporting a particular judge's view (for example, that of a concurring or dissenting judge), use *Judge* _______; for the United States Supreme Court and some state supreme courts, use *Justice* _______. (Note that *Mr. Justice* _______ is no longer used for United States Supreme Court justices. The "Mr." has been dropped in accordance with notice by Associate Justice Stevens to the clerk's office. *National Law Journal*, Dec. 1, 1980, at 55, col. 1, 2.)

2. Either *judge* or *court* may be used to refer to a court with a single judge, for example, for a trial court.

3. Do not substitute the name of a jurisdiction for *court*. For example, *California has held* is incorrect; it should be *the California court has held* if

reference is to the highest court in the state, or *a California court has held* if the reference is to other than the highest court.

4. Do not substitute *case* or *opinion* for *court* or *judge*. For example, *the Graham case so held* is incorrect; it should be *In the Graham case, the California court so held.*

criteria. *Criteria* is a plural noun. The singular is *criterion.*

deals with, as in *The federal regulation specifically deals with "cooperation" in obtaining support.* This phrase is often a fuzzy substitute for a more descriptive verb. Here, for example, the writer may have meant that the regulation *defines "cooperation,"* or *specifies when "cooperation" may be required.* The more precise explanation should be provided.

decide, decision. See **hold, holding**.

deed, quitclaim deed, title.

1. It is the *deed*, not the title that is *delivered and recorded.*

2. *Quitclaim* is correct, not *quick*claim. *Quitclaim* is not hyphenated.

defendant. See **parties in litigation**.

dicta, dictum.

1. *Dicta* is plural; a *dictum* is singular.

2. *Dicta* are statements in a court opinion that are not necessary to the court's resolution of the

problem before it, or, stated in another way, they are answers to questions not presented. Thus, the words *dicta* and *holdings* are mutually exclusive. Therefore, it is an error to say that a court *held in dicta*; rather a court *states in dicta*. If the correct characterization is in doubt, use an expression like *stated in what may be dicta* and explain the reason for doubt. *Binding dicta* is equally objectionable.

different.

1. Use *different from* rather than *different than* and you will usually be safe. Thus, a case may be *different from* a previously decided case.

2. Do not use "no" with *different from* as in this sentence: *The conclusion reached by the scholars is that the rule in defamation cases should be no different from the rule in other cases.* (Rather, *the rule in defamation cases should not be different from* or *should not differ from*.)

disinterested, uninterested. *Disinterested* means "free from bias and self-interest." *Uninterested* means "not interested or apathetic." The distinction must be observed in legal contexts. In an administrative proceeding, the hearing official must be *disinterested*; whether he or she is *uninterested* is usually not legally significant.

doubtless, no doubt, undoubtedly. *Doubtless*, as an adverb, and *no doubt* have lost the literal sense of "without doubt." Now they merely suggest probability or concession, as in *The court doubtless considered the possibility* and *No doubt other* *opinions exist*. To express the absence of doubt, use *undoubtedly*, *without a doubt*, or *beyond a doubt*.

due to.

1. *Caused by*, *resulting from*, or *because of* will be more precise expressions than *due to* in such sentences as these: *The court allowed the tenant to recover for personal injuries due to the landlord's negligent maintenance*. (Rather, *for personal injuries resulting from the landlord's negligent maintenance.*) *This reasoning will become more appealing in light of the injustice suffered by litigants due to extensive court delays*. (Rather, *in light of injustice suffered by litigants because of extensive court delays*.)

2. *Due to* is often superfluous in the statement of a reason, as in this sentence: *The reason for distinguishing the cases may be due to different characteristics of the two types of vehicles*. (Rather, *The reason for distinguishing the cases may be the different characteristics of the two types of vehicles*.)

easy, easily, readily. These are often whistling-in-the-dark words, as in *It is easy to argue that* or *It could readily be argued that*. Avoid such usages. State what you mean: That a point could be *persuasively* or *authoritatively* argued? That opposing counsel may be expected to argue it? That a careless attorney might make the argument?

effect. See **affect**.

enormity. This word refers to the quality of something, not the size.

establishment. This word is often either incorrectly used or used in an awkward way (even though used correctly to mean "an act of establishing" or "state of being established"). Examples: *The establishment of the disclosure violation may be difficult*. (Rather, *Establishing the disclosure violation may be difficult.) Plaintiff's claim for benefits was barred by Mary Lou's establishment of her claim as Joseph's legal widow*. (Rather, *The claim was barred by Mary Lou's having previously established her claim.) The Secretary is charged with establishment of standards for state programs*. (Rather, *The Secretary is charged with drafting or adopting standards.) The survey revealed that many deserting fathers could afford to make child support payments but do not—either through lack of establishment or lack of enforcement of obligations*. (Rather, *either because their duty is not established or is not enforced*.)

et cetera or *etc.* Avoid this word, either written in full or abbreviated, because it is vague. Identify what you intend to include in a list instead.

expect. See **anticipate, expect**.

explicit, implicit. Use these words in their literal, not their colloquial sense. *Implicit* means "implied, understood though unexpressed." Do not use it to mean "absolute, full, or complete," as in *implicit obedience*. The opposite of *implicit* is *explicit*. Do not use it to mean "absolute, full or complete," as in *the one explicit payment* or in *that explicit group of people*. The opposites, *implied* and *expressed*, have not acquired colloquial meanings and so may be the wiser choices for the legal writer.

fact.

1. The line between *fact* and *rule* may be indistinct, but it should not be ignored, as in this sentence: *This result is a reaction to the fact that the patent-child relationship alone is not sufficient to impute liability*. The writer was clearly noting the effect of a *rule*, not a *fact*.

2. *The true facts are stated in the record*. Strike *true*. *Facts* are true by definition. But a *statement of facts* may be untrue or inaccurate.

3. See **find, finding**.

farther, further. Distinctions between these two words seem to be disappearing. You will not be faulted, however, if you confine your use of *farther* to describe physical distance. *Thus, The court reasoned further that . . .*

feels, as in *The court felt that the result was justified* or in *I feel . . .*

1. A *court* does not *feel*, and we ordinarily cannot know how the *judges feel* about a case. Search for a more precise verb.

2. Search for a more precise word also if you are tempted to say, "I feel . . . " Usually you will realize that you *conclude, believe, assume, or infer*. Use *feel* only if you are making an intuitive or emotional statement.

few, fewer, less.

1. *Fewer* means "a smaller number," as in *fewer people* (not *less people*) and *fewer mistakes, fewer words. Less* as a comparative means "a smaller amount of," as in *less pay*.

2. Use *comparatively few*, not *a comparative few* or *the comparative few*.

find, finding. Courts may *find facts*. *Findings of fact* are a court's determinations of the facts. The *findings* may be included in a document stating those factual determinations and also stating legal conclusions. The title of the document is "Findings of Fact and Conclusions of Law." The document, signed by the judge, is commonly required in cases tried before a judge without a jury.

gratuitous. This word does not mean "additional." It means unearned or unwarranted as in a "gratuitous gesture," which is one not expected or deserved.

guilty, liable. *Guilty* carries stronger implications of blameworthiness than *liable.* It implies consciousness of crime or moral wrong. Hence, it is appropriate to say that a person is *guilty of a crime* but *liable for negligence* (or other civil fault).

heavily, as in *The court relied heavily on distinguishable precedents*. The word is imprecise. Did the court rely *exclusively*? *primarily? in part*?

hold, holding, decide, decision

1. *Holding* refers to the result reached by a court in resolving a case regularly and properly before it. That result may also be called a *decision* (though *decision* may also be used in a more general sense). A *holding* is unique because it can refer only to the result on the facts and for the parties in a particular case. Neither *holding* nor *decision* should be used to refer to a *rule*, which is a more general statement that explains many cases. (But see **rule, ruling** 3.) Example: *The court applied the rule that a violation of a zoning ordinance is not an encumbrance that renders title unmarketable. It then held that the violation of the Seattle ordinance that restricted use of the building on the defendant's property did not render the defendant's title unmarketable. Holding* may also refer to the result in a case in a procedural sense, as in *The court's holding that the complaint should be dismissed was in error.* These observations apply also to the verbs *hold* and *decide.*

2. Courts *hold.* Rules do not. Therefore, use of *holds* in the following sentence is both wrong and redundant: *Our client's position will be affected by the rule that holds that evidence of remarriage must not be admitted.*

3. Since *hold* and *holding* have a technical meaning, their use in general or non-technical senses should be avoided, as in *This argument does not hold* or in *The court holds [reasons] that such information would mislead the jury.*

idea. This word is used vaguely to express a number of "ideas" that should be more precisely identified, as in these sentences: *In McDonald the court directly addressed the assumption of risk idea.* (Assumption of risk *defense*?) *The Washington court deals unfavorably with the idea concerning public policy.* (Public policy *argument*?) *Analysis of the idea suggests that the Washington court would allow disclosure.* (Analysis of the *rationale*? the *criticism*?)

impact. As a noun, *impact* means "the forceful striking of one thing against another, a collision." Do not use it figuratively to mean "effect or influence" as in this sentence: *The impact of the court's decision cannot be predicted as this time.*

implicit. See **explicit, implicit**.

imply, infer. *Imply* means "to suggest or to say indirectly." *Infer* means "to surmise or to draw a conclusion from something written or spoken by someone else." Thus, a court may *imply* a conclusion in its opinion, but a reader will *infer* the conclusion from the court's opinion.

in terms of. This phrase is commonly used as a substitute for a precise identification of relationship or as a substitute for such prepositions as *at, by, as,* or *for*. The phrase is correctly used when one thing is being expressed *in terms of* another thing, as when a rule is discussed *in terms of* its economic effect. The phrase is loosely or incorrectly used in the following sentences: *This policy argument is strong in terms of our client's case.* (Is a strong argument for our client? Or for the opposition?) *If* *the doctor's words are construed in terms of a guarantee, the result will be different*. (Construed *as* a guarantee?)

interpretation. See **construction**.

irregardless. This means "regardless," so use that shorter word instead. The "ir" is redundant.

issue.

1. An *issue* is a question that can be answered in more than one way, a point of dispute or controversy. *Issue* should not be used vaguely or unnecessarily. For example, in *The issue of assignment is not disputed*, the word is used improperly. What is not disputed? The *existence* of an assignment? The *validity* of an assignment? In the following sentence, the introductory phrase is used unnecessarily: *The issue of whether the assignment was valid was decided without reference to the controlling precedent*. If the *issue* has been previously stated, the sentence may be correctly written without "*The issue of*" or even more concisely, *The assignment issue was decided without reference to the controlling precedent.*

2. The following phrases should be distinguished: *In issue* refers to points that are in controversy or disputed, particularly those issues that are properly before a court. *At issue* refers to issues that are ready for decision, ready to go to the trier of fact (judge or jury).

it is, there is. Sentences beginning with these words can often be rewritten more concisely and more directly. For example, *It is uncertain as to which procedure the agency must follow* can be more directly written as *Which procedure the agency must follow is uncertain*. The sentence *There is no provision in the statute for rescission if the notice is given* can be more concisely written as *The statute does not provide for rescission if the notice is given*.

judge, justice. See **court** 1.

judgment. When used to mean the terminal decision or document in litigation, *judgment* is spelled without the middle "e" in American legal materials, although use of that "e" ("judgement") is an accepted variant spelling in English legal materials and in other settings.

jurisdiction. This word is commonly used in two senses: to refer to a court system (for example, the federal *jurisdiction*) and to refer to the power of a court or a court system to hear and decide particular disputes. Do not use *jurisdiction* in the former sense when you are actually referring to a particular court. See **court** 3.

lawyer. See **attorney, counsel, counselor, lawyer**.

less. See **few, fewer, less**.

liable, liability.

1. See **guilty**.

2. *Liability* is *imposed on* a party to litigation, *not fastened on, placed on*, or *procured.*

like. See **as, like** and **as if, like**.

likely.

1. When *likely* is used as an adverb, it ought to be modified by a qualifying word like *quite*, *very*, or *most* as in *A decision will most likely be given within ten days.*

2. The colloquial misuse of *likely* instead of *probably* in the following examples is becoming too common: *There will likely be a change* and *Its validity as a contract will likely be challenged.*

ludicrous, as in *It is ludicrous to say that Congress intended this result in such a small class of cases.* This word means "inept, foolish, or exaggerated to the point of absurdity." To so characterize an opposing counsel's argument or a court's rationale is to over argue or overstate.

maintain. See **argue**.

memoranda, memorandum. The singular form is *memorandum*.

most and almost. Use carefully to avoid a casual tone. If you need to qualify a word or phrase, choose a more precise qualifier. Instead of "almost there," state the distance in time, space, or significance.

no doubt. See **doubtless, no doubt, undoubtedly**.

obtuse. See **abstruse, obtuse**.

opinion. A court *opinion* is the official written statement of a court's decision in a case and its reasons for reaching the decision. For appropriate usage, see **court** 4.

oral, verbal. *Oral* means "spoken or uttered." *Verbal* means "with words or consisting of words, either written or spoken." Thus, *whether in writing or verbal* makes no sense; it should be *whether written or oral*.

overrule, reverse.

1. A court *overrules* its prior decisions and the decisions of lower courts within its jurisdiction. A court reverses a lower court judgment in the specific case before it, for example, *After holding that the precedent on which the lower court relied should be overruled, the supreme court held that the judgment for plaintiff should be reversed*. See also **rule, ruling** 3.

2. A decision is *overruled* only when the subsequent decision is directly contrary to the earlier decision. If the later decision is not directly contrary, then the earlier decision may be *limited* or *modified*.

3. Dicta are *disapproved*, not *overruled*.

4. Courts also *overrule* objections.

5. *Overrule* is sometimes used with respect to motions (applications to courts for orders), but *deny* is the more accurate verb.

parol, parole. *Parol* is a noun or adjective meaning *oral*, as in *parol evidence* or *parol lease* or *proof by parol*. *Parole* is a noun or a verb meaning *conditional release of a prisoner*.

parties in litigation.

1. A suit may be commenced by a *plaintiff* or by a *petitioner*, the latter term being used in some equity proceedings and in applications for extraordinary writs, such as mandamus or quo warranto. The party sued is a *defendant* (spelled with an "ant," not an "ent").

2. One who appeals as a matter of right will usually be called the *appellant*. The other party may be a *respondent* (spelled with an "ent," not an "ant") or an *appellee*. The choice apparently depends on which term happens to be used in the controlling rules or statutes. One who seeks review that is discretionary with a court (see **appeal**) is a *petitioner*.

3. In text, capitalize the title of a party (*e.g.*, plaintiff, appellant) only if you are using it as a formal title or as a substitute for a proper name, omitting "the," for example: Plaintiff telephoned Defendant [or Defendant Jones] several times but failed to reach her. But: The plaintiff telephoned the defendant several times.

penchant, proclivity, propensity. Each indicates a strong liking, but with a different connotation. Penchant suggests an attraction; proclivity suggests a habit; and propensity suggests an inner urge or innate preference.

petitioner, plaintiff. See **parties in litigation**.

precedence, precedents. *Precedents* are court decisions that may be followed by courts in subsequent cases presenting the same legal problem. Precedence means "priority, the fact of preceding in time."

principal, principle. Remember the different spellings for three different meanings: The principal [primary] objection to the liability principle [general and fundamental rule] is that the agent's principal [one who employs another to act] escapes all liability.

question of. This phrase is often used to introduce something that is not a question or that should be stated as a "whether" clause. For example, *The question of protective payments depends on two determinations*. Either a more precise word should be selected (*the propriety of protective payments* or *the need for protective payments*) or the question should be stated, for example: *Whether protective payments should be made depends on two determinations*. Or, if the question has been previously stated, then, *The answer to the protective payment question depends on two determinations*.

quitclaim deed. See **deed**.

quote. Do not use this verb for the noun *quotation*. For example, *Both attorneys and law students tend to use too many quotes* [should be *quotations*] *in their briefs*.

re. *Re* means *in the matter of*. It is correctly used in the case title for certain kinds of legal proceedings (*In re* Jones) or in a non-textual introductory statement for a letter to identify the subject matter (preceding the text of the letter, thus: *Re: Jones v. Allen*). In text, use *regarding, about* or *concerning*, for example, *I am writing to you about the appeal in the Jones case.*

respective, respectively. Do not use these words unnecessarily as in *The lawyers presented their respective theories in extended oral arguments*. Rather, use them when necessary to clarify the relationships between sets of things and sets of their modifiers: *Under the will, Peter, Francy, and Kenneth respectively are to receive the antique shop, the farm, and the residue*. The alternative may, however, be more readable: *Under the will, Peter is to receive the antique shop, Francy is to receive the farm, and Kenneth is to receive the residue.*

response, as in **in response to**. This phrase is often used incorrectly without a verb, as in the following sentences: *The regulations were in response to the problem created by lack of definitions.* Rather, state that the regulations were enacted to resolve the problem. *Board Letter No. 829 was in response to an inquiry about disclosure of a security interest in all after-acquired property.* Rather, state that the letter addressed disclosure of a security interest.

rule, ruling.

1. See **hold, holding**.

2. Give thought to selection of a precise verb in describing what a court does with reference to a rule. For example, rules may be *reaffirmed* (if previously applied by the same court), *adopted,*

accepted, or *stated*. Use of *laid down, set down*, or *set forth* normally reflects lack of precision in legal writing.

3. **The court reversed the rule** is incorrect. *Judgments*, not *rules*, get reversed. (*Rules* are *no longer followed*.) A court's *ruling*, on the other hand, may be *reversed*. A *ruling* is a court's determination or order made during litigation, as in deciding pre-trial motions or points during trial. For example, a court may apply the hearsay *rule* in *ruling* that the evidence would not be admitted.

shall. This word has given rise to litigation to determine whether it means "must" or "may." A better practice is to avoid it for a term that clearly indicates whether something is mandatory or discretionary.

tenant, tenet. Do not confuse the spellings. A *tenant* occupies rented premises. A *tenet* is a doctrine regarded as true, particularly by a group.

there is. See **it is.**

this. This word accounts for much fuzzy legal writing. It has been used to refer indefinitely to entire paragraphs of a preceding discussion. It has been used to refer to ideas, arguments, reasoning, or things not previously mentioned. Avoid such indefinite references by following the simple rule never to use "this" without adding a word that identifies what "this" refers to. For a fuzzy example, *This opens the way for indiscriminate seizure. This is further substantiated in a case decided last year. This is what leads me to conclude that the Harold* *decision will be controlling*. Each "this" refers to a different word, which the reader has to guess.

title. See **deed**.

undoubtedly. See **doubtless, no doubt, undoubtedly**.

unique. *Unique* is an adjective meaning one of a kind. Do not use it to mean *unusual* or *remarkable*. A case is either *unique* or it is *not unique*: it cannot be *somewhat unique* or *most unique*.

verbal. See **oral, verbal**.

I. COMMON TRANSITIONAL WORDS AND PHRASES

Introducing

under these circumstances	in the first place
in order to	the first reason
to a certain extent	primarily
initially, first	viewed broadly
to begin, to begin with	in general

Concluding

to conclude	therefore
to sum up, in sum	consequently
in summary	as a result
to summarize	eventually

in review
to review
finally
up to this point
thus
in short
in brief
in particular
on the whole
as we have seen

Restating

that is
to clarify
in other words
in simpler terms
to simplify
more simply
to repeat
in brief
in short
in particular
on the whole
to put it differently
to be sure
as noted

Exemplifying

for example
for instance
to illustrate
that is
as an illustration
specifically
in particular
incidentally
namely

Emphasizing

of course	after all
to be sure	above all
indeed	actually
in fact	still
as such	especially
in effect	at least
certainly	normally
even, even so	notably
nonetheless	and rightly so
in other words	not only . . . but also

Contrasting

however	in contrast
but	nonetheless
as the same time	rather
nevertheless	in opposition to
on the contrary	opposing
contrary to	although
on the other hand	in place of
yet	conversely
and yet	actually
though	despite

alternatively
provided that
still
unlike x
otherwise
by contrast
although this may be true
actually
in spite of
regardless
instead
notwithstanding
even so
even though

Adding or Amplifying

again
first, second, third
once again
further
furthermore
moreover
too
additionally
similarly
also
besides
beyond this
in other words
equally important
of equal importance
incidentally
nor
analogously
that is
provided that
alternatively
in the same vein
after all
a further reason

Comparing

similarly
in like form, manner
likewise
by analogy
analogously
in the same way

Sequencing

first, second, third
finally
last
initially
next
then
in the first place
soon
after

Cause and Effect

therefore
then
thus
as a result
hence
accordingly
consequently
in consequence
since
because
for this purpose
to this end
thereupon
provided that
in effect

Time or Place

above	later, lately
below	initially
beyond	eventually
simultaneously	meanwhile
subsequently	since
this time	more recently
until now	adjacent to
hitherto	opposite to
elsewhere	at length
formerly	ultimately
afterwards	shortly
earlier	thereafter

Alternatives for Overworked Transitions

Therefore	*And, In addition*
then	again
thus	further
hence	furthermore
accordingly	moreover
as a result	also
consequently	too
	similarly

However, but
nevertheless
on the contrary
contrarily
on the other hand
yet
still
nonetheless
by contrast

besides
likewise

APPENDIX D

SELECTED SOURCES

GENERAL COMPOSITION AND GRAMMAR

John B. Opdycke, *Harper's English Grammar* (1983)

The most comprehensive and reliable guide to grammar available to the non-specialist. Available in paperback.

William Strunk, Jr. & E. B. White, *The Elements of Style* (4th ed. 1999)

A concise and widely used paperback guide to general writing. Useful as an introduction to popular discourse; parts of the style section not helpful for legal writing.

LANGUAGE

Michele M. Asprey, *Plain Language for Lawyers* (4th ed. 2010)

Reviews the history of plain language in legal writing, explains the cost-savings to the profession, and makes a convincing case for simplicity.

R. W. Burchfield, *Fowler's Modern English Usage* (Rev. 3rd ed. 2004)

The oracle of modern English usage.

William C. Burton, *Legal Thesaurus* (3rd. ed. 1998)

A useful source of inspiration for synonyms and associated legal concepts for more than 5,000 words in legal contexts.

J. Butterfield, ed., *Fowler's Dictionary of Modern English Usage* (4th ed. 2015)

An easy way to access the oracle of modern English usage, alphabetically.

Martin Cutts, *Oxford Guide to Plain English* (4th ed. 2013)

A style guide with real-life examples and 25 practical guidelines.

Wilson Follett, *Modern American Usage: A Guide* (1998)

Bryan A. Garner, *Garner's Modern American Usage* (4th ed. 2016)

Concise and sensible advice on American usage, with good bibliography.

Bryan A. Garner, *Garner's Dictionary of Modern Legal Usage* (1st ed. 1998)

Tailored to the language of the law, a useful reference for all legal writers.

David Melinkoff, *The Language of the Law* (1963)

A fine historical approach to legal language, written by a lawyer. Entertaining and instructive.

Richard C. Wydick, *Plain English for Lawyers* (5th ed. 2005)

The original authority on plain English for legal writers. Easy to read and easy to use.

LEGAL RESEARCH AND ANALYSIS

Morris L. Cohen & Kent C. Olson, *Legal Research in a Nutshell* (12th ed. 2016)

Linda H. Edwards, *Legal Writing and Analysis* (4th ed. 2015)

Stephan H. Krieger & Richard K. Neumann, Jr., *Essential Lawyering Skills: Interviewing, Counseling, Negotiation, and Persuasive Fact Analysis* (4th ed. 2011)

Richard K. Neumann, Jr. & Kristen Konrad Tiscione, *Legal Reasoning and Legal Writing: Structure, Strategy, and Style* (7th ed. 2013)

Marjorie D. Rombauer, *Legal Problem Solving: Analysis, Research and Writing* (5th ed. 1992)

CITATIONS AND MECHANICS

Association of Legal Writing Directors & Coleen M. Barger, *ALWD Guide to Legal Citation* (5th ed. 2014)

A legal citation textbook and guide for law students, practitioners, and scholars, designed to be "easy to use, easy to teach from, and easy to learn from . . . ."

The Bluebook, A Uniform System of Citation (20th ed. 2015)

Published and distributed by the Harvard Law Review Association, *The Bluebook* guides practitioners and scholars on the structure, content, and form of legal citations and on many rules of mechanics (e.g., abbreviations, numerals, symbols, italicization, capitalization, and court titles).

Antonin Scalia & Bryan A. Garner, *Making Your Case: The Art of Persuading Judges* (2008)

Advice on why, how, and where to cite.

RHETORIC

Edward P. J. Corbett, *Classical Rhetoric for the Modern Student* (4th ed. 1998)

A compilation of the classical techniques for persuasion and argument. Much of it is directly applicable to argumentative legal writing. Contains a section on judicial discourse.

Marshall McLuhan, *Understanding Media: The Extensions of Man* (1964)

Ruth Ann Robbins, Steve Johansen, & Ken Chestek, *Your Client's Story: Persuasive Legal Writing* (2013)

Antonin Scalia & Bryan A. Garner, *Making Your Case: The Art of Persuading Judges* (2008)

Wise and clearly written advice on how to persuade courts orally and in writing.

STYLE

Anne Enquist & Laurel Currie Oates, *Just Writing* (4th ed. 2014)

A clear and helpful guide on grammar, punctuation and style for legal writers.

Bryan A. Garner, *The Redbook: A Manual on Legal Style* (3rd ed. 2013)

A "exhaustive" but easy to use style guide for legal writers.

Tom Goldstein & Jethro K. Lieberman, *The Lawyer's Guide to Writing Well* (2d ed. 2002)

Practical and engaging advice from a professor of journalism and a professor of legal writing.

Ross Guberman, *Point Made: How to Write Like the Nation's Top Advocates* (2d ed. 2014)

Concise advice for advocates, illustrated with many fine examples from practice.

Noah Messing, *The Art of Advocacy: Briefs, Motions, and Writing Strategies of America's Best Lawyers* (2013)

Jennifer Murphy Romig, *Checklists for Powerful, Efficient Legal Writing*, Georgia Bar Journal, December 2011, at 50

Terry Jean Seligmann, *Why Is a Legal Memorandum Like an Onion*, 56 Mercer Law Review 729 (2005)

INDEX

Italics indicate references to explanations of word usages or to case names.

References are to Pages.
